- experiences
- opportunities
- exercises
- drills

Expand knowledge & [illegible] (process)

- [illegible]

Skill in using lang.—forms, styles etc.

Learn to practice in ways that benefit the writer.

what "they" want:

1) "Correct" use of lang.
- They assume knowledge of grammar & rules will do it.

To Compose

Questionnaire

How do you rate yourself as a writer?

1st GRADER ——————— HEMINGWAY

Ave. of grades through-out ed. career:

E ——————— A

One/main thing get out of this course:

To what extent is the knowledge of grammar important for effective writing?

NO IMP. ——————— VERY IMPORTANT

Dunnings "River Noise" = river as metaphor of the power and current of our past lives = dipping fingers to make you feel as though you are here = slip into the past (p. 121)

To Compose

Teaching Writing in High School and College

Second Edition

Edited by Thomas Newkirk
University of New Hampshire

Heinemann
Portsmouth, NH

Heinemann Educational Books, Inc.
70 Court Street Portsmouth, NH 03801
Offices and agents throughout the world

The editor and publisher wish to thank the following for permission to reprint previously published material: "Toward Righting Writing" by Arthur Daigon originally appeared in the December 1982 issue of *Phi Delta Kappan* and is reprinted by permission of the author. "A Way of Writing" by William Stafford originally appeared in the Spring 1970 issue of *Field* and is reprinted by permission of the publisher. "Write Before Writing" by Donald Murray originally appeared in *College Composition and Communication* 29 (December 1978). Copyright 1978 by the National Council of Teachers of English. Reprinted with permission. "Understanding Composing" by Sondra Perl originally appeared in *College Composition and Communication* 31 (December 1980). Copyright 1980 by the National Council of Teachers of English. Reprinted with permission. "How to Completely Individualize a Writing Program" by William A. Clark originally appeared in *English Journal* 64 (April 1975). Copyright 1975 by the National Council of Teachers of English. Reprinted with permission. "Teaching the Other Self: The Writer's First Reader" by Donald Murray originally appeared in *College Composition and Communication* 33 (May 1982). Copyright 1982 by the National Council of Teachers of English. Reprinted with permission. "Writer-Based Prose: A Cognitive Basis for Problems in Writing" by Linda Flower originally appeared in *College English* 41 (September 1979). Copyright 1979 by the National Council of Teachers of English. Reprinted with permission. "Dialogue with a Text" by Robert E. Probst originally appeared in *English Journal*, January 1988. Copyright 1988 by the National Council of Teachers of English. Reprinted with permission. "Looking for Trouble: A Way to Unmask Our Readings" by Thomas Newkirk originally appeared in *College English* 46 (December 1984). Copyright 1984 by the National Council of Teachers of English. Reprinted with permission. "Language Across the Curriculum: Examining the Place of Language in Our Schools" by Bryant Fillion originally appeared in the *McGill Journal of Education* 14:1 (1979). Reprinted with permission. "Journals Across the Disciplines" by Toby Fulwiler originally appeared in *English Journal* 69 (December 1980). Copyright 1980 by the National Council of Teachers of English. Reprinted with permission. "Guidelines for Using Journals in School Settings" originally appeared in *Slate*, June 1987. Reprinted by permission of the National Council of Teachers of English. "Breaking the Rules in Style" by Tom Romano originally appeared, in a shorter version, in *English Journal*, December 1988. Copyright 1988 by the National Council of Teachers of English. Reprinted with permission. Every effort has been made to contact the copyright holders and the children and their parents for permission to reprint borrowed material. We regret any oversights that may have occurred and would be happy to rectify them in future printings of this work.

Library of Congress Cataloging-in-Publication Data

To compose : teaching writing in high school and college / edited by
Thomas Newkirk.—2nd ed.
p. cm.
Includes bibliographies.
ISBN 0-435-08496-8
1. English language—Composition and exercises—Study and teaching
(Secondary). 2. English language—Rhetoric—Study and teaching.
I. Newkirk, Thomas.
PE1404.T6 1990
808'.042'071273—dc20 89-31484
CIP

Designed by C. J. Petlick, Hunter Graphics.
Printed in the United States of America.
10 9 8 7 6 5 4 3 2 1

Contents

Preface to the Second Edition

The first edition of *To Compose* contained twelve essays selected after extensive consultation with teacher educators. I was looking for selections that teachers in high school and college found useful, the ones that would be referred to long after the course was finished. I wanted selections that were vivid and well-written—serious without being solemn.

Almost all of that first edition is retained in this new edition. While I was pleased with the reception of the first edition, I was keenly aware of the almost complete absence of pieces by high school teachers (only two of the original twelve were by that group). I have tried to address that deficiency in this edition, and even the pieces written about college teaching are written from what Stephen North would call the "practitioner" point of view. This new edition is therefore richer in examples of student writing and student talk.

The essays are grouped into six sections:

Prologue. Arthur Daigon contrasts traditional instruction in writing with an approach centered around the writing process.

Getting Started. This section begins with two well-known writers, William Stafford and Robert Cormier, discussing their own writing processes. Stafford emphasizes the importance of receptivity in the early stages of composing, the willingness to accept an initial idea or impression and to see where it leads. Cormier touches on a range of topics, but he too keeps coming back to the importance of the writer trusting his or her instincts. Donald Murray, drawing on the testimony of published writers, explores the signals that help writers get started. Sondra Perl examines the ebb and flow of composing; the writer often must move backward and re-establish contact with what she calls "a felt sense" in order to move forward. In the last essay in this section, William Clark splits an infinitive and offers practical advice on beginning a writing program that allows students to truly function as writers.

Responding. This section has been expanded to include three new essays that take us inside the act of responding. Terry Moher discusses the ways she uses writing conferences in her high school classroom. Mary Fallon asks "What About Arthur?"—how can a teacher help a student with severe writing problems? And what standards should be used in evaluating such a student? Lad Tobin examines another difficult issue in holding conferences with students: how much advice is useful? Tobin argues that there are no easy answers to questions like this one. There are no set procedures that can assure effective response.

The final pieces in this section are more theoretical. Donald Murray develops the metaphor of the "other self," the self that looks over our shoulder as we write, cajoling, encouraging, evaluating, and keeping us on track. Linda Flower's classic essay, "Writer-Based Prose: A Cognitive Basis for Problems in Writing," is also included in this section. While a number of theorists have claimed that "expressive" writing is important, Flower, using an information-processing model, explores the cognitive processes that result in writer-based prose, language so close to the writer's mental exploration that it does not meet the needs of the reader.

Writing and Literature. All four of the essays in this section represent attempts to break away from traditional text-centered approaches to literature. Robert Probst presents a rich array of strategies for helping students respond to texts and develop these responses through discussion with other students. The remaining essays explore, in some detail, ways in which students can use writing to deepen their response to literature. Maureen Barbieri presents a case study of one student's use of a journal to respond to poetry, and Nancie Atwell shows how she established a dialogue with her students through letter writing. In my essay, I show how students can "look for trouble" in their reading, how they can use writing to work through the perplexities of reading poems.

Writing Across the Curriculum. If writing is a major instrument for learning, it should have a place in all subject areas. But how is writing used in schools? I've retained in this edition Bryant Fillion's survey of Canadian schools, which found that *copying* was the most common form of writing. More recent surveys, such as John Goodlad's monumental study *A Place Called School,* suggest that Fillion's critique is still timely. The other two essays in the section suggest alternatives that engage the student in thinking about subjects. Toby Fulwiler suggests ways in which journals can be used across the curriculum. John Ferguson describes ways in which teachers in high school have begun to use writing in their courses. Ferguson also suggests that implicit in the movement to integrate writing into courses is a more radical agenda: to transform traditional notions of what it means to teach. This section concludes with the National Council of Teachers of English statement on the use of journals in school settings.

Style and Grammar. In this final section, I have included Tom Romano's description of a unit he taught in which he encouraged students to consciously break the rules of correctness—to experiment with one-word sentences, labyrinthine sentences, the coining of new words.

In addition to these essays, I include after each section a "Time for Questions." Here I pose questions that are frequently asked in workshops, questions like:

1. How can I help students find something to write about?
2. How can I help students become more effective in responding to papers of their classmates?

In some cases I will refer to research in answering these questions, but for the most part I rely on my own experience as a teacher on the high school and college level.

At the end of each section I include a short list of suggested readings. By now the amount of material available on these topics is huge, so I have limited the lists to a few books and articles that are both easily available and highly readable.

I'd like to acknowledge, again, the help that I received in putting together the first edition. Thanks to my colleagues Bob Connors and Tom Carnicelli for their good advice. I also benefited from the suggestions of Nancie Atwell, Charlie Chew, Ted Hipple,

Jane Kearns, Judith Fishman Summerfield, Ann Gere, Sally Reagan, Arthur Daigon, Sheila Fitzgerald, James S. Davis, Nancy Wilson, John Mayher, and John Warnock.

Much of the credit for this book must go to Doug Fleming, who saw it through production. In August of 1985 I took the copy for the book to Ed Comeau, a typesetter living in a log cabin outside Exeter, New Hampshire, and went off to Hawaii for a year. Doug took the book through the production process as the Northeast Regional Exchange, his employer and the book's publisher, was going out of business. The project could have easily died at that point. Philippa Stratton of Heinemann managed to purchase the rights to this book (and to *Understanding Writing*) as NEREX was being liquidated. It's a small miracle that the book is now going into a second edition. Thank you, Doug and Philippa.

Introduction

The Writing Process—Visions and Revisions

It is hardly radical to claim that writing is a process. After all, what isn't a process? Sleeping, eating, talking, raising children, raking leaves—all are processes. All involve a series of actions, all occur over time, all are different for different individuals. We can understand the near revolutionary impact of the claim "writing is a process" only if we understand the teaching methods that writing process advocates attempted to dislodge.

In her influential research monograph, Janet Emig (1971) identified one enemy: the formulaic "essay," depicted in a recent Sandra Boynton cartoon as a triceratops—three horns (or points) in front, three longer versions of these spikes coming up from the back, and a long tail dragged over ground that has already been covered. Emig called this form the "Fifty-Star Theme":

> A species of extensive writing that recurs so frequently in student accounts that it deserves special mention is the five-paragraph theme, consisting of one paragraph of introduction ("tell what you are going to say"), three of expansion or example ("say it"), and one of conclusion ("tell what you have said"). This mode is so indigenously American that it might be called the Fifty-Star Theme. In fact, the reader might imagine behind this [theme] Kate Smith singing "God Bless America" or the piccolo obligato from "The Stars and Stripes Forever." (97)

The Fifty-Star Theme restricted the topics students could write about. At the time Emig completed her study virtually all student writing was writing about literature, invariably literature that was part of an unquestioned canon (Squire and Applebee 1968).

The "process" movement challenged the assumptions underlying this traditional approach—beginning with the almost self-evident claim that writing is a process. If writing is a process, does it make sense for the teacher to simply assign the topic and assess the product, providing no help during the activity of writing? Isn't this a form of chronic absenteeism? Donald Murray, Roger Garrison, and others argued for the writing conference as a way of helping students as they composed. James Moffett, Ken Macrorie, Peter Elbow, Ken Bruffee, and others showed how peer groups could read and respond to student work. In their attempts to help students discover and develop their topics, these innovators drew on sources as diverse as classical rhetoric and Eastern mysticism—from structured questions to meditation, from problem solving to Wordsworth's "wise passiveness."

A second challenge was to the limitations traditionally placed on what a student could write about. Why should literature dominate composition classes? Why should the literary critic be the ideal toward which students are directed? By what scale of values is it legitimate to comment on *Hamlet* and illegitimate to comment on the Boston Celtics? Proper for students to analyze Hamlet's character but not their own? Proper to read about Huckleberry Finn's adventures but not those of their classmates? But if students are to write convincingly, they need what all writers need—to work from abundance, to become authorities on their topics, to write about what they care about. Consequently, advocates of the writing process urged a shift away from literary topics assigned by the teacher to topics chosen by students. The teacher's job was to help the student discover, elaborate, and reflect upon these topics. The invitation was the one made by Thoreau in *Walden:*

> I, on my side, require of every writer, first or last, a simple and sincere account of his own life, not merely what he has heard of other men's lives; some such account as he would send to his kindred from a distant land; for if he has lived sincerely he must be in a distant land from me. ([1854] 1983, 46)

Even when the student writes about literature, the focus should not be on some text that exists separate from the reader. The poem is not an object but an event, a process, an experience. The student's role is not to declare timeless truth (backed up by the inevitable three examples) but to explore the experience of reading the text.

A third challenge was to the relation of language to thought implicit in traditional instruction. The student assigned the Fifty-Star Theme could hardly be expected to discover something in the actual process of writing because the structure of the entire paper was set in the concrete of the opening paragraph. The act of writing was an act of transcription, of transposing previously formulated ideas and plans into written text. Yet the testimony of writers is almost universal in claiming that writing is a process of discovery, that, as E. M. Forster noted, we can't know what we think until we see what we write. The formal school essay—with its quasi-assured tone, its absence of personal voice (and first person pronoun), its reduction of all complexity to a single assertion—was hardly the form students needed to explore a topic. The language needed had to be closer to talk. It needed to allow for digression, for contradiction, for personal expressions of delight, confusion, and irritation. The writing classroom was opened to a new language for learning—free writing, journal writing, open-ended responses to literature. Again Thoreau's reminder is timely: "We commonly do not remember that it is, after all, always the first person that is speaking" (47).

Implicit in all of these challenges was a changing role for the teacher. In the traditional approach the teacher was primarily—if not exclusively—an evaluator. The primary job of the teacher was to judge the quality of the writing, which often meant the noting of errors. In the writing process classroom, the teacher began to assume other roles: fellow writer, reader, coach, editor. The classroom became not a set of individuals vying for the benediction of the teacher, but a collection of writers who read, responded, and supported each other's efforts. Students were urged to write for this community and not for the teacher. To be sure, the teacher was hardly just another student, and in almost all classrooms the teacher did have to grade. But the evaluator role was minimized as much as possible by practices like portfolio grading (i.e., not every paper was graded), the use of informal exploratory writing, peer workshops, self-evaluation, and taking into consideration elements other than the quality of the writing (e.g., was the student a good peer responder? did the student revise his or her work effectively?)

The writing process movement reflects the political era in which it was born, the turbulent years between 1966 and 1975. True to those times, much of the process pedagogy has an anti-institutional bias. The student was portrayed not as someone entering the academy, learning the practices of academic writing; it was more common to view academic writing as the enemy because it seemed to suppress the individual voice of the writer. The movement was clearly a challenge to the literature specialists who controlled English departments; the attempt was to ask students to read their life experiences as texts rather than to restrict their attention to the literary canon. And it was a challenge to the authority structure of the classroom and the "transmission" model symbolized by the podium placed before rows of immovable seats.

The success of the writing process movement can be shown by the fact that even those who argue most strongly against it accept most of the positions stated above. Many of the pedagogical innovations such as journal writing, writing conferences, and non-lecture formats have been adopted not only in writing classes but, through the writing across the curriculum movement, in a variety of disciplines. But there are two lines of criticism that I would like to discuss: one is ideological and the other is instructional.

In terms of ideology, the writing process movement has been attacked from both the Left and the Right. Paradoxically, both begin from a similar premise: that no pedagogy can or should be politically neutral. The term *process,* however, seems to be a neutral term; Martin Luther King, Jr., employed a writing process, and so did Adolf Hitler. These critics would argue that of course we should teach the process of writing—but for what ends should the process be used? In other words, the emphasis on process may be technically useful, but it avoids the more critical issues of the ends of education.

The writing process movement can also be seen as politically neutral because students are urged to pick their own topics—in other words, no one topic is better or more appropriate for the composition course than another. Yet critics from the Left and Right would argue that all topics are not created equal, some are more worthy of being investigated than others. Many of these more worthy topics are not ones that students would spontaneously choose. Instead, when given a choice, students may decide to recount interesting or exciting experiences (in New Hampshire we get the inevitable ski trip papers). In other words, choice can limit the student, can push the student back into familiar modes of retelling experience.

Here the agreement between Left and Right ends. Conservatives view schools as preserving a common culture and therefore contend that writing should help students develop cultural literacy and that English courses should acquaint students with a core of centrally important works (see Hirsch 1984, 1987). As literary theorists have shown, all texts rely on *intertextuality:* none could exist in and of itself, and each depends on other texts for its meaning. On a basic level, Mark Twain assumes that the reader of *Tom Sawyer* knows the Bible; we are expected to laugh when Tom stands before the congregation and identifies David and Goliath as the first two apostles because we have enough biblical knowledge to recognize the absurdity of his answer. The conservative critic would claim that the divorce of writing from literature or "great ideas" takes the student away from the appropriate content of a writing course.

Leftists consider "cultural literacy" to be racist, sexist, and chauvinistic. The lists of great books that conservatives like William Bennett and E. D. Hirsch, Jr., draw up are almost exclusively those of white males. The critic from the Left (see, for example, Berlin 1988) would argue that the content of a writing course should be to help students become critically aware of the racism, sexism, and economic oppression that are part of our society. James Berlin (1988) claims that the relentlessly *individual* focus of writing process instruction, the focus on *personal* experience, limits the student's ability to be politically effective. The recounting of individual experience is important, but primarily as a step toward examining social forces that shape individual experience. The literature that students read should confront them with accounts of exploitation and oppression, and the goal is often to dispel the natural optimism that students, particularly middle-class students, bring to class.

Both Left and Right would agree that the writing teacher's classroom is not a neutral, value-free zone in which the teacher can pass authority over to the student. Both critiques assume that the teacher must have the authority to decide on the content and issues to be dealt with in the class. For the conservative this authority presents little problem because the conservative position assumes an authoritative set of texts, a literate tradition, that students need to be familiar with. The leftist position is more complex. It begins with the assumption that students are part of an exploitative political system that students need to examine and criticize. But what about students who don't accept this opening premise? What about students who take a more benign view of political institutions? Is that a viable position to hold in a radical classroom? And if it is not, won't the classroom itself become oppressive? Won't students become reluctant to speak against the orthodoxies of radicalism? There is a long history of radical movements that begin with arguments for liberation from oppression and that end by oppressing.

Within the classroom, the writing process approach may be at once less political and more transforming than the "radical" alternatives. There is no definable political agenda; the course is not a failure if there are still Republicans in it at the end. Terry Moher's essay in this collection tells of a conference with a student who is sorting through her autobiography. Terry asks, "What is the essence of Marangelli?" This question focuses the student's efforts. She begins to define herself, to show how she can resist the pressure to conform to the definitions that others offer for her.

Is that question "What is Marangelli?" a political one? I think it is more basic and important than that—it is a question that helps in the formation of an individual intellectual identity. If the question is political, it is in the sense that it promotes a decentralization of authority. It is a destabilizing question because it asserts that the responsibility for answering is the student's and not her guidance counselor's or teacher's or parent's or sister's. The role of the teacher is to pose the question, to raise the unexplored issue, and then to be silent. Should there be an implicit or explicit political agenda for the class, this silence is compromised.

The more pragmatic challenge to the writing process approach concerns the kind of support given to the writer. In his massive review of writing research George Hillocks (1986) claims that the "natural process" approach (which he identifies with Donald Graves, Lucy Calkins, Peter Elbow, and Janet Emig) is not particularly effective because the teacher assumes too passive a role and because strategies like "free writing" fail to provide students with the assistance needed for complex writing tasks. Hillocks claims that an "environmental" approach with carefully structured writing assignments can provide that necessary assistance. Paradoxically, many of the methods he recommends—particularly the use of small groups—were first developed by the educators he is criticizing.

I have argued elsewhere (Newkirk 1987) that the statistical proof Hillocks offers for the superiority of the environmental approach is not as powerful as he claims. Still, his criticism is an important one. The language used to describe the writing process almost invites misunderstanding. For example, it is almost a commonplace to claim that the student needs a sense of "ownership." But if the student "owns" the writing, what business do I, as a teacher, have asking him to change it? Since students should write for readers, don't the readers "own" it in some sense? I also hear about "giving control of the writing back to the writer." True to a point, but as a teacher I have expectations that interact with the student's intentions. I am more than part of a "facilitative environment"—I'm not a potted plant. I hope that the essays in this book, particularly those on the writing conference that I've added in this second edition, help illustrate the active role of the teacher.

Another area of contention is topic choice. If students have an unrestricted choice of topic and approach, it is possible and probably likely that they will choose forms they know and feel comfortable with—which usually means some version of personal narrative or fictional narrative (modeled after T.V. plots more than written fiction). The teacher clearly has a responsibility to expand this repertoire. Because students are not likely to attempt to write in forms they haven't read, the teacher needs to provide rich and diverse reading experiences. And the teacher may choose to assign a topic or form. In the Freshman English program I direct, students must do a research paper. While they can choose the topic, the paper itself is a requirement because we feel that it is an experience they should have. As we ask (or require) students to try new forms, we often need to provide more guidance for students—using many of the environmental techniques Hillocks describes. As students prepare to write the research paper, they may generate questions about it, they need to see and discuss model essays, they are shown how to conduct computerized searches, they may give oral presentations before writing, they will share drafts with classmates. This is hardly hands-off teaching.

A final shift of emphasis in the writing process movement concerns the distinction between process and product. In an early influential essay, Donald Murray urged teachers to "teach writing as a process, not product"—an injunction that became a rallying cry. Finished texts, after all, say nothing about how they were produced; we read a novel and experience the inevitability of language to the point where we cannot imagine that the text could be other than it is. As readers, we have difficulty moving from the seamlessness of reading to the messy process of composing, to the blank page (and now blank screen) that confronted the writer before major decisions had been made, when the wealth of options may have been paralyzing. This process cannot be inferred from the finished product, Murray claims in a famous metaphor, any more than a pig can be inferred from a sausage. The injunction had political use as well. If composition teachers identified their task as teaching the process of writing, they were separating themselves from literature teachers concerned about products.

This opposition of process to product, while useful to call attention to composing processes, is ultimately misleading. Every good writer that I've known has been an avid reader of products (though not all avid readers are good writers). By reading finished products we can see the completed performance of the writing process, and we need a sense of the completed performance to guide our own composing. A sense of type or genre guides our composing; we set out to write lyrics, or memos, or book reviews, or journal entries, and our understanding of these forms comes from having read them. We may not be able to infer the process from the product, but without the product as a rough guide for our efforts, the process will inevitably go awry. We can't shoot at a target we've never seen.

Literature can also provide a vantage point for interpreting personal experience. If we want students to go beyond reporting experience—if we want them to interpret or analyze that experience—they need more than their memory of the experience itself. If we are to interpret *x*, we need something that is not *x* to relate it to. Interpretation is the interplay between *x* and not-*x*; it can be the interplay between remembered experience and experiences rendered in literature. Literature provides a frame, a vantage point from which we can view ourselves. In Nancie Atwell's essay in this collection we see how one of her eighth graders drew on her reading of E. H. Hinton and Robert Frost to capture the special quality of an early morning sunrise:

> Sunday morning was special. The cats were under my bed at 4:15 doing something, I don't know how they got upstairs. I took them down and looked out the window. Low and behold, sunrise! But

> no, it did not rise. All I could see was a golden strip across the sky. I pulled up a chair and put my feet up. I said, "Nothing Gold Can Stay" in my mind without stumbling and found how Ponyboy could have felt in *The Outsiders.* After fifteen minutes when the sun didn't appear I went back to bed feeling new.
>
> We're really going to miss you.

The writer here is reading, first of all, her experience watching the sun rise, but the text of her experience is mingled with other texts that allow her to understand and feel the moment even more deeply. It is not an isolated event; it is connected to literary experiences that allow her to see a pattern—that there is a residual sadness in these moments caused by the awareness that they can't last. The last line, "We're really going to miss you," adds to this pattern, for the experience of working with a special teacher, like the sunrise, can't last.

Finally, literary criticism has shifted away from an exclusive focus on products to a position that more closely resembles those of writing process proponents. Attention has shifted from the formal properties of the literary text to the transactions (to use Louise Rosenblatt's term) that occur between reader and text—from the poem as object to the poem as event, from the poem as timeless to the poem as timebound, from meaning as grounded in the text to meaning as constructed by communities of readers. Attending to literature, then, is fundamentally similar to attending to our personal experiences. My late colleague Gary Lindberg (1986) has noted that

> [s]tories and poems show us people trying to make sense of their experiences—to name them, to fit them into orderly sequences, to find language fresh enough to catch what is too personal for stock phrases. We watch both author and characters making meanings out of what has happened to them, attributing motives to explain the odd conduct of others, and finding patterns within which their feelings count. In other words, the characters in stories and poems are busy doing exactly what we do as readers. We are all interpreters. (144)

In this description of what readers do—make sense of experience, assign motive for behavior, find patterns to explain behavior—Lindberg is describing what a writer does as well. The roles of author, character, reader merge. If reading is viewed in this way, it becomes more difficult to argue for the separation of composition and literature.

To Compose is a collection of essays designed to introduce classroom teachers to teaching the writing process. In order to compile this collection I have made use of the convenient fiction that I am speaking of a coherent body of work, that the "writing process movement" is composed of scholars and teachers working as a unit to change writing instruction. This is, of course, not the case. Janet Emig's life work has been to establish the theoretical roots of writing instruction, while Don Murray's has been to argue for the importance of using practicing writers as models for instruction. The conference method proposed by Roger Garrison is radically different from that of Don Murray—and both differ from the teacherless writing groups advocated by Peter Elbow. But this diverse group would agree on the danger of writing instruction becoming simply one other formulaic system of instruction with clearly labeled do's and don'ts. We can see the orthodoxies already: the writing teacher should be nondirective, the teacher must never assign a topic, all mechanical problems should be dealt with in the editing stage of writing, the student must always speak first in the conference.

I urge the readers of this book to be skeptical. Measure any advice against your own classroom experience. Trust your intuition. I suppose there are some teachers who teach "purely," who have a clear philosophy that guides every choice. I'm more of a scrambler, myself. The actual conditions of teaching cause me to be flexible and opportunistic. I may generally want the student to be the primary critic of her paper, but sometimes that doesn't work and I have to be more directive. I may generally want to deal with the content of a paper in early conferences, but in some cases I will spend some time on grammar and mechanics. While I tend to downplay grading and avoid the evaluator role, in some cases I need to confront a student with my low evaluation of his work. Nothing is tidy.

Consider also the images of successful teaching that we create. When people speak about the way they teach, I form a mental image of their classroom and compare it to my own. A dangerous business. I often find myself depressed by the reported success of others (and, of course, guilty about these feelings) because my own success seems much more incomplete or infrequent than other teachers'. Their writing groups, apparently, are always happily on task, but there is always one of mine that is either silent or talking about sports. Their students always eagerly proceed through multiple drafts, while some of mine hit periods of sluggishness that make me want to shake them and say, "Get to work!" Their semester seems to ride from success to success, while mine has these God-awful troughs.

These thoroughly successful classes may exist. But mine are different. Each semester there is a point where I think the course a failure, when I can't imagine the students will ever match the work of previous students, when I feel that all of the waiting, the encouragement, the questioning will not pay off. Even at the end of the semester, when my mood has improved, there are students who didn't progress as much as I had hoped and I reexamine my interactions with those students. Should I have been firmer, more encouraging? Did I become impatient?

I offer these observations (or confessions) as a caution: none of the suggestions in this book will produce an idealized classroom, where all students want to write all the time or where progress is steady and continually gratifying. I suspect I wouldn't like that classroom much anyway. I prefer the students I face. I prefer the difficulty.

References

Berlin, James. 1988. "Rhetoric and Ideology in the Writing Class." *College English* 50: 477–94.

Emig, Janet. 1971. *The Composing Processes of Twelfth Graders.* NCTE Research Report no. 13. Urbana, Ill.: National Council of Teachers of English.

Hillocks, George. 1986. *Research on Written Composition: New Directions for Teaching.* Urbana, Ill.: National Council of Teachers of English.

Hirsch, E. D. 1984. " 'English' and the Perils of Formalism." *American Scholar* 53: 369–80.

———. 1987. *Cultural Literacy: What Every American Needs to Know.* Boston: Houghton Mifflin.

Lindberg, Gary. 1986. "Coming to Words: Writing as Process and the Reading of Literature." In *Only Connect: Uniting Reading and Writing,* ed. Thomas Newkirk. Portsmouth, N.H.: Boynton/Cook.

Murray, Donald M. 1982. "Teach Writing as a Process Not Product." In *Learning by Teaching: Selected Articles on Writing and Teaching.* Portsmouth, N.H.: Boynton/Cook.

Newkirk, Thomas. 1987. Review of *Research on Written Composition: New Directions for Teaching. Teachers College Record* 89: 155–57.

Squire, James, and Roger K. Applebee. 1968. *High School English Instruction Today.* New York: Appleton Crofts.

Thoreau, Henry David. [1854] 1983. *Walden and Civil Disobedience.* Harmondsworth, England: Penguin.

Prologue

1

Toward Righting Writing

Arthur Daigon
University of Connecticut
Storrs, Connecticut

THE bell rings and soon the class settles down, prepared for the writing that Teacher had warned them they would do during this period—and possibly the next. They know the procedure. Last time they compared two characters in a story. Before that they wrote about "An Important Event in My Life," and before that about "Why Marijuana Use Should or Should Not Be Legalized." They wait for today's topic to be written on the board. They wait too for the reminders about complete sentences, about introductory and concluding sentences, about clarity and coherence, about the need for examples and detail, about punctuation and capitalization, and about how an outline will make writing easier. The paper is distributed, and after some perfunctory attempts at outlining they begin to write.

Some thirty minutes later, Teacher suggests that they finish and check their papers for errors—misspelled words, an omitted title, paragraphs that need indenting, and so on. In the time remaining they may begin copying their final drafts, to be handed in tomorrow.

At the next class meeting, Teacher asks them for the assignment. For a variety of reasons, several students have been unable to finish their compositions, but they promise to turn them in, probably the next day. The others hand their completed assignments to Teacher, who expresses the hope that these papers will be better than those written two weeks ago. Teacher then suggests that the class open their grammar texts to the section on correct usage and continue the work interrupted by the composition.

At the end of the day, Teacher brings the papers home, and a few days later begins to grade them. Teacher makes sure that no error is left uncovered. Error-free papers receive higher grades than those with mistakes. Longer, more complex sentences and unusual vocabulary add to the likelihood of a better grade. After several hours every paper has been corrected and graded. Brief comments accompany the grade at the top of the paper. Sometimes major flaws are noted; sometimes a student is urged to try harder on the next composition. Occasionally, Teacher congratulates a student for an "excellent piece of work."

A week has passed and Teacher is ready to return the papers. Once again, the usage exercises are put aside, and Teacher tells the class about several students who misunderstood the assignment, about failure to go beyond generalizations, about lack of support for positions taken, about misspelled words, and about the frequency of run-on sentences.

Then Teacher asks several students to read their A-rated papers aloud. These papers will then be displayed on the bulletin board as models of good writing. No one is surprised. These students have read their papers to the class before. After the readings, Teacher returns the compositions, requesting that each correction be noted and each misspelled word be added to the Misspelled Word List kept in each student's notebook. Some students smile; some frown as they consider the grades and the comments on their papers. When the bell rings, they gather their books and move toward the door. Teacher counts four compositions wadded into balls and thrown into the wastebasket—three fewer than the last time.

In an earlier time, Teacher would be universally commended for a job well done and reassured that the students' failure to improve their writing was to be expected. Teaching composition is a burdensome and frustrating task, but a necessary one. After all, don't teachers need to assign topics? Don't they need to warn students about errors in usage, spelling, punctuation, and the rest? Don't they need to read, correct, and grade everything written by students? Isn't that what they were trained and hired to do? How else are students going to learn to write?

Over the past decade, answers to all of these questions—and more—have filled the pages of the professional journals and dominated the programs at English/language arts conferences. Everyone involved in English/language arts education has been scrambling to transform what research reveals to be the most promising ways to teach composition into workable classroom practices.

Research and the practice of successful writing teachers tell us that virtually every assumption and action of Teacher in the scene above prevents or retards growth in writing competence. From assigning the topic to returning the graded papers, Teacher contradicts what we have come to know about how writing happens—or should happen—in school and out.

Writing specialists agree that writing is an immensely complex process. To produce a successful composition, a writer must find out what to say about a subject and how to arrange the saying. A writer must adjust the subject and the saying to the purpose of the writing, to the intended audience, and to his or her own rhetorical stance toward all of these. A writer must accommodate the conventions of his or her chosen mode of composition and the linguistic etiquette expected of those who write English.

These discoveries, arrangements, and accommodations that produce good writing are achieved through the performance of an intricate and demanding ritual—a continuous cycle of exploration, rehearsal, drafting, and revision that leads to new exploration, rehearsal, drafting, and revision. Attention to the demands of the composing process and to what teachers and peers can do to make it work is at the center of a revolution in the way writing is perceived and taught. The traditional pedagogy of *select the topic, correct the error,* and *expect improvement* is still widely practiced. But—given the failures of the old writing regime, the ardor of the insurgents, and the success of the reforms they propose—not for long.

Nearly all reservations about Teacher's way of teaching and the alternatives to it derive from the work of composition researchers and teachers known by their peers as major contributors to our knowledge about writing. The research of James Britton, Janet Emig, Donald Graves, and Sondra Perl and the commentary of Stephen Tchudi, James Moffett, and Donald Murray are essential to understanding the composing process and its application in the public schools.

The Assignment

The bell rings and soon the class settles down, prepared for the writing that Teacher had warned them they would do during this period—and possibly the next. They know the procedure. Last time they compared two characters in a story. Before that they wrote about "An Important Event in My Life," and before that about "Why Marijuana Use Should or Should Not Be Legalized." They wait for today's topic to be written on the board.

Teacher's assignment comes out of the blue, disconnected from any earlier event that might justify writing. Today is composition day on Teacher's schedule, and that, rather than any experience—personal or public, real or fictional, pragmatic or expressive—determines what students will be doing that afternoon. No case is made to or solicited from students for the topics presented to the class. Occasionally and for a special reason, a teacher might justifiably assign a topic "cold," but most writing assignments should progress logically from some earlier engagement.

Whatever the earlier engagement, the assignment should indicate the purpose of the writing, the intended audience, and the stance of the writer. This applies to writing that emphasizes personal experience as well as to more objective exposition. Consider two examples: Having created a small community store, a class of second graders was asked to write to candy companies requesting stock—a writing situation that proceeds logically from an earlier event with clearly defined rhetorical circumstances. A twelfth-grade class was asked to assume the role of a minor character in *Hamlet* and in a letter to the king assess Hamlet's behavior and its likely consequences. Here again, the assignment springs from an earlier encounter—an encounter with a literary text—and the assignment defines the purpose, the audience, and the voice of the writer.

Prewriting

They wait too for the reminders about complete sentences, about introductory and concluding sentences, about clarity and coherence, about the need for examples and detail, about punctuation and capitalization, and about how an outline will make writing easier. The paper is distributed, and after some perfunctory attempts at outlining they begin to write.

Teacher's routine reminders about linguistic and structural lapses can only distract students from more urgent claims on their attention. They need to consider the requirements of the assignment, to recall relevant experiences, and to connect them with their understanding of the task. They must determine the voice or tone that best suits the audience and purposes and consider the framework that might best hold the composition together. Finally, they need to rehearse all of these elements, singly and in combination, for the inner director who can "listen," judge, and help reshape each possibility. Reluctance to begin the physical act of writing may well be the inner director's signal that more exploration, planning, and rehearsal are necessary.

The teacher can help by providing time and suggesting ways to activate these processes before the pen touches paper. Discussing the subject, brainstorming, exchanging parallel experiences, role playing, referring to similar or contrasting events in the media—all of these help to generate and shape substance, to clarify rhetorical circumstances, and to suggest structural possibilities. To determine what comes first and what follows rarely requires a formal outline—a prewriting device that discourages the composing process and is ignored by most successful writers.

All of this tentative invention and organization is subject to the changes demanded by the internal director during the countless rehearsals that take place from pre-writing up to the moment that the paper, finally completed, leaves the writer's hands. Only after the prewriting activities have done their work and after the changes demanded by the inner director have been made and rehearsed does a writer set down that first reluctant string of words. And these are but the beginning of a first draft.

The cognitive foreplay of prewriting is essential to the writing act. Teachers need to provide time for it in their composition classes.

Drafting

Some thirty minutes later, Teacher suggests that they finish and check their papers for errors—misspelled words, an omitted title, paragraphs that need indenting, and so on. In the time remaining they may begin copying their final drafts, to be handed in tomorrow.

Teacher's warnings about various linguistic oversights are ill-timed. No one would presume to interrupt a playwright and a director as they sketch performance strategies with the leading actors. Decisions about seating arrangements, background music in the second act, and the color of the leading lady's costume would be set aside for a later time.

In the same way, details better attended to later should not be allowed to stymie the performance of the first draft of a composition. To burden a writer struggling over issues of substance and form with violations of linguistic etiquette can only retard or block altogether the flow of language onto paper. To encourage this flow, many teachers recommend "free writing"—a technique in which a writer sets down the words, phrases, and sentences suggested by a topic in a continuous stream, uninterrupted by attention to mechanical or grammatical blunders. Because the mind is focused on retrieving ideas and feelings and converts them almost automatically into language, the stream of words can be maintained. Finding and correcting errors at this critical time would squander a writer's planning and decision-making resources. Spelling, punctuation, capitalization, appropriate usage, and complete sentences *are* important and must be attended to. But this can be done more efficiently in a later draft.

Teacher assumed that students needed only thirty minutes to discover and shape their compositions and a few more minutes to "check their papers." That left only the final copying to be done. Too frequently this produces only a neater version of a first draft, shorn of a few of the grosser errors.

To grasp the near impossibility of composing without frequent opportunities to draft, revise, and draft again, Teacher need only try the assignment along with the students. The experience should persuade Teacher to provide time for these essential elements of composing.

Revising

Except for a virtually useless suggestion to check for errors, Teacher had made no provision for revising—a process many writers consider the *real* task of writing. Just as a play director deals with weaknesses revealed during the first run-through of a play, so must a writer respond to a first draft. Some words and sentences do not work on paper as anticipated. The argument that seemed so clear-cut when first approved by the inner director appears ragged on the page. The tone seems not exactly right for the intended audience. The opening sentence is vague and wordy and will need reworking. A word or a phrase suggests another line of inquiry that ought to be pursued. The transition between the second and third paragraphs is flawed. Too many embedded relative clauses cloud the last section. A new and more convincing resolution of the argument needs to be invented.

Revision, not to be confused with proofreading, is the effort to reconcile the scheme provisionally approved by the inner director with what has materialized as the first draft. A writer may find that the first draft omits or distorts elements in the original plan and thus requires structural revision. On the other hand, there may be unanticipated strengths in the first draft that should be retained and elaborated, thus requiring changes in the original concept. During revision, both draft and concept are modified through a recurring, overlapping, fugue-like process called into play during earlier writing stages. Words, sentences, and paragraphs undergo continuous rehearsal and revision—the one process blending into and becoming indistinguishable from the other. Not only the draft, but the plan, the rhetorical relationships, and, most interesting of all, the writer's understanding of the subject undergo the process of rehearsal and revision. Frequently, writers change their minds as well as their texts.

All of this may seem to apply only to accomplished writers. Can students find what has to be modified in a draft? Can they make the changes that will add cogency and clarity to their writing? Are their inner directors capable of passing informed judgment on suggested rearrangements?

Because students are least experienced and comfortable with revision, they need more help with this than with other phases of the composing process. They are generally unfamiliar with matters of adding, cutting, and rearrangement and must be taught. A critical audience recruited from outside the classroom offers the strongest incentive to learn. In the traditional role of grader, however, the teacher has proved ineffectual. Suggestions written on papers completed the previous week exert little influence on how students handle revision problems that surface during the next composing performance.

To improve students' revision, teachers will have to change from graders looking for improvement next time to working editors responding to drafts in progress. In their new role teachers will collect drafts and—at home, on hall duty, or in class—will scribble reactions, questions, and suggestions about subjects and their treatment. They will take time in class to work on common problems found in several of the drafts. They will conduct brief conferences with individual students while others are redrafting or meeting in groups. At other times teachers will circulate, looking over shoulders, asking questions, recommending changes. Sometimes whole compositions or excerpts will be read aloud or flashed on a screen or written on the board to give students practice discussing specific writing problems and their solutions.

Yet, if teachers are to survive the demands of a workshop setting, they will have to enlist the aid of other surrogate inner directors who can help with revision. Groups of three or four students can provide useful feedback about whether a piece of writing is working, where its strengths and weaknesses lie, and what can be done to make it better. This is likely to happen when a teacher initially suggests specific questions to be asked or elements to be considered. It is likely to happen when students are encouraged to respond as the intended audience would. It is likely to happen when students see their teacher as an editor and learn to ask similar questions and recommend similar remedies.

As a piece of writing approaches completion, proofreading becomes more important. The teacher may give lessons on proofreading problems common to the class. Students may become specialists in spelling or punctuation or capitalization and put their skills at the disposal of the class. The composition/grammar text is now useful as students consult it for correct usages and formats. Students may meet in groups to monitor one another's papers and recommend still more redrafting.

As students gain confidence and ability to conduct rehearsals and recommend revisions in drafts written by their peers, these new directing skills can be applied to their own drafts as well. This signifies the birth of an informed inner director capable of listening and judging.

Publication

Then Teacher asks several students to read their A-rated papers aloud. These papers will then be displayed on the bulletin board as models of good writing. No one is surprised. These students have read their papers to the class before.

Publication provides an audience for writing; it transforms a required exercise into a purposeful activity and stiff, flat prose into lively discourse. Having an audience other than a grade-dispensing teacher can act as a powerful incentive to work hard at writing well.

For the few with A-rated papers, Teacher provided a captive audience of students. Teacher intended these papers to be taken as models of good writing. For the student audience, however, these papers only confirmed what they have come to believe are their own inadequacies. Teacher could have involved other students by publishing, if not whole compositions, at least successful paragraphs or even sentences.

In classes where students draft, revise, and draft again until the best possible paper emerges, the teacher posts papers on bulletin boards and collects them in booklets for circulation throughout the school and the community. In such classes, what students write about their school, their community, their country is made available to appropriate readers—the principal, the mayor, the manager of the television station, the newspaper editor, the local legislator. Book reports are aimed at and delivered to other classes. Invitations, catalog orders, tourist information, and consumer complaints are directed to appropriate readers. When writers write for a specific audience, they internalize that audience and consult it as they write. In effect, the writer's conception of an audience acts as a visiting inner director.

Publication need not depend entirely on real audiences. For example, students may write advice, criticism, and commentary to the people they meet in fairy tales, myths, short stories, and novels. Because such messages cannot be delivered to the intended audience, other students can assume an appropriate role and write logical replies. To do this, student writers need knowledge of a character's situation, and thus they must engage in a closer reading of the story.

This technique is a good way to connect writing to another part of the English/language arts curriculum.

Evaluation

Teacher brings the papers home, and a few days later begins to grade them. Teacher makes sure that no error is left uncorrected. Error-free papers receive higher grades than those with mistakes. Longer, more complex sentences and unusual vocabulary add to the likelihood of a better grade. After several hours every paper has been corrected and graded. Brief comments accompany the grade at the top of the paper. . . .

A week has passed, and Teacher is ready to return the papers. . . . Teacher tells the class about several students who misunderstood the assignment, about failure to go beyond generalizations, about lack of support for positions taken, about misspelled words, and about the frequency of run-on sentences. . . . Teacher returns the compositions, requesting that each correction be noted and each misspelled word be added to the Misspelled Word List kept in each student's notebook. Some students smile; some frown as they consider the grades and comments on their papers. When the bell rings, they gather their books and move toward the door. Teacher counts four compositions wadded into balls and thrown into the wastebasket—three fewer than the last time.

For Teacher, evaluation means correcting and tallying errors and assigning a grade. Although such practices have been shown to produce no noticeable improvement in subsequent writing, Teacher is committed to correcting and grading everything put on paper. Teacher views all writing performances as final performances whose flaws must be noted and reckoned in a grade.

Teacher's colleague, the football coach, expects blunders from his players. He knows that practice sessions will work out the problems and turn rookies into competent performers. He does not penalize players during practice sessions (nor, for that matter, during games). He supplies concrete suggestions about how to improve passing, running, or blocking skills and makes time to work out problems—alone and with the team. Teacher would do well to consider such a model of instruction and evaluation.

A grade is a crude device to apply to the complex phenomenon that is a composition. What does a grade tell a writer about his or her writing? About invention? Organization? A sense of audience? Coherence? Clarity? Tone? Syntactic fluency? Usage, mechanics, spelling, handwriting? Which are most important? Do we presume to judge all composition traits with one grade? Two? Do we assign a separate grade for each? Should a grade report "achievement" or "progress" in a student's writing? Does the grade report competence relative to other writers in the class, in the district, in the state? Or does it report "absolute" competence? How reliable are grades anyway?

These questions and the reservations they imply have convinced many who teach composition that grading drains their time and energies without contributing either to improved writing or to accurate assessment of writing performance. Despite this widespread disaffection with grading, composition teachers—under pressure from parents, students, and administrators—will undoubtedly continue to defuse the worst misunderstandings that inevitably plague those who grade and those who are graded by adopting these alternatives to conventional grading:

- Keep a folder of each student's writing—including drafts and revisions. Inside the folder students record the nature of the writing task, the dates it was undertaken and completed, and comments by peers and by you about weaknesses to be addressed, strengths to be maintained, and relapses suffered. Periodic review of the folder can focus on progress made and progress still needed, rather than on the pattern of letter grades.
- Meet with each student in a brief conference and focus on particular elements crucial to the success of an assignment. A checklist of such primary traits takes the place of a letter grade and becomes the occasion for revision.
- Midway through a semester and again at its end, allow students to choose two or three pieces of writing to be graded. Thus the grades will reflect the best the students can do. Encourage students to grade these papers and to compare their grades and how they were determined with yours and how you arrived at them.
- Try open-ended grading. Encourage students to revise and rewrite a composition and possibly earn a higher grade.

Epilogue

Teacher's light is still burning. The stack of compositions, begun nearly two hours earlier, is dwindling. Teacher's red pencil has found its quota of errors and oversights and has duly recorded the consequences in a black grade book. After the last author has been urged to try harder and a grade assigned, Teacher sits back, weary but pleased with a difficult job thoroughly done, and murmurs, "They'll probably do better next time."

Selected Bibliography

Britton, James, et al. 1975. *The Development of Writing Ability, 11–18.* London: Macmillan.

Emig, Janet. 1971. *The Composing Processes of Twelfth Graders.* NCTE Research Report no. 13. Urbana, Ill.: National Council of Teachers of English.

Graves, Donald. 1981. "A New Look at Research in Writing." In *Perspectives on Writing in Grades 1–8,* ed. Shirley Haley-James. Urbana, Ill.: National Council of Teachers of English.

Judy (Tchudi), Stephen. 1981. *Explorations in the Teaching of English.* New York: Harper & Row.

Moffett, James. 1968. *Teaching the Universe of Discourse.* Boston: Houghton Mifflin.

Moffett, James, and Betty Jane Wagner. 1976. *Student-Centered Language Arts and Reading, K–13.* Boston: Houghton Mifflin.

Murray, Donald M. 1968. *A Writer Teaches Writing.* Boston: Houghton Mifflin.

———. 1980. "Writing Process: How Writing Finds Its Own Meaning." In *Eight Approaches to Teaching Composition,* ed. Timothy R. Donovan and Ben W. McClelland. Urbana, Ill.: National Council of Teachers of English.

Perl, Sondra. 1979. "The Composing Processes of Unskilled College Writers." *Research in the Teaching of English* 13: 363–69.

Getting Started

2

A Way of Writing

William Stafford
Lake Oswego, Oregon

A writer is not so much someone who has something to say as he is someone who has found a process that will bring about new things he would not have thought of if he had not started to say them. That is, he does not draw on a reservoir; instead, he engages in an activity that brings to him a whole succession of unforeseen stories, poems, essays, plays, laws, philosophies, religions, or—but wait!

Back in school, from the first when I began to try to write things, I felt this richness. One thing would lead to another; the world would give and give. Now, after twenty years or so of trying, I live by that certain richness, an idea hard to pin, difficult to say, and perhaps offensive to some. For there are strange implications in it.

One implication is the importance of just plain receptivity. When I write, I like to have an interval before me when I am not likely to be interrupted. For me, this means usually the early morning, before others are awake. I get pen and paper, take a glance out the window (often it is dark out there), and wait. It is like fishing. But I do not wait very long, for there is always a nibble—and this is where receptivity comes in. To get started I will accept anything that occurs to me. Something always occurs, of course, to any of us. We can't keep from thinking. Maybe I have to settle for an immediate impression: it's cold, or hot, or dark, or bright, or in between! Or—well, the possibilities are endless. If I put down something, that thing will help the next thing come, and I'm off. If I let the process go on, things will occur to me that were not at all in my mind when I started. These things, odd or trivial as they may be, are somehow connected. And if I let them string out, surprising things will happen.

If I let them string out. . . . Along with initial receptivity, then, there is another readiness: I must be willing to fail. If I am to keep on writing, I cannot bother to insist on high standards. I must get into action and not let anything stop me, or even slow me much. By "standards" I do not mean "correctness"—spelling, punctuation, and so on. These details become mechanical for anyone who writes for a while. I am thinking about what many people would consider "important" standards, such matters as social significance, positive values, consistency, etc. I resolutely disregard these. Something better, greater, is happening! I am following a process that leads so wildly and originally into new territory that no judgment can at the moment be made about values, significance, and so on. I am making something new, something that has not been judged before. Later others—and maybe I myself—will make judgments. Now, I am headlong to discover. Any distraction may harm the creating.

So, receptive, careless of failure, I spin out things on the page. And a wonderful freedom comes. If something occurs to me, it is all right to accept it. It has one justification: it occurs to me. No one else can guide me. I must follow my own weak, wandering, diffident impulses.

A strange bonus happens. At times, without my insisting on it, my writings become coherent; the successive elements that occur to me are clearly related. They lead by themselves to new connections. Sometimes the language, even the syllables that happen along, may start a trend. Sometimes the materials alert me to something waiting in my mind, ready for sustained attention. At such times, I allow myself to be eloquent, or intentional, or for great swoops (treacherous! not to be trusted!) reasonable. But I do not insist on any of that, for I know that back of my activity there will be the coherence of my self, and that indulgence of my impulses will bring recurrent patterns and meanings again.

This attitude toward the process of writing creatively suggests a problem for me, in terms of what others say. They talk about "skills" in writing. Without denying that I do have experience, wide reading, automatic orthodoxies and maneuvers of various kinds, I still must insist that I am often baffled about what "skill" has to do with the precious little area of confusion when I do not know what I am going to say and then I find out what I am going to say. That precious interval I am unable to bridge by skill. What can I witness about it? It remains mysterious, just as all of us must feel puzzled about how we are so inventive as to be able to talk along through complexities with our friends, not needing to plan what we are going to say, but never stalled for long in our confident forward progress. Skill? If so, it is the skill we all have, something we must have learned before the age of three or four.

A writer is one who has become accustomed to trusting that grace, or luck, or—skill.

Yet another attitude I find necessary: most of what I write, like most of what I say in casual conversation, will not amount to much. Even I will realize, and even at the time, that it is not negotiable. It will be like practice. In conversation I allow myself random remarks—in fact, as I recall, that is the way I learned to talk—so in writing I launch many expendable efforts. A result of this free way of writing is that I am not writing for others, mostly; they will not see the product at all unless the activity eventuates in something that later appears to be worthy. My guide is the self, and its adventuring in the language brings about communication.

This process-rather-than-substance view of writing invites a final, dual reflection:

1. Writers may not be special—sensitive or talented in any usual sense. They are simply engaged in sustained use of a language skill we all have. Their "creations" come about through confident reliance on stray impulses that will, with trust, find occasional patterns that are satisfying.

2. But writing itself is one of the great, free human activities. There is scope for individuality, and elation, and discovery, in writing. For the person who follows with trust and forgiveness what occurs

to him, the world remains always ready and deep, an inexhaustible environment, with the combined vividness of an actuality and flexibility of a dream. Working back and forth between experience and thought, writers have more than space and time can offer. They have the whole unexplored realm of human vision.

3

A Conversation with Robert Cormier

Tom Romano
Formerly of Edgewood High School
Trenton, Ohio

All I had was this burning desire to be a writer and all these emotions.

ROBERT Cormier is a premier novelist whose work crosses the boundary between adult and young adult fiction. His novels include *The Chocolate War, Beyond the Chocolate War, After the First Death, I Am the Cheese,* and *The Bumblebee Flies Anyway.* His collection of short stories is titled *Eight Plus One.* His most recent novel is *Fade* (Delacorte/Dell), published in the United States and England in the fall of 1988.

For secondary school English teachers, Cormier's fiction can be an indispensable second teacher in the classroom. His main characters are usually teenage boys, and the worlds they inhabit are contemporary, tough, sometimes brutal, always unsentimental. The books prove to be an effective lure to literacy for many students who resist reading.

Robert Cormier also serves as a model for those seeking to learn effective writing techniques through their reading. His plots are tight, his characterizations complex, his outcomes uncompromising. And he accomplishes all this with language that is vivid, richly metaphorical, and finely crafted.

During a summer of teaching and writing at the University of New Hampshire, I contacted Robert Cormier at his home in nearby Leominster, Massachusetts. Our conversation occurred August 13, 1987, at his home, and then moved to one of his favorite restaurants, One Cottage Square, in Fitchburg.

Romano: Where did you get the idea for *Fade?*

Cormier: It's based on something that happened in my family that's intrigued me and, in fact, haunted me for years. On my father's side I'm French Canadian. My mother's side is Irish with some French there, too. Her maiden name is Collins. My father's family came to New England from Quebec in 1910. They were attracted by the mills. They had large families, and farms were drying up in Quebec. My grandfather and his wife had five sons and five daughters and decided to come to the states.

To commemorate the occasion he had a photographer come from town and take a portrait of the family. Everything went fine. About two weeks later the photographer brought the picture to them. It was perfect, except for one thing: one of my uncles didn't emerge in the photograph. He was missing. It wasn't a flaw in the film or a ray of light or a streak. It's like he was transparent. You could see the house behind him, the clapboards, but he just didn't emerge. This picture has attained a legendary status in the family. I haven't seen it for years. My aunts now are very old—in their nineties and late eighties—they remember it. My mother remembers it vaguely. "Yes, the picture of your uncle in which he didn't appear."

So I started writing. I began in 1938 with a thirteen-year-old boy, much like myself at that time. He's known about the photograph; he's always been curious about it. The uncle who hadn't appeared in the picture is a hobo. In the thirties a lot of men went on the road like that. They would try to get jobs or work at a farmhouse for food. It's almost a cliché of the Depression. So he's become a wanderer, although some people in the family call him a bum. Some thought he should be in the factories working. He comes back that summer, and the boy meets him. That's where the novel starts. Then it leaps a generation from 1938 to 1963, and then there's a further leap into the present. The bulk of it, however, takes place in 1938.

Romano: In the 1985 *Horn Book* interview with Anita Silvey you said that one of your limitations was dealing with setting and inanimate things. How was it recreating 1938?

Cormier: You still won't find a lot of scenery in my books. My biggest fear in writing is losing readers' attention. Inevitably, they're going to put the book down at some point, but I try to keep that reader, grab that lapel and hold on. That's why I don't like description. I not only find it hard to write, but I don't like to hold up the story to describe a building.

I use similes and metaphors as description. There's a scene in the book that takes place in a meadow where people go to have picnics. I wanted to show the length of the meadow. I wrote something to the effect that there are barns in the distance, and they look like ancient animals pausing to rest. I attempt to capture an emotional response of a boy to his surroundings, rather than the surroundings themselves.

Romano: Do you have to work at those similes and metaphors or do they just appear when you need them?

Cormier: Some of them I have to work at. I'll put down, "He looked at the buildings like . . . " and I'll leave it blank. But other times the similes and metaphors come to me immediately. The magic often happens at the typewriter. But there are times when you get that terrific idea as you're looking out the window or driving your car. A lot of those similes and metaphors just come out of nowhere. But some you have to manufacture. You sit there and think, "I want to describe this thing. What does it look like?" Often I try to put myself in a childlike state of mind. How would a kid, without any preconceptions, look at it? How would it look to a little child?

Romano: In the dedication of my book, I thanked my daughter because when she was a child, she taught me how to see. Through her metaphorical language she made me look at the world all over again.

Cormier: That's the magic of children, really, the way they look at things, the way they talk. My daughter never called it Howard Johnson. She always called it Orange Johnson.

Romano: Orange Johnson, sure.

Cormier: And it was never an umbrella: it was a . . .

Romano: Rainbrella!

Cormier: Right.

Romano: Years ago I was trying to learn to smoke a pipe. One evening my daughter said, "Papa, get your pipe and blow doughnuts."

Cormier: Smoke rings, doughnuts. That childlike approach, not childish, but childlike.

Romano: Your readers would say that you have the ability of entering the adolescent mind, too. How do you do that?

Cormier: We've had teenagers around for the last twenty years. My oldest daughter will be thirty-six this year. My son is thirty-three, and I have a daughter, thirty, and one, twenty. Not only our children were around, but also their friends and the phone calls and the agonies. Then I go out to schools and talk to kids, and every year I get letters by the hundreds. I get phone calls all the time. That's what keeps me in touch with young people. I don't have to make any daring leap when I write about them. Maybe I'm an arrested adolescent. I think we carry the baggage of our adolescence with us through our lives.

Romano: I've been trying to sort that baggage in the fiction I've written in Don Murray's class.

Cormier: You're writing a young adult novel?

Romano: I don't know what it's going to be.

Cormier: I'm glad to hear you say you're not sure if it's a young adult or not. That's when the best writing comes. When you try to follow a trend or a market or when you're too much aware of censorship, that can cut down the creativity. It can be the death of creativity. Follow your instincts. The writing can always be adjusted later.

Romano: How do you protect your time from interruptions so that you get the writing done?

Cormier: Right now I'm very loose because I just finished a manuscript. But when I'm into a book, I'm ruthless about my mornings. And the traveling and speaking engagements I try to control, too, although I find them good. If I'm here every day pounding on the typewriter, I can lose my perspective.

But I am very protective of my time when I'm in the throes of a book. When I was finishing *Fade,* this place was a fiction factory for a few weeks. The way I write—I don't outline—something would happen in the last stages of the book that affected something at the beginning. My wife, Connie, was typing the first part of the book to send to New York. I was in the other room working on the end of it.

Sometimes I think I disappoint people, because I write these tough books, and they meet me and see I'm not that tough person. Yet there's part of me that is ruthless.

Romano: That's Archie.

Cormier: Yes, you're all your characters. The part of me that's Archie is really ruthless about writing and discipline. It's got to be that way. When you're on your own like this—free-lancing—you've got to have a certain discipline. That's more important than talent sometimes. If you have a minimum of talent, but you sit at that typewriter long enough, something will emerge. All I had was this burning desire to be a writer and all these emotions.

Romano: When did you develop that burning desire to write? Did you have it in school?

Cormier: For the first eight grades, I was in a parochial school where we had English in the morning and French in the afternoon. In ninth grade I went into junior high. I had not read anything special, really, except comic books and pulp magazines. As far as exposure to books is concerned, we just didn't have it. There was nothing to bridge me between *Wings Magazine* and Thomas Wolfe.

Romano: When did you get to Wolfe?

Cormier: In junior high. Fourteen years old.

Romano: Did you read him through an assignment or on your own?

Cormier: On my own. I went to the library almost every day, and I was never happy with the children's books. The adventure stories never satisfied me. I went through them quickly. I couldn't wait to get into the adult section. In junior high they finally gave me an adult library card. I went wild.

I went into the new fiction section, and I saw *The Web and the Rock.* I read the flap copy and it said that this was the story of a man's hunger in his youth for fame and fortune, a small-town boy who wants to be a writer. "That's me!" I said. "Somebody else in the world feels this way." And I devoured it.

Romano: What were your writing experiences like in high school English classes?

Cormier: Not great. We had a general course, a commercial course, and a classical course. If you were going to college, you took the classical course. Coming out of St. Cecilia's, we were advised to take the commercial course. The nun said, "You kids can't afford to go to college."

There I was, very art oriented—I loved music, I loved reading—and I was taking shorthand and bookkeeping. As soon as I got to high school, it was obvious to everyone that I wanted to be a writer. The teacher who taught classical English volunteered to have me come into her class, which consisted of reading mostly, Elizabethan.

Romano: Did you write in this classical literature class?

Cormier: No writing. I never had any writing experience in my high school English classes that I remember, except for Miss Ricker. She taught English and directed plays. I never had her for a class, but she learned I wanted to be a writer and she worked with me.

Romano: You were writing on your own, then—out of school?

Cormier: Oh yes, out of school. I was sending in stories to magazines when I was fifteen or sixteen. Miss Ricker took my stuff home on weekends. After school we would get together and go over it. She used the old blue pencil. I had fallen in love with words and similes and metaphors. I was going wild with figures of speech. She showed me the dangers of similes and metaphors when they go askew. And she was ruthless. But I knew she did it with love and care, and I wanted that toughness.

There was a need in me to write. Every week the local paper gave us a page for high school news, and I wrote a column about sports. But instead of writing about the hero, I wrote about the odd and peculiar. The column was called "Behind the Scenes," something like that. I remember looking for a kid who never got in a game. I was always seeking the human side.

So even in high school I had that initiative. Then a marvelous thing happened. I went to Fitchburg State College. At the time it was a teachers' college. I didn't want to be a teacher. I wanted to learn. It was the tail end of the Depression. I was going to classes days, and at five o'clock I'd go to work in a plastics factory until nine.

But there I was, going to this teachers' college, and I knew instantly—after only three days—that this was not for me. All of a sudden I was thrown into calculus. I'd never even had algebra. After a year, I left and got a job on a newspaper. I've been writing ever since.

But I had an art teacher at Fitchburg who read one of my compositions. She said, "This is great. Are you interested in writing?" Naturally, I said yes. I went home and wrote a story at the kitchen table with pen and paper, brought it to her the next day. She said, "I love this. Mind if I keep it a while?"

Two months later, a Saturday afternoon, she came to my house with a $75 check. She'd had the story typed, sent it to a magazine, and sold it. My first story. So I owe my success to teachers—Miss Ricker, Miss Colley, who invited me into the classical English, and Miss Conlon who sold my first story. Think of it—I had a teacher as an editor in high school and a teacher as an agent in college. In the seventh grade, Sister Catherine started it all by telling me I was a writer.

Romano: That extra interest a teacher can give, that going beyond is so important. Don Graves believed I could write a book and told his editor. Without his little push I'd never have thought I could write a book about teaching.

Cormier: That sense of caring. You come into a school and you're shy and introverted. Then a teacher brings you out. That's why I owe a debt to teachers.

Romano: You said you liked the toughness that Miss Ricker gave you when she worked with you after school. Can you tell me more about that?

Cormier: What I want is the truth about my writing, even if it hurts. That's why there's part of me that doesn't go along with manuscript reading by friends. They're going to be kind. If they say, "I like that," it's of no use to me. In my newspaper work,

I was being edited every day by editors who were ruthless. I have become accustomed to it.

Romano: Is there a time when you can't take that toughness? Does your manuscript have to be along to a certain point?

Cormier: I don't show the manuscripts to anybody until they're done. Right now the manuscript of *Fade* is in New York. I think it's too long. I'd like to cut it. The first thing I do is say to the editors, "Could you give me some suggestions about cutting this? Is there any place where you think I indulge myself?" I've had my fun, I want suggestions, but I don't want to destroy the integrity of what I've done. I like a nice, tight book. I want to make the best book possible for the reader. I let the editors know I'm open to anything. Some suggestions I reject; some really open my eyes. And some things they suggest I'm horrified at—I wouldn't touch for all the money in the world.

Romano: If you really resist something . . .

Cormier: You see, you're the boss. That's why it's good. Why not ask for these suggestions, as long as you can refuse them? But you can't indulge yourself. You might love a certain chapter, but it doesn't advance the plot. You can say, "I love this chapter. It's going in no matter what." But you have to think of the book and the reader. So you take the chapter out, even though it breaks your heart.

There's a danger, too, of leaving out too much, of being too ruthless, becoming a minimalist. But I love rewriting. I could tinker with a book forever. Somebody sent me a cartoon that I put above my typewriter. It shows a guy writing down in his cellar. He's got all these pages piled up. His wife is at the top of the stairs, and he's looking up at her. He says, "What do you mean, 'Finish it'?"

I could tinker with the writing forever. But then it reaches the point where you have to let go. *Fade* was 490 pages, and I have a supermarket shopping bag full of pages I rewrote three, four, five times.

Romano: How did you learn to be tough on yourself, to cut your writing to the bone?

Cormier: I think through the years of being edited in newspapers. The editor cuts your story. You think he's spoiled it, then you meet a guy on the street who says, "I loved that story." You realize that the reader doesn't see what you left out.

Romano: When were you able to quit your newspaper job and devote full time to writing?

Cormier: After I started the book that became *After the First Death,* I was having a hell of a time with it because I was given more responsibilities at work. I was an associate editor. On a small paper you're doing a dozen jobs. I was trying to write at night, and my energies were diminishing. If I could have six months, I thought I could finish the novel. So I asked for a leave of absence. They were very nice about it.

They said, "Bob, we're a small paper. Everybody does so many things here. How can we let anyone go for six months and keep the job open?" They also said, "You have four weeks' vacation now. We'll give you an extra two, and if you take two without pay, that will be eight weeks. How's that?"

I said, "I don't want eight weeks. I need six months." And I told them to forget it. I went home and told Connie the situation.

She said these magic words: "Why don't you quit? You're giving your energies to the paper. All your potential is in your writings."

Romano: That's real faith in you.

Cormier: Yes. I said, "But I'm a Depression baby. You don't cut the umbilical cord to the weekly paycheck. We have kids going to college."

"Listen," she said, "it will work out." She was a secretary at the telephone company.

So I quit the job. Never looked back. The irony is that I finished *After the First Death* in six months, and it had a great sale.

Romano: In 1983 when you visited Ohio, I told you that you saved three or four boys every year for me. I give them *The Chocolate War,* and suddenly they have a book they really like.

Cormier: It's thrilling. You may have opened the door to other books for them. I get letters once in a while from kids reading *The Chocolate War.* They say, "This is the first book I ever finished."

Romano: When had you published your last novel before *The Chocolate War* came out in 1974?

Cormier: 1965. I had written two novels in the late sixties and early seventies that were rejected. I wrote a civil rights novel in the sixties. I wondered what might have occurred if civil rights activity happened in a small New England town. But the material was outdated by the time I finished it. Then I wrote a novel with a religious theme that was also rejected.

Romano: You kept great faith in yourself. After civil rights and religion, how did you get to *The Chocolate War?*

Cormier: My son was in school and he came home with two shopping bags of chocolate to sell. He decided not to sell them. The emotions involved in that situation propelled me to write *The Chocolate War.* I knew nothing about the YA novel, didn't even know the genre existed. And as I was writing, I thought, "Who's going to ever read this? Who cares about a bunch of high school kids selling chocolates?" But, you know, it felt right to me, it felt good. When the book was finished, I still thought nobody would want to read it. *The Chocolate War* was rejected by four publishers who wanted me to change the ending, to have Jerry win. Jerry couldn't win.

Romano: There's no way he could win.

Cormier: That's what I told them. One day the phone rang around supper time. My agent, Marilyn Marlow, said, "There's a publisher who loves *The Chocolate War.* She's ready to give you a $5,000 advance, promotion, advertising. But she wants you to change the ending so Jerry wins."

I told Marilyn I couldn't do that, because I would have to rewrite the book. We turned it down. That happened four times. I wasn't being heroic, because Marilyn had faith that it would sell eventually. It went through four major publishers, promising all kinds of things. But we stuck to our guns, and finally Fabio Coen at Pantheon/Random House accepted it with no changes.

Romano: In the *Horn Book* interview you talked about how kids wanted a sequel to *The Chocolate War.*

Cormier: They badgered me. That's why I wrote *Beyond the Chocolate War.*

Romano: And that book leaves many doors open. The next year at Trinity with Janza, the thug, in a position to manipulate the inexperienced Bunting, there will be corruption without any restraints.

Cormier: I know. That next year is going to be chaos. I don't know if I'll do anything more with the material. I thought I'd closed the doors, but I guess they were left open. If I ever did anything more, I think I would probably go ten years into the future, then use a flashback to that year, following the events of *The Chocolate War.*

Romano: You've said that *The Catcher in the Rye* is on your list of best books.

Cormier: One of the landmark books. I was wondering how it strikes people today.

Romano: It still works with teenagers. They get caught up in that voice.

Cormier: Voice is so important. You know, it's funny. I don't mind reading first person, but I don't like to write in first person. I find it too limiting. Yet this book I just finished is in first person. Form must follow function. The material cried out for first person, kept shouting at me, "This is it. This is it." So I did it.

I Am the Cheese was written in first person. The bike ride was first person, present tense, in fact. But that's all right. You have to follow the voice, the inclination. I felt it was right for the material in *Fade.* But then, toward the end of the book, I switched to third person for a certain character.

"Wait a minute," I thought. "I have this whole thing in first person. Suddenly I'm switching." But the switch felt right. That's what I mean by instinct. It broke the rules, but you often break the rules on purpose for dramatic effect.

My second novel, *Little Raw Monday Mornings,* was from the viewpoint of a thirty-eight-year-old woman who is pregnant, a widow.

Romano: Was that hard to do, getting inside her mind?

Cormier: Living with a woman, having daughters, I wasn't even aware of what I was doing until suddenly I realized I had thirty thousand words from a woman's viewpoint. I think we are everything. We're both men and women.

Romano: That Walt Whitman thing. Androgyny.

Cormier: Yes. I suppose there are some people strongly male, but I think the purpose of writing is to be everything.

Romano: I noticed that you work on a typewriter.

Cormier: An old Royal.

Romano: You never gave in to a word processor?

Cormier: Eight thousand people have tried to convert me. At this stage, with Connie typing my stuff, I can get on my green machine and roll.

There has to be a certain amount of obsession in this lifestyle. Writing every day. You don't know whether what you write will be accepted or not. I remember having a novel returned to me years ago after going to fourteen publishers. I was working full time at a newspaper. The day the manuscript came back, that night, I went to the typewriter, writing after supper.

Connie came into the room and said, "What are you doing?"

I said, "I'm writing."

She said, "Your novel just came back today. You spent two and a half years on it, and you're writing tonight?"

"That's what I do," I said.

It has nothing to do with acceptance or rejection. You write.

Acknowledgments

The author wishes to thank Donald Murray for his encouragement, The Poynter Institute for Media Studies in St. Petersburg, Florida, for its financial support, and Robert Cormier for his generosity and patient teaching.

4

Write Before Writing

Donald Murray
University of New Hampshire, Emeritus
Durham, New Hampshire

WE command our students to write and grow frustrated when our "bad" students hesitate, stare out the window, dawdle over blank paper, give up and say, "I can't write," while the "good" students smugly pass their papers in before the end of the period.

When publishing writers visit such classrooms, however, they are astonished at students who can write on command, ejaculating correct little essays without thought, for writers have to write before writing.

The writers were the students who dawdled, stared out windows, and, more often than we like to admit, didn't do well in English—or in school.

One reason may be that few teachers have ever allowed adequate time for prewriting, that essential stage in the writing process which precedes a completed first draft. And even the curricula plans and textbooks which attempt to deal with prewriting usually pass over it rather quickly referring only to the techniques of outlining, note taking, or journal making, not revealing the complicated process writers work through to get to the first draft.

Writing teachers, however, should give careful attention to what happens between the moment the writer receives an idea or an assignment and the moment the first completed draft is begun.

We need to understand, as well as we can, the complicated and intertwining processes of perception and conception through language.

In actual practice, of course, these stages overlap and interact with one another, but to understand what goes on we must separate them and look at them artificially, the way we break down any skill to study it.

First of all, we must get out of the stands where we observe the process of writing from a distance—and after the fact—and get on the field where we can understand the pressures under which the writer operates. On the field, we will discover there is one principal negative force which keeps the writer from writing and four positive forces which help the writer move forward to a completed draft.

Resistance to Writing

The negative force is *resistance* to writing, one of the great natural forces of nature. It may be called The Law of Delay: that writing which can be delayed, will be. Teachers and writers too often consider resistance to writing evil, when, in fact, it is necessary.

When I get an idea for a poem or an article or a talk or a short story, I feel myself consciously draw away from it. I seek procrastination and delay. There must be time for the seed of the idea to be nurtured in the mind. Far better writers than I have felt the same way. Over his writing desk Franz Kafka had one word, "Wait." William Wordsworth talked of the writer's "wise passiveness." Naturalist Annie Dillard recently said, "I'm waiting. I usually get my ideas in November, and I start writing in January. I'm waiting." Denise Levertov says, "If . . . somewhere in the vicinity there is a poem, then, no, I don't do anything about it, I wait."

Even the most productive writers are expert dawdlers, doers of unnecessary errands, seekers of interruptions—trials to their wives or husbands, friends, associates, and themselves. They sharpen well-pointed pencils and go out to buy more blank paper, rearrange offices, wander through libraries and bookstores, chop wood, walk, drive, make unnecessary calls, nap, daydream, and try not "consciously" to think about what they are going to write so they can think subconsciously about it.

Writers fear this delay, for they can name colleagues who have made a career of delay, whose great unwritten books will never be written, but, somehow, those writers who write must have the faith to sustain themselves through the necessity of delay.

Forces for Writing

In addition to that faith, writers feel four pressures that move them forward towards the first draft.

The first is *increasing information* about the subject. Once a writer decides on a subject or accepts an assignment, information about the subject seems to attach itself to the writer. The writer's perception apparatus finds significance in what the writer observes or overhears or reads or thinks or remembers. The writer becomes a magnet for specific details, insights, anecdotes, statistics, connecting thoughts, references. The subject itself seems to take hold of the writer's experience, turning everything that happens to the writer into material. And this inventory of information creates pressure that moves the writer forward toward the first draft.

Usually the writer feels an *increasing concern* for the subject. The more a writer knows about the subject, the more the writer begins to feel about the subject. The writer cares that the subject be ordered and shared. The concern, which at first is a vague interest in the writer's mind, often becomes an obsession until it is communicated. Winston Churchill said, "Writing a book was an adventure. To begin with, it was a toy and amusement; then it became a mistress, and then a master. And then a tyrant."

The writer becomes aware of a *waiting audience,* potential readers who want or need to know what the writer has to say. Writing is an act of arrogance and communication. The writer rarely writes just for himself or herself, but for others who may be informed, entertained, or persuaded by what the writer has to say.

And perhaps most important of all, is the *approaching deadline,* which moves closer day by day at a terrifying and accelerating rate. Few writers publish without deadlines, which are imposed by others or by themselves. The deadline is real, absolute, stern, and commanding.

Rehearsal for Writing

What the writer does under the pressure not to write and the four countervailing pressures to write is best described by the word *rehearsal,* which I first heard used by Donald Graves of the University of New Hampshire to describe what he saw young children doing as they began to write. He watched them draw what they would write and heard them, as we all have, speaking aloud what they might say on the page before they wrote. If you walk through editorial offices or a newspaper cityroom you will see lips moving and hear expert professionals muttering and whispering to themselves as they write. Rehearsal is a normal part of the writing process, but it took a trained observer to identify its significance.

Rehearsal covers much more than the muttering of struggling writers. As Graves points out, productive writers are "in a state of rehearsal all the time." Rehearsal usually begins with an unwritten dialogue within the writer's mind. "All of a sudden I discover what I have been thinking about a play," says Edward Albee. "This is usually between six months and a year before I actually sit down and begin typing it out." The writer thinks about characters or arguments, about plot or structure, about words and lines. The writer usually hears something which is similar to what Wallace Stevens must have heard as he walked through his insurance office working out poems in his head.

What the writer hears in his or her head usually evolves into note taking. This may be simple brainstorming, the jotting down of random bits of information which may connect themselves into a pattern later on, or it may be journal writing, a written dialogue between the writer and the subject. It may even become research recorded in a formal structure or note-taking.

Sometimes the writer not only talks to himself or herself, but to others—collaborators, editors, teachers, friends—working out the piece of writing in oral language with someone else who can enter into the process of discovery with the writer.

For most writers, the informal notes turn into lists, outlines, titles, leads, ordered fragments, all sketches of what later may be written, devices to catch a possible order that exists in the chaos of the subject.

In the final stage of rehearsal, the writer produces test drafts, written or unwritten. Sometimes they are called discovery drafts or trial runs or false starts that the writer doesn't think will be false. All writing is experimental, and the writer must come to the point where drafts are attempted in the writer's head and on paper.

Some writers seem to work more in their head, and others more on paper. Susan Sowers, a researcher at the University of New Hampshire, examining the writing processes of a group of graduate students found

> a division . . . between those who make most discoveries during prewriting and those who make most discoveries during writing and revision. The discoveries include the whole range from insights into personal issues to task-related organizational and content insight. The earlier the stage at which insights occur, the greater the drudgery associated with the writing-rewriting tasks. It may be that we resemble the young reflective and reactive writers. The less developmentally mature reactive writers enjoy writing more than reflective writers. They may use writing as a rehearsal for thinking just as young, reactive writers draw to rehearse writing. The younger and older reflective writers do not need to rehearse by drawing to write or by writing to think clearly or to discover new relationships and significant content.

This concept deserves more investigation. We need to know about both the reflective and reactive prewriting mode. We need to see if there are developmental changes in students, if they move from one mode to another as they mature, and we need to see if one mode is more important in certain writing tasks than others. We must, in every way possible, explore the significant writing stage of rehearsal, which has rarely been described in the literature on the writing process.

The Signals Which Say "Write"

During the rehearsal process, the experienced writer sees signals which tell the writer how to control the subject and produce a working first draft. The writer, Rebecca Rule, points out that in some cases when the subject is found, the way to deal with it is inherent in the subject. The subject itself is the signal. Most writers have experienced this quick passing through of the prewriting process. The line is given and the poem is clear; a character gets up and walks the writer through the story; the newspaperman attends a press conference, hears a quote, sees the lead and the entire structure of the article instantly. But many times the process is far less clear. The writer is assigned a subject or chooses one and then is lost.

E. B. White testifies, "I never knew in the morning how the day was going to develop. I was like a hunter hoping to catch sight of a rabbit." Denise Levertov says, "You can smell the poem before you see it." Most writers know these feelings but students who have never seen a rabbit dart across their writing desks or smelled a poem need to know the signals which tell them that a piece of writing is near.

What does the writer recognize which gives a sense of closure, a way of handling a diffuse and overwhelming subject? There seem to be eight principal signals to which writers respond.

One signal is *genre.* Most writers view the world as a fiction writer, a reporter, a poet, or an historian. The writer sees experience as a plot or a lyric poem or a news story or a chronicle. The writer uses such literary traditions to see and understand life.

"Ideas come to a writer because he has trained his mind to seek them out," says Brian Garfield. "Thus when he observes or reads or is exposed to a character or event, his mind sees the story possibilities in it and he begins to compose a dramatic structure in his mind. This process is incessant. Now and then it leads to something that will become a novel. But it's mainly an attitude: a way of looking at things; a habit of examining everything one perceives as potential material for a story."

Genre is a powerful but dangerous lens. It both clarifies and limits. The writer and the student must be careful not to see life merely in the stereotype form with which he or she is most familiar but to look at life with all of the possibilities of the genre in mind and to attempt to look at life through different genres.

Another signal the writer looks for is a *point of view.* This can be an opinion towards the subject or a position from which the writer—and the reader—studies the subject.

A tenement fire could inspire the writer to speak out against tenements, a dangerous space-heating system, a fire-department budget cut. The fire might also be seen from the point of view of the people who were the victims or who escaped or who came home to find their home gone. It may be told from the point of view of a fireman, an arsonist, an insurance investigator, a fire-safety engineer, a real-estate planner, a housing inspector, a landlord, a spectator, as well as the victim. The list could go on.

Still another way the writer sees the subject is through *voice.* As the writer rehearses, in the writer's head and on paper, the writer listens to the sound of the language as a clue to the meaning of the subject and the writer's attitude toward that meaning. Voice is often the force which drives a piece of writing forward, which illuminates the subject for the writer and the reader.

A writer may, for example, start to write a test draft with detached unconcern and find that the language appearing on the page reveals anger or passionate concern. The writer who starts to write a solemn report of a meeting may hear a smile and then a laugh in his own words and go on to produce a humorous column.

News is an important signal for many writers who ask what the reader needs to know or would like to know. Those prolific authors of nature books, Lorus and Margery Milne, organize their books and each chapter in the books around what is new in the field. Between assignment and draft they are constantly looking for the latest news they can pass along to their readers. When they find what is new, then they know how to organize their writing.

Writers constantly wait for the *line* which is given. For most writers, there is an enormous difference between a thesis or an idea or a concept and an actual line, for the line itself has resonance. A single line can imply a voice, a tone, a pace, a whole way of treating a subject. Joseph Heller tells about the signal which produced his novel *Something Happened:*

> I begin with a first sentence that is independent of any conscious preparation. Most often nothing comes out of it: a sentence will come to mind that doesn't lead to a second sentence. Sometimes it will lead to thirty sentences which then come to a dead end. I was alone on the deck. As I sat there worrying and wondering what to do, one of those first lines suddenly came to mind: "In the office in which I work, there are four people of whom I am afraid. Each of these four people is afraid of five people." Immediately, the lines presented a whole explosion of possibilities and choices—characters (working in a corporation), a tone, a mood of anxiety, or of insecurity. In that first hour (before someone came along and asked me to go to the beach) I knew the beginning, the ending, most of the middle, the whole scene of

> that particular "something" that was going to happen; I knew about the brain-damaged child, and especially, of course, about Bob Slocum, my protagonist, and what frightened him, that he wanted to be liked, that his immediate hope was to be allowed to make a three-minute speech at the company convention. Many of the actual lines throughout the book came to me—the entire "something happened" scene with those solar plexus lines (beginning with the doctor's statement and ending with "Don't tell my wife" and the rest of them) all coming to me in the first hour on that Fire Island deck. Eventually I found a different opening chapter with a different first line ("I get the willies when I see closed doors") but I kept the original which had spurred everything to start off the second section.

Newspapermen are able to write quickly and effectively under pressure because they become skillful at identifying a lead, that first line—or two or three—which will inform and entice the reader and which, of course, also gives the writer control over the subject. As an editorial writer, I found that finding the title first gave me control over the subject. Each title became, in effect, a pre-draft, so that in listing potential titles I would come to one which would be a signal as to how the whole editorial could be written.

Poets and fiction writers often receive their signals in terms of an *image.* Sometimes this image is static; other times it is a moving picture in the writer's mind. When Gabriel García Márquez was asked what the starting point of his novels was, he answered, "A completely visual image . . . the starting point of *Leaf Storm* is an old man taking his grandson to a funeral, in *No One Writes to the Colonel,* it's an old man waiting, and in *One Hundred Years,* an old man taking his grandson to the fair to find out what ice is." William Faulkner was quoted as saying, "It begins with a character, usually, and once he stands up on his feet and begins to move, all I do is trot along behind him with a paper and pencil trying to keep up long enough to put down what he says and does." It's a comment which seems facetious—if you're not a fiction writer. Joyce Carol Oates adds, "I visualize the characters completely; I have heard their dialogue, I know how they speak, what they want, who they are, nearly everything about them."

Although image has been testified to mostly by imaginative writers, where it is obviously most appropriate, I think research would show that nonfiction writers often see an image as the signal. The person, for example, writing a memo about a manufacturing procedure may see the assembly line in his or her mind. The politician arguing for a pension law may see a person robbed of a pension, and by seeing that person know how to organize a speech or the draft or a new law.

Many writers know they are ready to write when they see a *pattern* in a subject. This pattern is usually quite different from what we think of as an outline, which is linear and goes from beginning to end. Usually the writer sees something which might be called a gestalt, which is, in the world of the dictionary, "a unified physical, psychological, or symbolic configuration having properties that cannot be derived from its parts." The writer usually in a moment sees the entire piece of writing as a shape, a form, something that is more than all of its parts, something that is entire and is represented in his or her mind, and probably on paper, by a shape.

Marge Piercy says, "I think that the beginning of fiction, of the story, has to do with the perception of pattern in event." Leonard Gardner, in talking of his fine novel *Fat City*, said ,"I had a definite design in mind. I had a sense of circle . . . of closing the circle at the end." John Updike says, "I really begin with some kind of solid, coherent image, some notion of the shape of the book and even of its texture. *The Poorhouse Fair* was meant to have a sort of wide shape. *Rabbit, Run* was kind of zigzag. *The Centaur* was sort of a sandwich."

We have interviews with imaginative writers about the writing process, but rarely interviews with science writers, business writers, political writers, journalists, ghost writers, legal writers, medical writers—examples of effective writers who use language to inform and persuade. I am convinced that such research would reveal that they also see patterns or gestalts which carry them from idea to draft.

"It's not the answer that enlightens but the question," says Ionesco. This insight into what the writer is looking for is one of the most significant considerations in trying to understand the free-writing process. A most significant book based on more than ten years of study of art students, *The Creative Vision, A Longitudinal Study of Problem-Finding in Art,* by Jacob W. Getzels and Mihaly Csikszentmihalyi, has documented how the most creative students are those who come up with the *problem* to be solved rather than a quick answer. The signal to the creative person may well be the problem, which will be solved through the writing.

We need to take all the concepts of invention from classical rhetoric and combine them with what we know from modern psychology, from studies of creativity, from writers' testimony about the prewriting process. Most of all, we need to observe successful students and writers during the prewriting process, and to debrief them to find out what they do when they move effectively from assignment or idea to completed first draft. Most of all, we need to move from failure-centered research to research which defines what happens when the writing goes well, just what is the process followed by effective student and professional writers. We know far too little about the writing process.

Implications for Teaching Writing

Our speculations make it clear that there are significant implications for the teaching of writing in a close examination of what happens between receiving an assignment or finding a subject and beginning a completed first draft. We may need, for example, to reconsider our attitude toward those who delay writing. We may, in fact, need to force many of our glib, hair-trigger student writers to slow down, to daydream, to waste time, but not to avoid a reasonable deadline.

We certainly should allow time within the curriculum for prewriting, and we should work with our students to help them understand the process of rehearsal, to allow them the experience of rehearsing what they will write in their minds, on the paper, and with collaborators.

We should also make our students familiar with the signals they may see during the rehearsal process which will tell them that they are ready to write, that they have a way of dealing with their subject.

The prewriting process is largely invisible; it takes place within the writer's head or on scraps of paper that are rarely published. But we must understand that such a process takes place, that it is significant, and that it can be made clear to our students. Students who are not writing, or not writing well, may have a second chance if they are able to experience the writers' counsel to write before writing.

5

Understanding Composing

Sondra Perl
Herbert Lehman College
City University of New York
New York, New York

Any psychological process, whether the development of thought or voluntary behavior, is a process undergoing changes right before one's eyes. . . . Under certain conditions it becomes possible to trace this development.

L. S. Vygotsky

It's hard to begin this case study of myself as a writer because even as I'm searching for a beginning, a pattern of organization, I'm watching myself, trying to understand my behavior. As I sit here in silence, I can see lots of things happening that never made it onto my tapes. My mind leaps from the task at hand to what I need at the vegetable stand for tonight's soup to the threatening rain outside to ideas voiced in my writing group this morning, but in between "distractions" I hear myself trying out words I might use. It's as if the extraneous thoughts are a counterpoint to the more steady attention I'm giving to composing. This is all to point out that the process is more complex than I'm aware of, but I think my tapes reveal certain basic patterns that I tend to follow.

Anne
New York City Teacher

ANNE is a teacher of writing. In 1979, she was among a group of twenty teachers who were taking a course in research and basic writing at New York University.* One of the assignments in the course was for the teachers to tape their thoughts while composing aloud on the topic, "My Most Anxious Moment as a Writer." Everyone in the group was given the topic in the morning during class and told to compose later on that day in a place where they would be comfortable and relatively free from distractions. The result was a tape of composing aloud and a written product that formed the basis for class discussion over the next few days.

One of the purposes of this assignment was to provide teachers with an opportunity to see their own composing processes at work. From the start of the course, we recognized that we were controlling the situation by assigning a topic and that we might be altering the process by asking writers to compose aloud. Nonetheless we viewed the task as a way of capturing some of the flow of composing and, as Anne later observed in her analysis of her tape, she was able to detect certain basic patterns. This observation, made not only by Anne, then leads me to ask "What basic patterns seem to occur during composing?" and "What does this type of research have to tell us about the nature of the composing process?"

Perhaps the most challenging part of the answer is the recognition of recursiveness in writing. In recent years, many researchers including myself have questioned the traditional notion that writing is a linear process with a strict plan-write-revise sequence (see Emig 1971; Flower and Hayes 1980; and Sommers 1979). In its stead, we have advocated the idea that writing is a recursive process, that throughout the process of writing, writers return to substrands of the overall process, or subroutines (short successions of steps that yield results on which the writer draws in taking the next set of steps); writers use these to keep the process moving forward. In other words, recursiveness in writing implies that there is a forward-moving action that exists by virtue of a backward-moving action. The questions that then need to be answered are, "To what do writers move back?" "What exactly is being repeated?" "What recurs?"

*This course was team-taught by myself and Gordon Pradl, Associate Professor of English Education at New York University.

To answer these questions, it is important to look at what writers do while writing and what an analysis of their processes reveals. The descriptions that follow are based on my own observations of the composing processes of many types of writers including college students, graduate students, and English teachers like Anne.

Writing does appear to be recursive, yet the parts that recur seem to vary from writer to writer and from topic to topic. Furthermore, some recursive elements are easy to spot while others are not.

1. The most visible recurring feature or backward movement involves rereading little bits of discourse. Few writers I have seen write for long periods of time without returning briefly to what is already down on the page.

For some, like Anne, rereading occurs after every few phrases; for others, it occurs after every sentence; more frequently, it occurs after a "chunk" of information has been written. Thus, the unit that is reread is not necessarily a syntactic one, but rather a semantic one as defined by the writer.

2. The second recurring feature is some key word or item called up by the topic. Writers consistently return to their notion of the topic throughout the process of writing. Particularly when they are stuck, writers seem to use the topic or a key word in it as a way to get going again. Thus many times it is possible to see writers "going back," rereading the topic they were given, changing it to suit what they have been writing or changing what they have written to suit their notion of the topic.

3. There is also a third backward movement in writing, one that is not so easy to document. It is not easy because the move itself cannot immediately be identified with words. In fact, the move is not to any words on the page nor to the topic but to feelings or nonverbalized perceptions that *surround* the words, or to what the words already present *evoke* in the writer. The move draws on sense experience, and it can be observed if one pays close attention to what happens when writers pause and seem to listen or otherwise react to what is inside of them. The move occurs inside the writer, to what is physically felt. The term used to describe this focus of writers' attention is *felt sense.* The term "felt sense" has been coined and described by Eugene Gendlin, a philosopher at the University of Chicago. In his words, felt sense is

> the soft underbelly of thought . . . a kind of bodily awareness that . . . can be used as a tool . . . a bodily awareness that . . . encompasses everything you feel and know about a given subject at a given time. . . . It is felt in the body, yet it has meanings. It is body *and* mind before they are split apart.

This felt sense is always there, within us. It is unifying, and yet, when we bring words to it, it can break apart, shift, unravel, and become something else. Gendlin has spent many years showing people how to work with their felt sense. Here I am making connections between what he has done and what I have seen happen as people write.

When writers are given a topic, the topic itself evokes a felt sense in them. This topic calls forth images, words, ideas, and vague fuzzy feelings that are anchored in the writer's body. What is elicited, then, is not solely the product of a mind but of a mind alive in a living, sensing body.

When writers pause, when they go back and repeat key words, what they seem to be doing is waiting, paying attention to what is still vague and unclear. They are looking to their felt experience, and waiting for an image, a word, or a phrase to emerge that captures the sense they embody.

Usually, when they make the decision to write, it is after they have a dawning awareness that something has clicked, that they have enough of a sense that if they begin with a few words heading in a certain direction, words will continue to come which will allow them to flesh out the sense they have.

The process of using what is sensed directly about a topic is a natural one. Many writers do it without any conscious awareness that that is what they are doing. For example, Anne repeats the words "anxious moments," using these key words as a way of allowing her sense of the topic to deepen. She asks herself, "Why are exams so anxiety provoking?" and waits until she has enough of a sense within her that she can go in a certain direction. She does not yet have the words, only the sense that she is able to begin. Once she writes, she stops to see what is there. She maintains a highly recursive composing style throughout and she seems unable to go forward without first going back to see and to listen to what she has already created. In her own words, she says:

> My disjointed style of composing is very striking to me. I almost never move from the writing of one sentence directly to the next. After each sentence I pause to read what I've written, assess, sometimes edit and think about what will come next. I often have to read the several preceding sentences a few times as if to gain momentum to carry me to the next sentence. I seem to depend a lot on the sound of my words and . . . while I'm hanging in the middle of this uncompleted thought, I may also start editing a previous sentence or get an inspiration for something which I want to include later in the paper.

What tells Anne that she is ready to write? What is the feeling of "momentum" like for her? What is she hearing as she listens to the "sound" of her words? When she experiences "inspiration," how does she recognize it?

In the approach I am presenting, the ability to recognize what one needs to do or where one needs to go is informed by calling on felt sense. This is the internal criterion writers seem to use to guide them when they are planning, drafting, and revising.

The recursive move, then, that is hardest to document but is probably the most important to be aware of is the move to felt sense, to what is not yet *in words* but out of which images, words, and concepts emerge.

The continuing presence of this felt sense, waiting for us to discover it and see where it leads, raises a number of questions.

Is "felt sense" another term for what professional writers call their "inner voice" or their feeling of "inspiration"?

Do skilled writers call on their capacity to sense more readily than unskilled writers?

Rather than merely reducing the complex act of writing to a neat formulation, can the term "felt sense" point us to an area of our experience from which we can evolve even richer and more accurate descriptions of composing?

Can learning how to work with felt sense teach us about creativity and release us from stultifyingly repetitive patterns?

My observations lead me to answer "yes" to all four questions. There seems to be a basic process that skilled writers rely on even when they are unaware of it and that less skilled writers can be taught. This process seems to rely on very careful attention to one's inner reflections and is often accompanied with bodily sensations.

When it's working, this process allows us to say or write what we've never said before, to create something new and fresh, and occasionally it provides us with the experience of "newness" or "freshness," even when "old words" or images are used.

The basic process begins with paying attention. If we are given a topic, it begins with taking the topic in and attending to what it evokes in us. There is less "figuring out" an answer and more "waiting" to see what forms. Even without a predetermined topic, the process remains the same. We can ask ourselves, "What's on my mind?" or "Of all the things I know about, what would I most like to write about now?" and wait to see what comes. What we pay attention to is the part of our bodies where we experience ourselves directly. For many people, it's the area of their stomachs; for others, there is a more generalized response and they maintain a hovering attention to what they experience throughout their bodies.

Once a felt sense forms, we match words to it. As we begin to describe it, we get to see what is there for us. We get to see what we think, what we know. If we are writing about something that truly interests us, the felt sense deepens. We know that we are writing out of a "centered" place.

If the process is working, we begin to move along, sometimes quickly. Other times, we need to return to the beginning, to reread, to see if we captured what we meant to say. Sometimes after rereading we move on again, picking up speed. Other times by rereading we realize we've gone off the track, that what we've written doesn't quite "say it," and we need to reassess. Sometimes the words are wrong and we need to change them. Other times we need to go back to the topic, to call up the sense it initially evoked to see where and how our words led us astray. Sometimes in rereading we discover that the topic is "wrong," that the direction we discovered in writing is where we really want to go. It is important here to clarify that the terms "right" and "wrong" are not necessarily meant to refer to grammatical structures or to correctness.

What is "right" or "wrong" corresponds to our sense of our intention. We intend to write something, words come, and now we assess if those words adequately capture our intended meaning. Thus, the first question we ask ourselves is "Are these words right for me?" "Do they capture what I'm trying to say?" "If not, what's missing?"

Once we ask "what's missing?" we need once again to wait, to let a felt sense of what is missing form, and then to write out of that sense.

I have labeled this process of attending, of calling up a felt sense, and of writing out of that place, the process of *retrospective structuring.* It is retrospective in that it begins with what is already there, inchoately, and brings whatever is there forward by using language in structured form.

It seems as though a felt sense has within it many possible structures or forms. As we shape what we intend to say, we are further structuring our sense while correspondingly shaping our piece of writing.

It is also important to note that what is there implicitly, without words, is not equivalent to what finally emerges. In the process of writing, we begin with what is inchoate and end with something that is tangible. In order to do so, we both discover and construct what we mean. Yet the term "discovery" ought not lead us to think that meaning exists fully formed inside of us and that all we need do is dig deep enough to release it. In writing, meaning cannot be discovered the way we discover an object on an archeological dig. In writing, meaning is crafted and constructed. It involves us in a process of coming-into-being. Once we have worked at shaping, through language, what is there inchoately, we can look at what we have written to see if it adequately captures what we intended. Often at this moment discovery occurs. We see something new in our writing that comes upon us as a surprise. We see in our words a further structuring of the sense we began with and we recognize that in those words we have discovered something new about ourselves and our topic. Thus when we are successful at this process, we end up with a product that teaches us something, that clarifies what we know (or what we knew at one point only implicitly), and that lifts out or explicates or enlarges our experience. In this way, writing leads to discovery.

All the writers I have observed, skilled and unskilled alike, use the process of retrospective structuring while writing. Yet the degree to which they do so varies and seems, in fact, to depend upon the model of the writing process that they have internalized. Those who realize that writing can be a recursive process have an easier time with waiting, looking, and discovering. Those who subscribe to the linear model find themselves easily frustrated when what they write does not immediately correspond to what they planned or when what they produce leaves them with little sense of accomplishment. Since they have relied on a formulaic approach, they often produce writing that is formulaic as well, thereby cutting themselves off from the possibility of discovering something new.

Such a result seems linked to another feature of the composing process, to what I call *projective structuring,* or the ability to craft what one intends to say so that it is intelligible to others.

A number of concerns arise in regard to projective structuring; I will mention only a few that have been raised for me as I have watched different writers at work.

1. Although projective structuring is only one important part of the composing process, many writers act as if it is the whole process. These writers focus on what they think others want them to write rather than looking to see what it is they want to write. As a result, they often ignore their felt sense and they do not establish a living connection between themselves and their topic.

2. Many writers reduce projective structuring to a series of rules or criteria for evaluating finished discourse. These writers ask, "Is what I'm writing correct?" and "Does it conform to the rules I've been taught?" While these concerns are important, they often overshadow all others and lock the writer in the position of writing solely or primarily for the approval of readers.

Projective structuring, as I see it, involves much more than imagining a strict audience and maintaining a strict focus on correctness. It is true that to handle this part of the process well, writers need to know certain grammatical rules and evaluative criteria, but they also need to know how to call up a sense of their reader's needs and expectations.

For projective structuring to function fully, writers need to draw on their capacity to move away from their own words, to decenter from the page, and to project themselves into the role of the reader. In other words, projective structuring asks writers to attempt to become readers and to imagine what someone other than themselves will need before the writer's particular piece of writing can become intelligible and compelling. To do so, writers must have the experience of being readers. They cannot call up a felt sense of a reader unless they themselves have experienced what it means to be lost in a piece of writing or to be excited by it. When writers do not have such experiences, it is easy for them to accept that readers merely require correctness.

In closing, I would like to suggest that retrospective and projective structuring are two parts of the same basic process. Together they form the alternating mental postures writers assume as they move through the act of composing. The former relies on the ability to go inside, to attend to what is there, from that attending to place words upon a page, and then to assess if those words adequately capture one's meaning. The latter relies on the ability to assess how the words on that page will affect someone other than the writer, the reader. We rarely do one without the other entering in; in fact, again in these postures we can see the shuttling back-and-forth movements of the composing process, the move from sense to words and from words to sense, from inner experience to outer judgment and from judgment back to experience. As we move through this cycle, we are continually composing and recomposing our meanings and what we mean. And in doing so, we display some of the basic recursive patterns that writers who observe themselves closely seem to see in their own work. After observing the process for a long time we may, like Anne, conclude that at any given moment the process is more complex than anything we are aware of; yet such insights, I believe, are important. They show us the fallacy of reducing the composing process to a simple linear scheme, and they leave us with the potential for creating even more powerful ways of understanding composing.

References

Emig, Janet. 1971. *The Composing Processes of Twelfth Graders.* NCTE Research Report no. 13. Urbana, Ill.: National Council of Teachers of English.

Flower, Linda, and J. R. Hayes. 1980. "The Cognition of Discovery: Defining a Rhetorical Problem." *College Composition and Communication* 31 (February): 21–32.

Gendlin, Eugene. 1978. *Focusing.* New York: Everest House.

Sommers, Nancy. 1979. "The Need for Theory in Composition Research." *College Composition and Communication* 30 (February): 46–49.

Vygotsky, L. S. 1978. *Mind in Society*, trans. M. Cole, V. John-Steiner, S. Scribner, and E. Souberman. Cambridge: Harvard University Press.

6

How to Completely Individualize a Writing Program

William A. Clark
Public Schools
Machias, Maine

TALKING to students about writing doesn't make them better writers.
Students learn to write by writing.
Therefore: Students should write more.

The more students write, the more papers teachers have to correct.
It is hard to motivate students to write anyway.
Therefore: Students don't write very much.

These syllogisms catch the great dilemma of teaching writing in a nutshell. The predicament cries out for an approach that is simple, is relatively convenient, and works. Maybe anyone who splits an infinitive, right in the title, has no business suggesting an approach. Especially if he seems to consistently do it. Double-especially if he is an *ex*-English teacher now defected to the ranks of administration. But I have used the approach that follows several times, with groups of high ability, low ability, mixed abilities, and seemingly no ability.

With all of them it works, if you will accept my rigorously unscientific measures of effectiveness:

Students write more, much more, than they ever did before during an equivalent span of time.

They do it with little hassle, at least compared to groups I have taught in more traditional ways.

The writing is more interesting to read.

With this approach I found myself consistently looking forward to reading papers, a luxury that I, for one, have enjoyed all too seldom during my teaching career. Perhaps many teachers would not consider this as evidence of success. I once heard a distinguished writing professor say only half-facetiously that when a student submits a dull paper, the teacher should ask the student to come in and read the paper back aloud while the teacher yawns. An extreme move, I admit. But the fact is that students know when they're writing interesting stuff—they're interested in it and excited about it themselves.

Best of all, students are enthusiastic. Perhaps the only scientific way of judging students' enthusiasm is to wrap blood-pressure straps around their arms and monitor the dials. But teachers are a supersensitive lot, and every one I've met (me included) has hairy little antennae that pick up classroom vibrations with split-second speed. I *know* when something is working in my classroom.

To begin a writing program, you take each student where he is. Most teachers will subscribe to this starting point, without being very clear about what it means. I'm afraid that to many teachers it means placing each student's writing on a continuum from *Perfectly Awful* to *Supergood.* Then the goal is to move the student along the continuum. One catch among many is that judgments of *Good* and *Bad,* and of student placement in between, are based on the *teacher's* perceptions. And we've all done those little experiments in which a group of teachers read the same composition and come up with wildly different assessments of it.

A writing program has to start with the *student's* perception of where he is. Therefore, the early stages have to emphasize the importance of the individual student's uniqueness and the teacher's willingness—even determination—to accept it. On the first day, I "lecture." I take students for a ten-minute walk outside the school building. I point out things that interest me and move me to verbalization: cars in the student parking lot, the uniform rows of school windows looking out from uniform rows of classrooms, the students inside staring at us outside, the absence of student activity outside the building, the flag on the pole, etc. I suggest how these things trigger off associations that are significant to me and that I would like to write about. Each student of course sees things I don't see and makes connections that no other person would make, and I encourage anyone who feels like it to do so as we walk. The point of the tour is that any ten-minute observation period in anyone's day will provide raw materials for completely personalized associations.

Back inside, they do the first (and last) canned writing assignment: Write a quick (five-minute) description of the view outside the classroom window. A description of anything else would do as well, as long as everyone describes the same thing. Then I read each one aloud, divulging no author's name, commenting about how each individual perceived the scene in a unique way. This one sees geometric patterns, another catalogues the phenomena methodically from left to right, still another puts the description in a framework of it's-beautiful-out-there-and-we're-stuck-in-here. Every description comes naturally out of the author's way of looking at this piece of his world. No mention is made of the quality of the writing. Every way of perceiving is valid, and no one perception is more valid than another.

Whether or not a teacher uses this particular strategy of reading back descriptions, I cannot overemphasize the importance of the process of validating each student's uniqueness. Importance, that is, to the teacher, because it commits the teacher to a public stance. (How the students take it depends on your subsequent actions: they are conditioned to play it cool and see if the teacher lives up to his promise.) Faced with a batch of papers, many teachers have a tendency to classify (Good and Bad; A, B, or C; those that need a lot of revision, those that don't; etc.)—that is, to match them against some standard. But the validation process asks the teacher to avoid mental subsets of any kind and to consider each student's vision as unique. Incidentally, it's surprisingly easy to read back papers and articulate the unique point of view without any preparation. After a while you can read back the papers of five classes, thirty students each, and report 150 different ways of seeing the same scene. If a student tries to record the unique way he perceives things, he is writing "individually." He is into an individualized writing program.

So far all this has been preparatory. The day-to-day work of the course depends on whether this is a course in writing only or a "Kitchen Sink" English course. I've done it both ways, and while I prefer the writing-only course, this approach can be woven in and around literature, spelling, grammar, speech, and all the other pieces that once led me to put up a horrendous bulletin board display entitled "English Is a Many-Splendored Thing." In the writing-only course, students write a predetermined number of rough drafts, say ten in a half-year course. They use any writing modes they wish, any subjects they wish. This freedom is hard for students to handle at first. "I can't think of anything to write about." (Translation: What do you really want me to write about?) I make suggestions, and plenty of them. I even give specific "assignments," complete with examples, instructions, advice—always ending with, "But you don't have to write that if you don't want to."

It is important, I think, to persist in not telling students what to write about or what mode to use. Once you succumb to the pressure, the student flips back to the same old please-the-teacher channel and both of you are licked. Persist and you will find that one by one most students will accept their freedom and finally exult in it. Since there is almost no group instruction, the teacher is free to walk around and confer. But these early "what-do-I-write-about conferences" must reinforce the idea that the student is to write out of his perceptions, not yours. The teacher has to find out what the student has been doing and thinking about lately, maybe to have him recall, if necessary, one of his recent ten-minute walks. Using this as raw material, the teacher helps the student discover his own topic. And he has to write about *his* topic; the zappiest topic you pick out of the air to hand him will be your topic, not his. Some students find it helpful to write a detailed account of that ten minutes from their day. Out of that the teacher can help the student find other subjects and suggest alternate ways of handling those subjects (poetry, sketch, interior monologue, etc.).

The early goal, then, is to churn out rough drafts. Emphasis is clearly not on quality but on finding one's own voice, finding out what one wants to say. Drafts are incomplete, tentative, just barely legible enough for someone else to read. They are not graded.

Periodically (usually at the end of a marking period) we invoke the delightful strategy offered by Don Murray. The student selects a few of his papers that *he* thinks are most promising and polishes them for a grade. Between the drafts and the hand-ins comes the nitty-gritty of revision.

Students are encouraged to get off a number of rough drafts before revising any of them. Since they know that in the end only a few of their papers will be graded, and then only after plenty of revision, a beautiful thing happens: they begin to feel free to experiment with their rough drafts. If they want to try a crazy stream-of-consciousness technique or imitate Salinger or write a parody, they are free to try it. If an experiment doesn't work out, there is no penalty—they just won't select it later for handing in.

It is frequently hard for a teacher to accept (in any sense of the word) some of the experimental efforts, especially when an effort somehow doesn't come off. In some papers it's hard to know what the student was trying to do, especially when he didn't really *do* what he was trying to do. After I read a student's rough draft I invariably ask him the same question: What do you think is the best thing about this paper? The question is intentionally ambiguous. It might be interpreted to mean, "What do you like best about it?" or "Which section do you think is best?" or "Which idea in it do you really like and were you trying to get at?"

A few years ago I was in a small group of experienced writing teachers at an NDEA Institute. We had all written a quick, short paper on anything we liked, with no time for revision. Sitting around a table, we all read dittoed copies of everyone's drafts. The leader asked us to suggest ways each paper could be improved. I had already figured the way I wanted to improve mine. What surprised me was that not one of those experienced and competent teachers suggested what I was thinking of. Their suggestions were good, but those teachers weren't *me*, and they couldn't possibly have figured out what would be the most appropriate direction for me.

So I ask the students, "What do *you* think is the best thing about your draft?" And whatever they say (incredibly, they almost always *do* say), whether I see any possibilities in their selection or NOT, I accept it and try to help them build on it. One boy wrote a paean to his girl friend, with two pages of delicious and loving physical description of her, and a final innocuous sentence or two about how he felt when he was with her. Yet he told me he felt the ending was the best part. I was surprised, even disappointed, but apparently the description part wasn't what he wanted to write. Perhaps he thought papers about people *should* start with a physical description—I don't know. Anyhow, we talked for a while about how he felt when he was near her, and he seemed relieved and happy to go back and redo the paper the way *he* wanted it. As it turned out, he did include portions of the physical description in his final draft, but in a context that was his own creation.

One of the ironies of teaching writing is that most teachers give of their expertise when the student needs it least. They give a lot of help before the student starts to write, and after the student has written, but too little during the process. Once the student has done a rough draft and has freely committed himself to doing a revision, he then truly needs (and wants) a teacher's help. At least most students do. When you individualize there are precious few generalizations you can make that apply to all students in a class. Some want help infrequently, and then only with pressing problems. Some want help with wording, some with grammar or spelling, some with organization. Some want no help at all. So I spend most of the class time sitting with students providing on-the-spot help. There are even some who want a draft completely red-penciled in the good old-fashioned way. I invite them to submit a second draft, still in pencil, for this service.

Of course you can sneak in some unsolicited advice at times, if it somehow is in the context of something the student has solicited. An interesting phenomenon is that a student's requests will change as time goes on. If the door is left open, he will tend to ask for the type of help he feels himself ready for. A typical pattern for many—though not all—is to ask for increasingly more help with mechanics, as concerns grow for "getting it just right."

A problem that arises in every class I have taught is the boy who wants to write only about cars. But why discourage him? That's clearly where he's at, at this stage of his life, for perfectly understandable psychological and sociological reasons. (I remember during my first year of teaching all I thought about or read about or wrote about was school.) The teacher can suggest different ways of writing about cars. The student can, for instance, write for audiences with varying knowledge of cars, from his car-ignorant teacher to his car-sophisticated friends. He may enjoy writing a glossary of technical car terms, to flaunt his special knowledge and get some control over a world so fascinating to him. But if his world is mainly populated with cars, then he ought to write about them.

Many experts on the teaching of writing place great emphasis on having students "correct" each other's papers. Moffett suggests dividing a class into small groups in which students read their papers and provide mutual feedback. An excellent idea, though I must confess I've never had much success at making it work. The groups seem to be either unduly tough on each other, or unduly accepting of everything they read. I prefer the constant informal swapping of papers that inevitably goes on when the teacher walks around the room talking with individuals and the atmosphere is not one of control from the front. Students, especially those who are beginning to build confidence in their own perceptions, hunger for supportive advice, and they know which classmates will provide it and which ones probably won't. Of course there should be periodic "publishing" of student writing. My favorite way is the dittoed class "literary magazine," which includes at least one selection by each student and is distributed just within the class (with extra copies for the students to hand out to anybody else). A copy to each administrator in the school is a dandy move.

I don't mean to suggest that the teacher should spend all his class time walking around talking to students. Sometimes he has to read papers. And he should himself do some writing, for a lot of reasons that I guess are obvious. One that may not be so obvious is that he really gets to know what students are going through. Teachers do scandalously little writing, except for term papers, and it won't be term papers these students are writing. (Though a perfectly legitimate activity in this class is for a student to write a term paper for another class.) Ask a student or two to read your drafts and react. It feels good later on when inevitably you find a student is having a problem you had, and you can say how you solved it.

As the end of the marking period approaches, all energies are focused on revising a few drafts for official "handing in." The revision of some papers may have started way back near the beginning of the term and has gone through several stages. Before a paper is ready, the student can exhaust the possibilities for advice and suggestions from teacher and classmates and can be reasonably sure that his final draft represents the best work he is capable of. There will be no surprises when he gets it back. When he finally does hand it in, all the learning about writing he is to do during the program will be completed, so that by the act of submitting the paper for a grade he is merely paying his respects to a grading system he is stuck with. This is the only time of real work for the teacher, because there is suddenly a big pile of papers to read all at once. But there is little commenting to be done, and the grades should be delightfully high.

I haven't said much about quality in the students' writing. The quality of their papers does improve, markedly so, but not in ways I could have predicted or planned for with any accuracy. Behavioral objectives would be absurd for such a program. Certainly this approach won't insure that a student gets a balance of experience in writing essays, short stories, book reports, and all the other types of writing, or that a student will learn all the elements of composition in the rhetoric handbook. One eleventh-grade girl spent a whole term working on one long, long short story. It wasn't a very good story even by the standard of the class, though it was a much better story at the end of the term than at the beginning. But she found her voice. She felt a new confidence in her ability to use that voice as she went on to other courses which demanded other kinds of writing.

Writing, it seems to me, cannot be "learned" in the same sense as one can learn square roots or punctuation or typewriting. One never really completes the process of learning to write. The technical skill is intimately tied up with one's self-confidence, self-image, and self-growth. Somewhere in the school experience, every student needs to have the chance to experience that kind of growth.

Time for Questions

What can I do for students who say they don't have anything to write about?

Students can mean many things when they say this. They may mean that they don't have "appropriate" topics; they can mean that they're afraid that if they invest energy in writing, they will be criticized; they could mean that they don't have *enough* to write about on any topic.

One way to help students discover topics and information about topics is to have them make lists. Here's a sequence you can go through:

1. Ask students to write an "authority list"—twenty-five (or any other number you choose) possible topics: experiences, hobbies, opinions, things that annoy them, people they admire, places they've visited, books they've read, movies they've seen, sports they play, and so on.

2. Once the list is completed put a star beside the topic the student likes best.

3. Students should pair up and ask each other questions about the topic each has chosen.

4. After the interviews, each student should make a list of key words—details, names, quotes, examples, physical descriptions that he or she might use to write about the topic.

5. Write about the topic.

This procedure slows down the composing process for students. Too often students have little to write about because they do not take time to inventory their own knowledge—they don't yet know what they know.

This procedure also gets the student talking about his or her topic, and talking helps students know what they know. But if students are to talk teachers must be willing to listen, and there are volumes of research studies to show that we don't do it well. I find that I get the best results when I begin with a general invitation to talk: "Could you tell me more about X?" The student will often begin with a rambling kind of list; then something will click, there will be animation in the voice; and the student senses that an oral text is being created, one that can be transformed into a written text.

My most vivid memory of this process involved a student of mine who had worked diligently for half a semester and had produced nothing that anyone would want to read. This particular week she had written on her hometown in Vermont, and the paper was like the ones she had written before, mechanical and lifeless. I asked her to tell me something about her hometown, and she talked for a while, but nothing clicked, nothing was added that could enliven her paper. Near the end of the conference, she picked up a postcard and said, "Look what I bought in the bookstore." It was Norman Rockwell's picture of Rosie the Riveter painted during World War II. "That's my mother."

It literally was her mother, who had posed for Rockwell. Not only had her mother posed, but many others in her town had also posed. And in typical New England fashion many of these people still lived in the hometown so dully described in her paper. So her next paper involved interviews with these people, their memories of Rockwell. A splendid paper she had talked her way into.

Sometimes when I encourage students to pick their own topics they don't choose well. They may pick topics they have no real investment in. What can I do?

I find that college freshmen often write more effectively on topics that are not recent. Perhaps our memories work to give shape and meaning to less recent experiences, while more recent ones are still undigested. While I do not assign topics, I encourage students to explore various topics during in-class focused writing. For example, I find that students often write well about work experiences. Their first jobs are often eye-openers. They leave the relatively sheltered world of school and meet people with different values, life-styles, and even language. I may read sections from Studs Terkel's *Working* to get them thinking about the topic—or I may use a student paper on the topic. I then have them list significant details they may want to include, and finally give them time to write.

I call these in-class pieces "attempts"—the original meaning of the word "essays." The student can explore what he or she has to say about the topic. After twenty-five to thirty minutes of writing the student can determine if it's worthwhile continuing. Many continue to write on the topic, working it into one of the weekly papers. Others decide the topic isn't working and choose to write on another topic for their papers.

I have students who can find topics, but their writing is painfully slow. What can I do about it?

Many students labor over their writing because they try to get it right the first time. I had a student describe her process as follows:

> I decided to write about my grandfather. "Grandfather was a woodsman," I began. Was he? Actually he was also an applepicker and a carpenter. I added those to the line. Now it was too long. I should concentrate on one subject, I said to myself. Was it "woodsman" or "woodsmen?" I looked it up in the dictionary. "Woodsman" was correct. I reread the first sentence; it sounded OK. Now for number 2.

It's painful to imagine someone continuing this way. William Stafford, the poet, offers some good advice for students who put themselves under this kind of pressure: "If I am to keep writing, I cannot bother to insist on high standards. I must get into action and not let anything stop me, or even slow me much."

One way for students to "get into action" is to ask them to free-write regularly. Initially I ask my students to write for ten minutes on any topic, and when the time is up I ask them simply to count the number of words they have written. Many are surprised that they can write the equivalent of a typed page in ten minutes. As the term progresses I regularly ask them to write at the beginning of class—sometimes on a topic I assign, sometimes on a topic they choose.

Many students lack fluency because they have not had to compose regularly. Bryant Fillion, in a later article in this collection, reports that the amount of writing students do can vary wildly from year to year. And Mina Shaughnessy (in *Errors and Expectations*) estimates that many basic writers do almost no writing. They are caught in a powerful dilemma: because they have difficulty writing they are not asked to do much, and because they are not asked to do much writing, it becomes increasingly more difficult. As students write more frequently, they not only develop more ease in writing, they also begin to write when they are not writing. They think about what they might write when they ride the bus or walk the dog. They begin to resemble James Thurber, who would sometimes mumble incomprehensibly at the dinner table. If guests were present, Thurber's wife would turn to them and explain, "You'll have to excuse him. He's writing."

What kind of prewriting activities would help students with expository or informational writing?

It's often useful to try a variation on the listing activity above. But this time students might be asked to write lists of questions about the topic—not just a few, but a large number. The first questions on the list will be the obvious ones; the later ones are likely to be more interesting.

Bruce Ballenger, a teacher in our Freshman English program, has an even more elaborate method for generating questions. He begins by taping huge pieces of newsprint around the room—one for each student. The student then writes the research topic and three or four main questions. Students then circulate around the room adding to the questions already on the paper. In a final step students might meet in small groups with their newsprint sheets, now covered with questions, and determine which from that list of questions are the most interesting ones. These questions can provide a focus for the information collecting that the student does.

Many students have also found mapping to be useful in showing the relationships among ideas. To construct a map the writer circles the key word of the piece. If I were writing a chapter on helping students to begin writing, I might begin by writing the words "getting started" and circling them. Then I would create some branches:

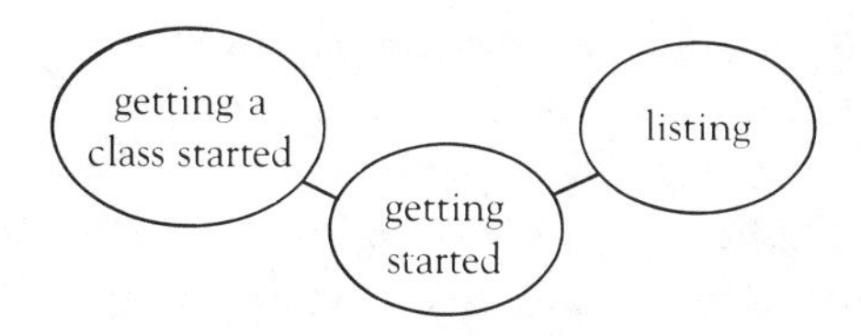

Then I would note areas or points that connect with each of these branches:

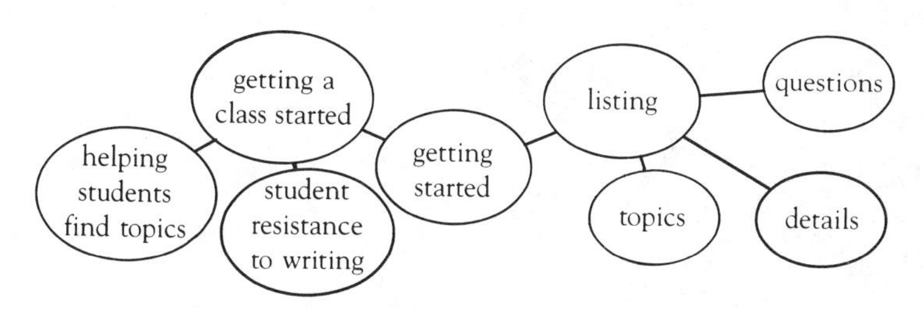

And so on. Not every branch will be used in the writing, but the method helps lay out possibilities and connections in a way that an outline does not. (For a more extensive description of this method see Donald Murray's *Write to Learn.*)

How can I get students to write term papers that don't bore me to tears?

Most term papers are too long; the student has to stretch to make the assigned length and as a consequence uses almost all of the information gathered. There is no selection process—no throwing away. Six to eight typewritten, double-spaced pages should be a maximum length.

But the biggest problem with research papers is the inability of students to transform researched information into their own language. After all, their sources say it so much better than they can. There are two things you can do to deal with this problem. At points in the writing ask students to write "What I Have Learned" papers, quick free writings without benefit of notes, where the student says in his or her own words what has been learned from the research. In this way, the student is freed from the language of the sources.

Students can also be encouraged to select topics where they can interview an expert. A student interested in emergency medicine could interview an ambulance attendant; someone interested in farm foreclosures could interview farmers or loan officers of banks. Good advice on interviewing can be found in William Zinsser's *On Writing Well.* I would also suggest Kenneth Macrorie's *Searching Writing,* which has excellent ideas for an I-Search paper, where a student moves into the community to gather information.

Suggestions for Further Reading

Elbow, Peter. 1973. *Writing Without Teachers.* New York: Oxford University Press.

———. 1981. *Writing with Power.* New York: Oxford University Press.

Emig, Janet. 1983. *The Web of Meaning: Essays on Writing, Teaching, Learning, and Thinking.* Portsmouth, N.H.: Boynton/Cook.

Flower, Linda. 1984. *Problem-Solving Strategies for Writing.* 2nd ed. New York: Harcourt Brace.

Flower, Linda, and John Hayes. 1980. "The Cognition of Discovery: Defining a Rhetorical Problem." *College Composition and Communication* 31 (February): 21–32.

Fulwiler, Toby. 1987. *Teaching with Writing.* Portsmouth, N.H.: Boynton/Cook.

Irmscher, William. 1979. *Teaching Expository Writing.* New York: Holt, Rinehart, and Winston.

Kirby, Dan, and Tom Liner, with Ruth Vinz. 1988. *Inside Out: Developmental Strategies for Teaching Writing.* 2nd ed. Portsmouth, N.H.: Boynton/Cook.

McClelland, Ben, and Timothy Donovan. 1980. *Eight Approaches to Teaching Writing.* Urbana, Ill.: National Council of Teachers of English.

Macrorie, Kenneth. 1984. *Searching Writing: A Contextbook.* Portsmouth, N.H.: Boynton/Cook.

———. 1985. *Telling Writing.* 4th ed. Portsmouth, N.H.: Boynton/Cook.

Moffett, James. 1981. *Active Voice: A Writing Program Across the Curriculum.* Portsmouth, N.H.: Boynton/Cook.

Murray, Donald. 1982. "Writing as Process: How Writing Finds Its Own Meaning." In *Learning by Teaching: Selected Articles on Writing and Teaching.* Portsmouth, N.H.: Boynton/Cook.

———. 1985. *A Writer Teaches Writing.* 2nd ed. Boston: Houghton Mifflin.

———. 1987. *Write to Learn.* 2nd ed. New York: Holt.

Romano, Tom. 1987. *Clearing the Way: Working with Teenage Writers.* Portsmouth, N.H.: Heinemann.

Rose, Mike. 1980. "Rigid Rules, Inflexible Plans, and the Stifling of Language: A Cognitivist Analysis of Writer's Block." *College Composition and Communication* 31 (December): 389–401.

Stafford, William. 1978. *Writing the Australian Crawl.* Ann Arbor: University of Michigan Press.

Stillman, Peter. 1984. *Writing Your Way.* Portsmouth, N.H.: Boynton/Cook.

Welty, Eudora. 1984. *One Writer's Beginnings.* Cambridge: Harvard University Press.

Zinsser, William. 1983. *On Writing Well: An Informal Guide to Writing Nonfiction.* 3rd ed. New York: Harper & Row.

Responding

7

Listening Beyond the Text

Terry A. Moher
Exeter AREA High School
Exeter, New Hampshire

ON my way to close the classroom door, a ritual I performed as class was about to begin, MaryEllen stepped in front of me, hands flailing. "I'm so frustrated, Mrs. Moher. I wrote three and a half pages last night and—and I'm not even there yet!"

I was a little flustered; I wanted to start class. I suggested what came to mind first. "Why don't you just start 'there.' Start writing at that point." She sighed, thought a moment, and went back to her seat. I resumed my ritual, shut the door, and suddenly realized that class had already begun. I'd already had one conference.

It was a successful one, because MaryEllen had returned to her writing. That's the purpose of the writing conference, to get the student writer to think about what she has to say and to consider the choices she has for saying it most effectively.

I remember MaryEllen because she was one of the hundreds of students who has taught me how to have an effective writing conference. It didn't happen with a carefully prepared repertoire of questions, though I did collect them at first. It developed as I listened and interviewed the writers themselves. Giving authority to my student writers changed my role in the conference. I learned to listen better, and they learned to trust their own responses to the writing when they began to assume the responsibility. The quick, tentative conference that MaryEllen and I had became the norm. Conference time became shorter as I discovered its real purpose. But it didn't happen all at once. I took risks, and the students had to learn to take them as well.

Rich was one of the few students at the beginning of a semester who said he felt comfortable with writing. He made it clear he didn't have any problems or anxieties and didn't need to do drafts. Like many "good writers," Rich was wary, and he avoided meeting me at the conference table. For confident writers, writers who have met with some success before, the risk is greater, the criticism more devastating. Rich threw his first paper on my desk and walked away, announcing that he had "completed the assignment."

I wasn't sure how to deal with that, so I took the paper home that night and just as warily read it. Twelve pages on the Grateful Dead, on every conceivable aspect he could think of, from standing in line for tickets to naming members of the group, a little of their history, and on and on. Around page nine a phrase caught my eye: "their musical evolution." I circled it, the only mark I made on the paper, and called him to the conference table the next day.

His body language let me know that he didn't want to hear anything critical about his piece. I know this feeling from personal experience, and my purpose is not to be critical in a negative way—certainly not until the writer has become comfortable about the worth of his writing. For some student writers, that point takes months to achieve. I talked with Rich about my observations, said I'd learned some things about the Grateful Dead from the paper, that I knew many students who liked the Dead. I just talked. He waited.

Finally he said, "Are you going to ask what it's about?" He'd heard the question before.

"Go ahead. Tell me what you intend it to be about."

"It's obviously about the Grateful Dead."

"Yes. But what about them?"

He was ready: "Their concerts!"

I ignored him. "It seems to me one of the most significant ideas in this piece, here on page nine, is this idea of 'musical evolution.' It struck me as pretty interesting. It seemed to say something, though I'm not sure what."

He was listening. I continued.

"Is it something, an important idea for you?"

He looked sideways at me, skeptical of what I was trying to do.

"Yeah. But you mean I have to rewrite twelve pages?"

It was an accusation. But I was ready for him.

"No. This short section alone offers a wonderful subject. Seems to me you could just focus more on that. What do you think?"

He was quiet for a moment.

"Yeah. Good idea," he mumbled, and left.

Rich went on to revise those pages, developing that specific focus. More importantly, he began to trust the conferences because he saw the meaning of them: finding ways to improve what he had to say, not what I wanted him to say. I listened as a reader who wants to know, not as a "teacher."

It was Rich who later brought up the term "school essay." He labeled and defined it. "You know, the kind you write that means nothing and says nothing, but is well written!" The class laughed. They all knew what he meant. They even came up with a formula for it. It was the kind of meaningless writing Rich was good at and that, unfortunately, had given him good grades. For the first time Rich was attempting to go beyond the formula, and the writing he began to do for himself rather than for the teacher was more risky, more revealing, and far more real.

Meaning is often tied to perception of the writer's audience. Getting student writers to think about different audiences helps them revise their writing in new and unexpected ways.

April came to the table without a paper and began to talk about the piece she was writing, about a friend involved with drugs. She started crying as she expressed her frustration that she could do nothing. I suggested that she write to an audience that would include her friend and others like him, and tell them just that, about her frustration. Her real piece began with a purpose. In the process of looking at her subject through this perspective, April uncovered poignant insights into issues beyond the friend's behavior:

> In school, if you even attend your classes, you just sit looking blankly ahead, never learning anything. You avoid homework and simply forget to study for tests.
>
> Your friends notice your unheeding attitude and realize that there is a definite problem. If they are true friends they even wish they could change you back into the person they used to know.

> Your brothers and sisters, under sort of a sibling oath know what's happening but would never tell. Your parents notice the change and wonder where they've gone wrong being unable to comprehend your silent plea.
>
> I'm seeing your life crumble apart and part of mine is going with it.

As often as I can I cash in on real purposes for writing. I walked by Mike's desk one day and noticed an application for something official-looking in a crumpled heap. I picked it up and saw that it was an application for the Vocational School program. Mike was a sophomore applying for the carpentry program for his junior and senior years. The form was done in pencil and was barely legible; he was about to hand it in. On the part of the application that asked for an explanation of why carpentry was his first choice and how it related to his career plans, Mike had written:

> I think that after high school there will be alot of carpentry jobs around you can just look at Stratham and see the construction going on know. So I figure that in two and a half or three years the demand for housing will be doubled.
>
> One of the major advantages of knowing this trade we be to know how to build your own house.

Mike was a bright kid, but not an academically oriented one. He had no confidence and thought this was the best he could do. I asked him to think about being on the committee that read the applications. "If there were twenty applications and only twelve openings, would you choose this Mike based on this application?" He shook his head.

"Why carpentry, Mike?" I asked him to talk to me a little about his responses to that question. As he spoke, I jotted down a few of his phrases. I asked him to try taking on his own words and writing out his ideas. He was reticent about writing. I wasn't sure he'd even try. Next day I checked in with him. He had written:

> I like carpentry because I like to put things togeather like tables forts and houses and I like working with my hands and I think I am pretty good at it to. The shaping and forming of wood is fun to make it smoth and fit right and when you have finished, knowing you have done a good job.
>
> Woodworking and a little carpentry is what I'm good at and I would like to learn how to become a good and secessful carpenter.

"OK!" I said. "How did you learn carpentry?" He talked about being in a course in the high school and mentioned that he was a foreman. I showed my respect and interest. I asked him to write all that down, explaining that the information would be a good reference, and that he should explain what qualifications he had as a foreman.

Each draft was painfully slow for Mike, but getting him talking just long enough to recognize that he had something worthwhile to say helped push him further. A paragraph a day was a good amount for Mike, and I gave him reinforcement. The next day he had addressed my question.

> There are many skills in woodworking and a few in carpentry that I have learned well. After taking Advanced Woods, I was put in the position of a foreman in Carreers in Building Trades. I am good at handling power tools, have a good imagination, and like to take charge. I am steady at machines and very careful.

Throughout this process, Mike looked at me in funny ways. He didn't quite know where all this was taking him and was concerned, I'm sure, about putting it all together, as are most students who begin to gather an unwieldy amount of writing. It is intimidating, but I coax them along, telling them not to worry. How to put the pieces together usually becomes apparent to them as they begin to discover what they have to say.

The next day I confronted Mike with another problem. "What about the second part now? You've explained why you chose carpentry. What about 'career plans'?"

Mike decided he'd already answered that question in the beginning, so he set out to put it all together. With four days invested in the writing already, he went about making some careful decisions. The organization had become apparent to him as the piece developed. He needed no help.

Mike took painstaking care to write out his essay on a new application and completed what was for him a long week of writing. I complimented his work and tried to impress on him the fact that he had written it. I had only asked questions. I'm not sure he believed me, but he was accepted to the program and has since graduated.

I try to approach each student writer with a sense of wonder and genuine interest in who she is and what she is trying to say.

Not judge or edit or correct. Just listen for what is going on behind the text.

Sue had written all period and came up to me as the bell rang. She said she had been writing about her experience in junior high school. She had two older sisters whom many of the teachers had known, and her father was a coach in the school.

She wasn't sure what to do with it all. She felt "something missing." Sue and I had earlier identified one of her writing problems. She could easily write twenty pages, but couldn't seem to shorten anything. On a whim, I asked her to define "Marangelli," her last name. "Assume I know exactly what you went through, all the facts. See if you can define the essence of Marangelli. I don't know what will come of it. Try it!" She seemed to like the idea. Next day she announced to the class she wanted to read her piece.

> Marangelli is a term that has stereotyped me many times. Besides being my last name it is a definition of what I'm SUPPOSED to be like. A Marangelli must be academically strong as well as socially popular. She must be an over-achiever and actively involved in music.
>
> Of course, she MUST enjoy football and various other sports.
>
> When I was in junior high I hated being a Marangelli. I couldn't live up to many of the standards. Now I am slowly gaining my individuality. I don't need to live in shadow of my last name. I can be a Marangelli without expecting a stereotype. I am my own person, Marangelli or not.

She was excited. She had successfully written a short piece, and the class had responded well. She was ready to write. In conference we talked, mainly about focus—what it was she was learning about her own feelings. She hadn't recognized at first that some of her feelings about her family name were negative, and once she did she began to explore those feelings. Her next draft addressed those issues:

> By simply mentioning that I belong to the family, I have the potential to gain respect. But "Potential" is a confusing term. In the past I had never thought of myself as respected or equal. I always assumed I had to live in the shadows of my older sisters, never living up to my potential. I used to think I had to be musically active and involved in sports. Many of my teachers expected me to be as gifted as my sisters seemed to be at everything. I went through junior high as "Marian's baby sister," "Mar-

> tha's photocopy," "the coach's daughter." It was hard to see who I really was. Now, when I look back on my life, I see myself constantly trying to improve myself. I have become the achiever my oldest sister was, not because I had to be her photocopy, but because I wanted to better myself through the reaching of my own goals. I try to be as witty as my other older sister, as well as her musical equal. But I still have my own techniques and serious moments. I have become an avid football spectator and can finally boast a thorough understanding of the game. I can say I reached this plateau by myself. He didn't need to teach me. I learned on my own.
>
> I am my own person, Marangelli or not. I am proud of my family and their accomplishments. I am also glad I can be the youngest in an easily recognized family and still be free to experiment with my own uniqueness and individuality.

As do many student writers, Sue began with an account of the situation. Moving from the situation to its meaning is an evolution for a writer, a tough process. Sue moved beyond a simple narrative in the process of thinking about her situation and evaluating its meaning to her. The most important questions I ask are questions of meaning. And the answers are usually surprising. They aren't mine. Sue was the only one who could discover that meaning.

Becky came to the conference table with a piece with which most students would have been satisfied. In her writing, she had tried to define her reasons for wanting to get a teaching degree, but she said she didn't like it. She'd written about her experiences in a day-care center and wondered if it was too idealistic. I noticed the line ". . . those first couple months of duties helped me realize it wasn't all glory." I laughed and asked her what she meant. She began talking about a handicapped child with whom she'd worked. Instead of letting her talk on, I asked her to go write about him. Ten minutes later she'd written several pages. Becky liked this writing but wasn't sure how it would work into her original intention. After several attempts, she finally wrote the piece, entitled "My Life Was Touched By His Determination." Her new lead began:

> He swung peacefully on the swing, his legs rythmically going back and forth, as he ascended. He gazed into the sky and seemed transfixed by the brilliant sun. His back was slouched and his arms trembled as if they were unsure of their ability to hang on.

> The other children gathered together on the other side of the playground as they let Timmy swing silently on by himself.

Through that moving portrait, Becky was able to express her feelings about teaching. She arrived at conclusions about her experience that had not been clear in the earlier drafts:

> My dream of becoming a teacher and my personal opinions became more substantial and more stable for the first time in my life. I owe my growing and maturing to five year old Timmy who taught me the simple things in life. . . . My life has not noticably changed since those days at the center, but my outlook on life, attitude about people and basic self esteem changed immensely.

I ask student writers to add what I call a "process piece" to each completed piece of writing. I believe it is an important part of their learning to look closely at the development of the writing and become aware of their own decision making. Becky commented, "I think this paper has a real focus and is directed through Timmy. I learned how to use drafts better and get clearer with my ideas and feelings."

Conferences have no closure. I listen to the students, we talk, until a discovery happens, an idea emerges, a problem presents itself, a question comes up, and then I shoo them away to write again. The purpose of the conference is to get them to try stretching their ideas, trying out unfamiliar techniques. "What if . . . ? Try it. See what happens. Then come back." These are tentative trials in a joint venture, as one student said, "to realize who and why I am." I merely assume they can explore more about their subject, focus, audience, purpose, meaning, language, organization, and they do. Revision, in this perspective, becomes less of a step to avoid and more of an exciting personal quest. My acting as mediator between the student writer and her subject, in a nonjudgmental, encouraging, questioning way, helps the writer search more deeply about her own thinking, and we use the writing to test that.

My conference strategies have become as varied as my students and their attempts to write. I am directive, and I'm Rogerian; I read the papers and I refuse to (too soon); I move around the room, and I sit at a conference table; I'll write their words down for them; I'll take their words away, actually pry papers loose when they're too attached to the text; I'll ask what they want to do, and demand that they try something once; I make them cut it up and get lost in it; whatever. The point is that I follow the student writer much like a conversation. I am without an agenda. I listen.

So many students feel powerless about their own thinking and even more so about their writing, a far more permanent and gradable entity. Teaching them how to take control of their writing means helping them learn how to make decisions. When they discover they have the power of choice, they have to begin to take responsibility for what their writing does or does not do, and they can no longer disclaim any connection to the writing.

Vinnie had written an assignment for me early in the semester. It was an exercise for students to write about a phase in their lives.

> There was a phase in my life during the 7th and 8th grade. That summer before 7th grade I got a job feeding the young calves at a farm in my town. That was a good summer. it was the first real job I had. I always wanted to milk the big cows with the owner of the farm. The next summer that is what I got to do. I wanted to be a dairy farmer from 7th grade up to the beginning of 9th. I milked the cows 3 ½ hrs. every night and I got $10. a week.

Vinnie didn't hide the fact that he had not invested a great deal of time or thought in the assignment. An apathetic junior, he was doing minimal work. Later in the semester, however, he returned to this piece. He added more details, about the work, about the farmer and the farm.

I was moving around the room when I spotted his piece. A quick glance gives me lots of information. Vinnie was evidently involved in this writing. I commented that the piece told a lot about his job, about the farmer, and about the farm, and I asked him which one he meant to focus on. He hesitated a moment and admitted that he hadn't thought about it. Before I left him, I asked him to remember me. I explained that, having come from the city, I'd had a rather romantic view of farming, and how my husband had laughed when I'd told him how delightful it must be to live on a farm. Vinnie was laughing. He began talking about the farmer's life. Before I left he said, "Well, I thought I was writing about my summer job, but I think it's really about the farmer." He wrote again, exploring the details of the man and his farm.

> He had kind of a pot belly and his pants were baggy and dirty. He was always working around the farm. He had a few horses and some geese and many cats. He looked very old but I don't think he was. His face was weathered and had many wrinkles.

> But it looked so kind and soft. He had the kind of voic that when you here it you will never forget it. He didn't talk much and when he did it was usually a joke. Little changed from day to day he did almost the same things every day. . . .

Vinnie had consciously focused on the farmer and his farm. I met him in conference again and asked what he needed to do next. He knew. "It's not organized." I asked him to tell me how he might do that, and we looked at the physical descriptions of the man and the descriptions of the farm. He said he wasn't sure how he would organize it yet. He went back to the writing.

In his next draft, Vinnie had titled it "The Farmer." He had made a choice about his focus and organization: "the order: The man, a description, personality, and then related to the farm." It was no accident. Once Vinnie began to make decisions about what he wanted the piece to do, it took its course.

The Farmer

> The man I worked for at the end of the 6th grade was a farmer. He was an old yankee type man. I looked around the farm and I was surprised at how messy and unkept it was. At that time I had no idea of how much work there was and how merciless the farm could be.
>
> The man I worked for, the owner of the farm milked cows. He did most of the work and his sons did the rest. My second year I got to work with him all summer. He had kind of a pot belly and his pants were dirty and baggy. He always wore a hat and black runner boots over his work boots. His face was dark and it had many wrinkles. It look very soft and kind. the man looked very old but I don't think he was. He had a voice that once you heard it you never forget what it sound like. He was one of the kindest most concederate people I ever met.
>
> Little changed from day to day and I liked the man even more as I got to know him. He did not talk much and when he did it was usually a joke about the work that a farmer has to do. I think it was his way of relieving the stress of working all the time. One job after another.
>
> Every day when I arrived I saw him plowing out the yard. He looked like he enjoyed this part of the work. I think he liked riding on the tractor. He had alot of equipment and he took very good care of it, but the farm itself always had an unkept look about it. The animals and equipment need so much attention that there was no time to clean the place up.
>
> Very rarly did he lose his temper and get mad but when he did he had the worst temper. The cows would break something

> or they would not move or just cause trouble. He would hit them and yell at them. The farm was like the man that way. It was so peaceful most of the time but when things started to break even the simple jobs or the ones that he enjoyed became a pain. One time the tractor broke and he had to clean the yard by hand. I have never seen him so unhappy. Aanother time the hay ladder broke and we had to throw the bails up. It was no fun and haying is a fun part of the job. There was so much work to be done and with broken equipment it was impossible. He was at his worst then but he was always kind. He would do anything for you if you asked him.
>
> Things always got fixed and the man and the farm returned to their quiet selves. It took time because the man could get so mad.
>
> He still did not talk. There was so much work there was no time to talk.

The piece evolved because Vinnie was interested in the subject enough to take the time, which in turn brought commitment and more interest in what he would learn each time he wrote. And he was willing to write because I made no "corrections" from the beginning. Once the process of correcting and editing and polishing begins, the writing stops.

The original idea of Vinnie's "summer job" finally left this draft, and the piece became clearly focused. Vinnie's concept of the "merciless" farm came to him as he worked his way through the draft. There was no such clearly defined and articulated statement in the earlier drafts, no sign of these connections between the farm and the man. I could never have suggested such an insight. The discoveries happen to the student, and I have a good time observing them.

The development of Vinnie's paper defines the development of Vinnie as a writer. "No one ever said my writing was good before!" was his comment about his years as a student. He resented what had not been done for him. When we look at the history of our student writers, many of them nonwriters, we can learn a lot about how to teach writing, about encouragement and true coaching; about asking questions rather than giving answers; about the nature of learning.

Writing conferences are simple. They have to be. Neither my students nor I can handle much. In conferences I learned to listen beyond the text, behind the writer's own words, for his questions, not my own. It happens best when we are both caught off guard, unprepared for the process in which we engage ourselves.

Teachers often complain that there is never enough time to see everyone, to read all the papers, to address all the problems. And that's true. We need to stop trying to do it all for them and learn to exploit the adolescent demand for greater responsibility and freedom to extend boundaries. Their own choices and decisions will lead them away from reliance on our answers toward becoming more independent thinkers, able to understand and trust their own processes for learning.

In a final evaluation of the writing course, Burt wrote: "I learned from the conferences that you don't do a thing! All you really do is help us realize ourselves what the problem is. So if I ask myself the same questions, hopefully I'll get some helpful answers."

Burt is right. But I do work hard at getting students to go to the core of their thinking. It's not easy. It takes patience and trust on both our parts. I watch for those breakthrough pieces, watch to see that each writer recognizes even the smallest development in his writing. I work to get them to think further and longer and deeper and more convincingly than many of them have taken the time to do before.

It has taken time for my teaching to evolve, and I still learn from my students. I recently asked my classes to write what they have learned in these first few weeks of the semester. I wanted them to write the progress reports that their parents would read, another way of giving validity to their own awareness of their learning. After they had shared aloud their insights, Peter, the joker of the class, confronted me with a question. "What have you learned, Mrs. Moher?" I looked up, wondering how to respond to his laughter. I was surprised to see him looking at me, waiting seriously for an answer. I was pleased.

8

What About Arthur?

Mary M. Fallon
Brewster Academy
Wolfeboro, New Hampshire

ARTHUR sits in the first row in my Freshman Comp class. He appears relaxed and confident. His left ankle rests on his right knee. He leans back in his chair and absently rocks a pencil back and forth in his fingers. Arthur is listening. He is watching. He is at ease with the world. The image is important. But when Arthur speaks or offers his observations and opinions, a noticeable tremor appears at the corners of his mouth. The words shoot out in rapid-fire clusters, as if he must stop to reload, to charge himself with courage and momentum before he can proceed again.

On the first day of class, when my students paired off to introduce each other, Arthur was presented as a returning D.C.E. (Division of Continuing Education) student who had come back to school so that he wouldn't "blow his life off." The rest of the students laughed. Arthur smiled self-consciously.

The first assignment my students did was a brief, in-class composition in which I asked them to express their feelings and their concerns about being in Freshman Comp. They didn't have to sign their papers. And since it was the first day of class, and I had no experience with their handwriting, they could remain anonymous.

They all chose to leave their compositions unsigned, and I carried away twenty-four handwritten statements of hopes, frustrations, expectations, and apprehensions about English 401. Some of their responses were honest, open, and sincere expressions of their feelings. Some of them were written for me, giving me as a teacher what they felt I wanted to hear.

But there was one response that was totally unlike the rest. It was written in handwriting that Mina Shaughnessy, in her book *Errors and Expectations* (1977), describes as "so crabbed or slanted or blurred as to force the reader into puzzling out the shapes of the letters" (15). Words were misspelled. The same words appeared with different spellings. At first glance, capitalization seemed to be totally capricious. Capital and lowercase letters were mixed unpredictably. The script was obviously labored and difficult. There was no consistency in the slant of the letters or their distribution on the page. They seemed to come out in rapid-fire succession, to change contour and shape with the changing idea.

At first, I felt a mild twinge of middle-class-teacher indignation. I was teaching freshman classes at a state university, and I had to contend with someone who had not even mastered penmanship. How did he ever (I assumed it was a he) get into my class? But there are no prerequisites for D.C.E. students, so I was stuck with the situation. It would be up to me to decide whether he would remain in Freshman Comp or not. And so, I began to read his paper.* My prejudice and arrogance soon faded.

> my wrighting is the row edge
> of my soule. all the hate
> and anger in me comes
> out in it, that is why
> I fear it, and I fear what
> people will think of me
> when I show them this side
> of me.

I knew immediately that he was the student in the front row who didn't want to "blow his life off," who was reaching out to me

*The handwriting samples presented in this chapter are reduced in size from the originals.

as a first step on the way. His spelling was somewhat nonstandard, and, since I was familiar with my seven-year-old son's struggles to write, I was able to decipher Arthur's message. Locked in isolation, Arthur saw writing as a bridge to the outside and to communication with other human beings. His request was simple and direct. He needed access to words on paper. He needed to be able to spell and punctuate and form letters on the page.

*confidance in spell-
ing would would make
a world of differance*

And how did Arthur feel about being in English 401?

in a word terified

I had to make a choice. I could get rid of him now. I could tell him that he didn't have the necessary preparation to take my course. And, in truth, his writing revealed that he didn't meet even minimum freshman standards for written expression. Further, the course design was based on the assumption that I would be teaching a fairly homogeneous group. I had assumed my students would all be "college material" and would have mastered certain basic writing skills so that we could all proceed together in the direction in which the writing process leads—that is, to fuller, more confident self-expression. My goal was to establish a supportive environment in which my students could begin to free themselves from some of the inhibitions and self-consciousness about writing that many had developed as a result of writing experiences that had focused mainly on formal correctness.

But what about Arthur? Was there a place for him in my class? Could I refuse him? Could I ignore this request for help? I decided to ride out the situation for at least a few weeks and learn a little more about the person behind the twisted script and labored words.

And I learned a great deal! In the first few weeks of the course, Arthur wrote for me, and he wrote compositions about himself and his struggle. I learned that he had not come back to the university, as I had first thought, to pursue a degree in a pragmatic, employment-bound profession, such as engineering or computer science. That's not what he meant when he said that he didn't want to "blow his life off." Sure, Arthur wanted an education. But he also had a more intimate and personal purpose. He had come back to school, to my class, to win his dignity. He could no longer tolerate being "the butt of the joke." For too long his penmanship and spelling had been the targets of office humor. Now, at the age of twenty-three, Arthur wanted to establish himself as a self-respecting and respected adult. And for him, learning to write was a vital part of this process.

At our first conference, I suggested to Arthur that he audit my course the first time around. We could then work throughout the semester on developing his basic transcription skills, and he could take the course again the following semester for credit. But Arthur was determined to finish Freshman Comp. He had his own agenda and his own time schedule. He felt that he had already wasted too much time in setting and pursuing his goals in life.

> When you say to me "pass on this class art. take it for the experience." Time is not on my side, it is my nature to do things when I sense my destine. I have a clear goal in life to be a photographer. I will never be rich or that famous. still I will have adventure travle and danger. all the things that make life worth living.

At our second conference, Arthur and I talked about his mechanical difficulties. Being a conscientious academician, I tried to warn him that I couldn't in conscience pass him on to do the writing that would be required of him in future university courses unless he could master some of the mechanics of writing. It wouldn't fulfill my obligation to the University. More importantly, it would be a disservice to him. Together, we agreed that if, by the end of the semester, through the process of revision, Arthur could produce four clearly stated, well-developed papers that achieved an acceptable standard of formal correctness, he would get a C in the course. Our contract was made. The facts were established. Arthur was my student; I was his teacher.

At first, my approach to helping Arthur master the basics was to have conferences with him paper by paper, error by error, having him correct and rewrite, make spelling lists, and learn some simple rules of punctuation. However, I soon began to feel that my efforts were disjointed, that they were hit or miss. There seemed to be no carryover from one mistake to another. By the end of the first six weeks of the course, I was beginning to feel overwhelmed by Arthur's writing problems.

Then, I happened to read Mina Shaughnessy's book *Errors and Expectations* (1977). It was in those pages that I found Arthur. I saw him described in Shaughnessy's introduction as the third type of open admissions students "who had been left so far behind the others in their formal education that they appeared to have little chance of catching up, students whose difficulties with the written language seemed of a different order from those of other groups, as if they had come, you might say, from a different country, or at least through different schools, where even very modest standards of high-school literacy had not been met" (2). Arthur was one of these students. "He is aware that he leaves a trail of errors behind him as he writes. He can usually think of little else while he is writing" (7). But now Shaughnessy was pointing to me a way of helping Arthur in his struggle. By applying the process of error analysis elaborated in her book, I felt I could develop a more systematic approach to Arthur's mistakes.

First, I began to distinguish some patterns in his spelling errors and to break them down into categories. For example, many of Arthur's spelling mistakes occurred in the middle rather than at the beginning or the end of words. When he discussed these errors, Arthur confirmed that he based his spelling on his speech and that, when speaking, he tended to slur over the middle syllables of his words. By slowing down his mental "speech" as he wrote, Arthur began to "hear" some of the syllables and sounds he had previously either confused or left out altogether.

Still other errors in his spelling were caused by Arthur's unfamiliarity with certain spelling rules, such as in the pluralizing of words ending in *y* (as in the word *familys,* which appeared in one of his papers). After discovering this source of difficulty, we began to routinely practice the application of some of these rules with special, prepared exercises.

In addition to the insights I had gained into Arthur's spelling problems, I also began to see some patterns and logic in his punctuation errors, which at first had seemed so capricious to me. For example, in the writing samples shown in Figures 8–1 and 8–2, Arthur exhibits an understanding of what constitutes a clause as, in Figure 8–1, he separates "for photographers" from "images are

Figure 8–1

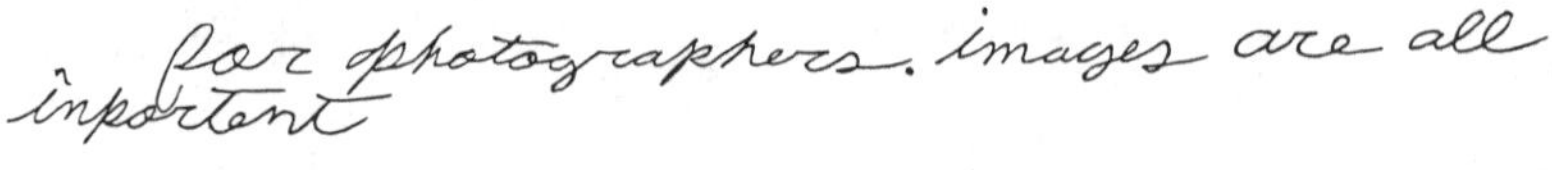

for photographers. images are all inportant

Figure 8–2

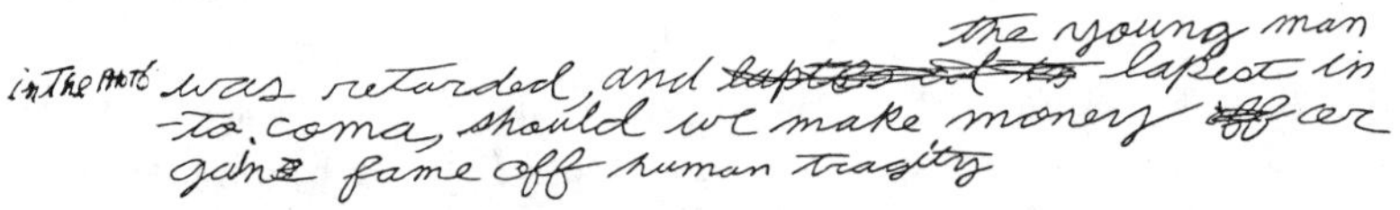

in The photo was retarded, and ~~[struck out]~~ the young man lapest in to. coma, should we make money ~~off~~ or gane fame off human tragity

all important" with a period, and, in Figure 8–2, "the young man in the photo was retarded, and lapest into coma" from the question "should we make money or gain fame off human tragity" by the use of a comma.

Since Arthur understood the basic patterns of English syntax, some of his confusion about punctuation was cleared up by examining and practicing the different functions of commas, periods, and question marks.

But there were other problems with Arthur's writing that were not so easy for me to understand or articulate at first. His compositions were often incomprehensible to me because, although I could usually intuit what Arthur was trying to do in a piece, I would often note large gaps, jumps, or empty spaces in his writing when he would abruptly leave one idea he was just beginning to develop and move on to the next without making connections or clarifying meanings for the reader. For example, in the following sample, Arthur was responding to an editorial in the *Boston Globe* about the Reagan Hot Line, which had been established between hospital nurseries and the federal government so that any suspected failure to give life-supporting care to impaired or defective infants could be immediately reported to federal authorities.

> In regards to your recent editorial on "The Reagan Hot Line," and its 24 hour-a-day number, (It's an old line but it seems to fit) Just how meanly tax dollars is this "Squeal Line" costing the American People? Another point is the fact that nursing is a

> highly competitive field. What better tool than a hot line A hot line where rumors coulf be started. It has shades of witch hunt about it.

In this sample, Arthur raises the first issue with a question, "Just how meanly tax dollars is this 'Squeal Line' costing the American People?" However, he fails to develop this line of thought any further and, instead, moves on abruptly to "another point." Again, when raising this second point, Arthur does not explain *how* the Hot Line could be used as a tool of competition in the nursing profession. In both instances, he merely implies his meanings and leaves the elaboration and the conclusions to the reader. As Shaughnessy (1977) notes, basic writers often have difficulty suspending closures until ideas are fully expressed and worked out. They tend instead to see each sentence as a closed and finished unit (227).

In his narratives, Arthur would sometimes begin a piece right in the middle of the action without identifying characters or giving background information so the reader could understand what he was writing about. The following lines are from the first paragraph of a piece in which he wanted to describe the early influence of "Star Trek" on his life:

> The show starts out with the captain and Spock as very young officers As the voyage open the ship is juct about to leave the known universe when they came apon and old-style destress beacon it warns Them of doom still they press on they have a job to do Then comes the negitiv energy barriar

Assuming that the reader shares the same background information about the series, Arthur does not explain who the Captain and Spock are, where they are traveling, what a negative energy barrier is, what ship they are on, and so on. Further, he makes several vague pronoun references in the piece that are confusing for the reader.

When I asked Arthur in conference to fill in the missing information or to explain or elaborate ideas that were there in his papers in germinal form, he would often respond with surprise. It surprised him that I didn't know what he was trying to say or couldn't make connections and read meanings into his work. I then began to realize that Arthur was attempting to write his compositions as if he were talking to intimates. It was speech written down, elliptical, unelaborated, full of extratextual references, and based on a set of projected knowns, mutual experiences and shared information about people, places, and events. My job then became a little clearer to me. What I had to do was help Arthur project an audience that was not intimate so that he could understand the need to elaborate and make connections in the text of his writing.

We were beginning to make progress. But progress was slow and difficult. For one thing, the very act of forming letters on paper was arduous for Arthur. When I asked him about his problems with penmanship, he told me that in the second grade, his teacher had forbidden him to write with his left hand, for which he had shown a natural inclination. Instead, he was forced to use his right hand for penmanship exercises. Subsequently, Arthur became a right-handed writer. But he had never been able to overcome a feeling of awkwardness and inadequacy in manipulating a pen or pencil. When I recommended a typing course, Arthur at first rejected the idea. He felt it was a cop-out. He insisted that he wanted to master the skills he had missed, not skip over them. It was important to his sense of progress and self-esteem. However, I was finally able to convince him that since he had been left at a great disadvantage in his early schooling, he needed to take advantage of any means available to make up the deficit that had been left by his early education.

In many of his compositions, Arthur trusted me with the story of that education, of his experience with public schools. It is upsetting. I felt anger and sadness when I read those pained narratives.

> You have asked "how and why this gap has devalepted." My early life in school was very traditional. I was passed on, I was considered a problem child. I was hyperactive I am dislexic I *was* considered retared untill the fifth grade, then I had my eyes tested and "they" found out I needed glasses. I was your stereotype "fat kid", allways in the "slow class", allways the butt of the jok this as you might expect made me very introverted. THEY could see wrighting. It was something they could point at.

Arthur described his time in internal suspension in his later school years, when he sat alone for days in a grey room learning to turn inward for sustenance and meaning:

Being alone frightens
some people. It is my natural
element. I all ways got a laugh when they
(they being the school) gave me internal
SUSPENSION. You would sit in a SMALL GRAY room all day.
"So what?" I'd just bring some sandwiches
a quart of orange juces and a bunch of magazine
es. I learned to
be alone and to like it. Mabey because
it was the only time I was in controle of
my life.

Arthur felt especially vulnerable in the area of written expression.

> Writing was a target for their ridicule, and scorn because it was so personal and close to me they knew it was a weak SPOT although I could keep my thoughts private my hardwirting made me a target of ridicile

Adrienne Rich, the poet and writer, taught with Mina Shaughnessy in the program for open admissions students at City University. In her book, *On Lies, Secrets, and Silence* (1979), she speaks of the debasing experiences many minority students and other "troublesome" or "nonconforming" or "different" students had in their early years in schools in which students were rewarded for conformity and passivity and punished for uniqueness. They were often, she affirms, victims of tracking and were channeled out of programs for middle-class peers, peers who were "teachable" (56). As in the case of the students described by Rich, the schools didn't reach Arthur. They didn't deal with him at all. Arthur didn't fail in school; school failed him.

In recent years, there has been a great deal of talk about the need to raise the standards of education in our colleges and universities. And I must confess, I too used to cluck my tongue and shake my head over the "deplorable" lack of excellence in higher education, which I felt had resulted from our more liberal admission policies. I firmly believed that entrance requirements needed to be upgraded so that only capable, well-prepared, and high-achieving students would be admitted to college programs. Besides, as a teacher of English, I wanted to work for "higher" goals—to help my students gain an authentic voice in their writing, to give them practice with different rhetorical forms, to guide them in developing their skills of abstraction. I certainly didn't want to be burdened with students who hadn't mastered the basics.

But now, what I have to keep asking, because the question is so present to me, "What about Arthur?" Arthur, who is my student? who doesn't want to "blow his life off"? who cries for what I have to give him, what I received so gratuitously as a white, middle-class, docile, conforming and highly verbal student, who mastered the fine motor skills early, who learned penmanship and participated in spelling bees and diagramed sentences and wrote compositions that were sold at student auction in grammar school, and who had success after success with the written word? And now, here is my student who does not have these tools, the so-called basics, and is locked inside himself.

Arthur has meaning. Meaning is not his problem. While the most frequent complaint of the majority of my English Comp students is that they have nothing to write about, nothing to say, Arthur is bursting with ideas and feelings, opinions and insights. After some initial hesitation and self-consciousness, he contributed enthusiastically and intelligently in class discussions. He enriched our classroom exchanges with observations from his broader experiences in the working world. In his papers, he has little trouble getting in touch with what matters to him and in expressing himself in a vigorous, authentic voice. In fact, he insists on that authenticity.

> When I first started to wright this paper it was a high sounding pretezous bore, when I remembered the best shots are simple clean and strong. Stright to the point

Arthur writes with commitment and a strong personal voice. For example, when he felt that the profession he wished to pursue after college was being attacked by an offhand remark of one of the class members, he passionately defended the photographer's right to remain artistically detached from the event being recorded:

> Suddenly the reality in my life was being threatened, and it was up to me to defend it, to prove to them and myself I was right, The attack came the other day, in my English class, A student raised the question of what responsibility a photographer has. With zeal we are condemed. "Should we help or get the shot"?
>
> As a young photographer, just at the beginning of what I hope will be a long and noteworthy career, this question looms

> befor me. All my life I have tried to do what was honorable. I ask "What can be more honorable than recording life in all it's aspects, good and bad?"

Further, he displays a highly developed aesthetic sense and uses sophisticated metaphors and the more complex syntax of the written code with apparent ease. For example, he ends a book review of *Dune* with the following paragraph:

> I would be a lier if I were to say that this is even an introduction to "*Dune*" for all my skill at speach I fail when it come to the telling of this tail. So perfect is it woven that no one part can be taken out to show the whole. Just as a finely woven fabraic can not be discribed by only showing the threds

But every composition is handicapped, weighted down with labor, the labor of undeveloped and unpracticed handwriting, the labor of looking up every word in a dictionary,, the labor of placing periods and commas correctly so that meanings can be understood, and the labor of learning to write in the elaborated code of literacy.

Near the end of the semester, Arthur was still working hard. He revised and recopied each piece of writing over and over again, working tirelessly with a friend/tutor who helps him with spelling and punctuation so that he can untangle the mysteries of the written word and mold and form it into the tool of his self-expression. I saw progress in his work. For example, the following revised piece of writing is legibly written, correctly punctuated, and has no spelling errors:

> Being alone frightens some people. It is my natural element. I always got a laugh when they (they being the school) gave me "internal suspension". You would sit in a small, gray room all day. So what? I'd just bring some sandwiches, a quart of orange juice and a bunch of magazines. I learned to be alone and to like it.

Still, Arthur has not been able to produce those four acceptable papers for his passing C. Together, we decided that he should take an incomplete in the course, and we would work throughout the summer concentrating on the full development of his ideas, the use of transitions, and the effective, clear organization of his compositions. He will also enroll in a typing class.

I am optimistic that Arthur will achieve his goals.

For me, the rewards of working with Arthur have far outweighed the tedium and time commitment. I feel my old sense of academic elitism beginning to crumble. It is being replaced by a refreshing and newfound humility based on my experience with this one student. I feel that I will never again be guided in my teaching by an arbitrary set of standards or impersonal dogma. Like Arthur, my students all have faces now.

If Arthur has learned from me, I have certainly learned from him. First, I have learned about courage and dignity through his determined struggle to overcome a severe educational handicap. Second, I have gained firsthand insight into the failure of our public education system, which often rewards conformity and punishes uniqueness. Third, I have acquired a new respect for the skills of written communication and the power of the written word. And finally, I have developed a special sense of reverence for my chosen profession as a teacher of writing. Arthur has helped me see, on a very personal level, the broad implications and the profound consequences of what I do each day in the classroom. The teaching of writing has now taken on political dimensions for me. As Adrienne Rich affirms, "when we teach our students to write, we are giving them power and dignity, and we are giving them freedom" (56).

References

Rich, Adrienne. 1979. *On Lies, Secrets, and Silence.* New York: W. W. Norton and Co.

Shaughnessy, Mina P. 1977. *Errors and Expectations.* New York: Oxford University Press.

9

Productive Tension in the Writing Conference

Studying Our Students and Ourselves

Lad Tobin
St. Anselm College
Manchester, New Hampshire

IT is Micki's third conference, and she looks pleased. "I brought in a revision of that essay about my job at the grocery store. I think I'm about done with it. I think it's better than the last draft. I still might change a few things. I'm not really happy with some of the words I used and stuff. But basically I think it's done. I think I'm going to start on my second essay this week." I read the introduction in silence.

> During the summer I worked in a grocery store as a cashier. This is a great opportunity for anyone who enjoys observing the behavior of people.

Already I feel uncomfortable. This is exactly how her last draft started. Is the point of her "about done" essay that she has observed people shopping?

> In my observations I noticed how many shoppers decided to shop at the same time and at the most awkward hours. The strangest hours are usually the busiest. What is frustrating is that while you are ready to leave for home there is a mad rush for last minute groceries. And customers can become very irritating at times, too.

Now my fears are almost confirmed: this is not the revision that I hinted at last week, that I thought we had agreed she would try to write. How can she feel the essay is done? I glance down the page to the conclusion.

> Most customers enjoy a cheerful greeting from a cashier, but when a cashier has been dealing with difficult people all day it is hard to be polite. Working in a grocery store has opened my eyes to the fact that there is not much emphasis on person to person dealings in the business world.

That paragraph sounds vaguely familiar and I remember why: in her last conference, Micki had brought in a draft organized loosely around her personal observations of shoppers. She had started *that* conference in a very different way: "I know this isn't really a good topic, but I can't think of anything to write about. I never really did this kind of writing in high school." She went on to say that her high school teacher gave her "rules and examples" to follow and that in a way she liked that better. "At least you knew what you had to do." Because she seemed discouraged and anxious, I tried to build up her confidence, to make her feel that she did have something to write about and the authority to write about it. I asked her why she didn't like her job, and she told me about rude customers. I asked her why she thought they behaved that way. She didn't know. I asked her if she was especially sympathetic to cashiers when *she* shopped in grocery stores. She laughed, "No. I'm kind of like the people who come into the store where I work." And so I encouraged her: "You do have things to write about. You're an expert on this subject; you've seen it from both sides. And since everyone has had some of the experiences you describe, readers will recognize your expertise and will want to understand what really goes on. Now what interests *you* about that relationship? What do *you* want to know more about?"

And so in that way I had led Micki to this decision to look at "person to person dealings," to this attempt to find meaning in her observations. But I had hoped for much more than this.

"Let me just look at your introduction again," I mumble, stalling for time, looking at the words on the page but thinking about what I should say. How should I respond to this draft? Certainly Micki seems to feel better about her writing (and better about herself) in this conference. But *I* am feeling worse. I am feeling anxious. I see potential here, but it is still basically unrealized, and I am not comfortable with her confidence in the essay, with her decision to move on to another draft.

I am tempted just to tell her what is wrong, but I hesitate. I am aware that Micki and I are not the only ones in this writing conference. Don Murray (1985) is here, too, reminding me that writers need the time and the encouragement to find their voices and their meaning. I hear Brannon and Knoblauch's (1982) argument about students' rights to their own texts. And I can't stop thinking about Ferguson McKay's (1987) case studies, which clearly demonstrate his thesis that "confidence is a writer's central need" (100). But there are other voices in the room as well: Thomas Carnicelli (1980) insists that I must accept my "professional obligation" (116) to give my opinion of each student essay; Pamela Richards (1986) argues that writers need to hear the truth because "the feeling that someone is humoring me [as a writer] is more damaging to my sense of self than outright attack" (118); and my colleagues, chairperson, dean, former teachers, and conscience all tell me that standards are important, that this draft needs to be revised, that Micki has not pushed herself hard enough.

I finally speak: "So you are happier with this draft?" A non-question. I am still stalling. She has already told me that she is. But I want some time to think, and I have learned that getting students to do the talking in these situations is essential. Often, when pushed just a little, students who claim to be finished with a draft will admit that the draft still needs work, that they still have questions and doubts, and sometimes that they even know what is wrong and how to fix it. But I have no such luck today.

"Yeah, I am." I wait to see if she will give up anything at all. Finally she asks directly, "Is it OK?" Her tone has changed now; she is sounding much less confident, aware that I am not satisfied.

"Well . . . I definitely see progress from your last one. . . . I am interested in the point about the impersonal environment of the store. Could you tell me more about that?"

She doesn't answer; instead she picks up her essay and begins reading as if she hasn't seen it before.

"I mean, is that really your central point, that the atmosphere in the store makes people behave in a certain way?"

Damn. Why can't I ever let long silences remain? As soon as I answer one of my own questions, I always remember Graves's (1983) point about the value of silence and patience in writing conferences; but with a struggling student sitting there I often can't take it. I just keep thinking I have got to get them, get us, over these uncomfortable moments. But that's the problem. Am I helping *them* by talking or helping *me?*

"I guess I could try to focus more on my point about how the atmosphere of the store makes people—the customers and the cashiers—act a certain way and they don't even realize it."

"Fine. Why don't you try that?"

As Micki gets up to leave, I worry once again about whether I talked too much, too little, or some of each.

I do not present Micki's conference as a model for teacher training. In fact, I would argue that there is no such thing as a model or typical conference. Like writing itself, the writing conference is a process—not static, not a noun, not a thing, but rather active, dynamic, organic. It changes with each student and each teacher and each second, and although there is value (even necessity, I think) in developing a logical theory and approach, we need to learn to work with students to "write" the conference as well as the essay, to learn when our response should dictate the process and when the process should dictate the response.

But while the specifics of Micki's conference may not be typical, the issues her conference raises are. When and how should we respond to a student's writing? And how should we deal with the tension that writers *and* teachers often feel in writing conferences? In many "first generation" writing conferences—Roger Garrison's (1974) early conferences would be an example—teachers set the agenda: "Here is what is wrong; here is how you can fix it." But "second generation" conference teachers (following Murray's lead) focused more on questions than on answers, more on structural issues than superficial problems. Still, however, this process approach to conference teaching became ritualized in its own ways—"Always start by offering encouragement," "Focus on only one or two things in each conference," "Do as little of the talking as possible," and "Never take over a student's essay."

If we want to understand how writing conferences work (and why some fail) we need to move beyond a set of rigid rules for writing conference teachers to an approach that takes into account the dynamic aspects of each writing conference: the student's relationship to the text, the teacher's relationship to the text, and the student and teacher's relationship to each other. To be effective, conference teachers must monitor the tension created within and between these relationships and strive to keep that tension at a productive level—for their students and for themselves.

The level of tension is productive only if it keeps the writing and reading processes alive. When the tension level is too high, writers freeze, panic, resist, retreat, telling themselves either "I really don't have anything to say" or "I have a lot to say but I can't get it down on paper." When the level is too low, they lack the interest, curiosity, desire, even pain, that compels someone to keep writing effectively. But the student's tension is only half of the picture. When the tension level is too high—that is, when they fear that their students are not making progress or lack the skills to produce a successful essay—teachers also panic and retreat: they revert to "objective" assignments, frequent grading, direct instruction. When the level is too low, they lack the curiosity and desire that compel them to read and respond effectively. For writing conferences to work, teachers must establish a level of tension that is productive not only for the students but also for themselves.

I do not mean to suggest here that tension is an end in itself; rather I am suggesting that we focus on tension—our students' and our own—because it will help us to make practical decisions about when and how to intervene in any individual conference. When a student seems tense, stuck, frustrated, we encourage, support, and question; when a student seems self-satisfied, refusing to go beyond his first superficial responses to a complex topic, we push, provoke, and question. But what about when *we* are feeling self-satisfied or stuck or tense? Whether we are aware of it or not, our expectations, frustrations, and associations, our responses and nonresponses, also shape the student's level of tension, the dynamics of the conference, and the direction of the subsequent revision.

But these two levels of tension—the student's and the teacher's—are interrelated not only because they each change in response to the other, but also because the frustration and tension that a writing conference teacher experiences is similar to the frustration and tension that a writer experiences. The trick is in negotiating the tension so that the student and teacher believe not only that the student has the potential to achieve her goals in the essay but also that those goals are worth achieving.

Unfortunately many teachers seem to fear tension and often try hard to reduce or eliminate it. These teachers have good intentions: they know that many students have been traumatized by writing and writing teachers and they also know that too much tension is debilitating, even paralyzing for a writer. But while we can decrease tension in certain areas of the process, we cannot (and should not try to) make writing or teaching writing entirely painless. We should not strive to make everyone in the writing class "as comfortable as possible," a goal appropriate for terminally ill patients, but not for teachers and writers. Rather than wasting time trying to dissipate tension, we need to expend more energy finding ways to use that tension productively. And in the final analysis, we can do that only by carefully studying our students and ourselves.

In the following case studies, I have tried to look carefully at the role tension played in my students' writing and my conference teaching. These case studies reveal at least as much about me as a conference teacher as they reveal about each of these student writers. They reveal, for example, my tendencies to offer editorial (and sometimes extremely directive) comments as if they were questions, to push students to write introspective, almost confessional essays, and, most of all, to try to sustain a relatively high level of tension in each conference. The research was conducted in a freshman composition course in which students were asked to "finish" three essays in fifteen weeks. No topics were assigned. No drafts were graded. Students were asked to write one personal narrative, one argument or analysis of a written work, and one essay analyzing some aspect of their own writing process. During the semester each student had a weekly conference in which he or she was expected to bring an essay to discuss (either a new draft or a revision). Generally students worked for five or six weeks on an essay and then moved on to another.

Denise

Conference 1

I read Denise's draft while she sits quietly. Her thesis: "I never knew that there were so many preparations that go into getting ready for a wedding. But now that my sister is getting married next month I am getting a chance to see how much work is really involved." From there she went on to list everything—ordering flowers, sending out invitations, and so on. I am struck by one section of the paper: "I am not sure why, but I am not really that excited about the wedding yet. I keep getting this kind of empty feeling. I am sure I will be excited, though, when the event comes." But she then returns to a list of the preparations. She ends the draft by stating that in spite of all the work involved she still believes in marriage.

In the middle of the conference, she said that she was "sort of happy" with the essay but that she "felt stuck" about how to revise it.

"Well, what interests you most in this essay?"

"I don't know."

"Did anything surprise you in writing this?"

"Not really."

"Did you learn anything new about weddings or about how you feel about this one?"

"Not really. What do you mean?"

"Well, what about this paragraph about the empty feeling?" Long pause. "It seems different to me. Does it to you?"

"Well, it is about feelings and the rest is just a list of facts."

"Yes. Do you want to write more about that?"

"I guess so. It's just that there is so much to do for a wedding. There's like ten showers and when I was home last week I had to spend almost an entire day doing stuff for the shower we're giving. I didn't really mind but I was just home for two days."

"So will you write more on this?"

"I don't know. What interests you most?"

"That paragraph because it is different. There is more tension there, more unanswered questions, don't you think?"

"So maybe I should write more about that?"

"I think so, but I don't want to be pushy. It is your essay, not mine."

"No. I need the help, the advice. In high school I never had to write this kind of paper before. We also got assigned topics about books and we always wrote five-paragraph essays. I don't know how to do this."

As usual, I feel good about some parts of this conference and bad about others. I see an essay here before Denise does. It is better than what she has, but I can tell that she does not see it herself. So I directed her attention to it. But that's all. I didn't interpret it, though I do have an interpretation: she is jealous of her sister and all of the attention she is getting. That is what I think she really feels. And I am thinking that she could write a great essay about how weddings and other big events are supposed to make us feel good but often they don't because we all bring our own emotional baggage. "Did you ever wonder why so many people cry at weddings?" That is how I would start it. But it isn't my essay. I knew Denise needs to get the details down on paper, write her way through that phase before she can (or dares to) shape it, interpret it. Students writing about painful experiences—the death of a family member or the breakup of a friendship—have taught me that. Give her time to find her point. Am I directing too much already? I need to be patient. I need to shut up. But I also need to reassure her (and me) that teaching and learning are going on here.

Conference 2

In her next draft, Denise explores her feelings of ambivalence. She does raise the question of jealousy over all of the attention her sister is receiving. But, she says, her "empty feeling" isn't caused by jealousy: "I will get my turn to have a big wedding someday." Then she raises the question of worry for her sister, but she says it couldn't be that either because "I like my sister's fiancé. I know he will be good for her." She concludes that her emptiness is probably nothing significant. "I can't wait till it is over, though, so we can get back to normal."

In the conference she expresses frustration again with the revision process. I keep pushing her, hoping that she will decide to take up the problem of her ambivalence. Finally, I ask directly about her negative feelings. "I don't know. I'm not sure what it is.

I mean, I am excited about the wedding, but there is something. . . . " I hesitate. She says nothing. The she shrugs and laughs nervously. "I really don't know."

I hesitate again. Finally I speak up: "Maybe before you revise it next time you should just write down ideas and feelings you associate with the empty feeling. You know, just list anything that comes to mind. Want to try that?"

God, I am feeling lousy about this. She just doesn't seem to get this "sight to insight" idea (Annie Dillard's [1985] description of writing). Maybe I just need to show her what I mean. There is a good paper here about jealousy, about feeling lousy when you are supposed to feel happy. But if I tell Denise that is the paper then she is not writing the paper in the sense that writing is thinking and seeing. I am making the breakthrough, not she. Again I have to remember Murray's advice about patience and faith: faith that the student on her own will find meaning and that that meaning will be worth finding. I don't know if Denise is capable of it.

Conference 3

In the next conference Denise brings her revision in which she again runs through all of the stuff that can't be causing her empty feeling and then says, "First there was my parents' divorce two years ago and then I went away to college and now my sister won't even have the same last name. Sometimes I wish that I could be back in the middle school when our whole family was living together under one roof." So, she suggests, "Maybe my sadness is because the wedding is the last step in my nuclear family splitting apart." Yet, she concludes by stating, "I still am excited for my sister and still look forward to the day that I am walking down the aisle."

I am immediately struck by how much stronger this draft is. In fact, when I read that paragraph about her family's disintegration and how that made her feel, I experienced as a reader the kind of "felt sense" that Sondra Perl (see her essay in this volume) associates with writers when they discover their meaning and voice and purpose. Denise seems to feel better about her essay, but she is not sure why or what to do next. I want her to keep working on this draft, to focus and organize her ideas more effectively, but I also want her to leave knowing what she has accomplished. And so, after some discussion of specific aspects of her revision, I say: "This is a much stronger draft, don't you think?"

"Yeah, I do."

"Do you see how this thesis—about why you have that empty feeling—is a different kind of thesis than your other ones?"

"Yeah. It's more about why I feel that way. Before I just had a lot of facts. Now I think I have more of a point."

That was a great conference. Or a great essay. Or both. I was so sure about the jealousy issue and so smug about that. And worried that I would have to tell her in the end, "Look. Write this." And then she comes in and writes this essay that is so much better, that really goes much further with the topic in a way that shows her thinking, not mine. Well, maybe it shows my way of thinking, my bias towards introspective, epiphany essays. But the epiphany itself came from her, not from me.

Conference 4

Denise brings in a revision with a few minor editing changes, no substantial changes. I ask her if she plans to keep working on this essay and she says, "No, I want to start on my second one." So we discuss her ideas for her new essay.

In some ways I am a little disappointed. The essay took such a leap last week I hoped that it would just keep getting deeper and deeper and better and better. Also, I hoped that Denise would pick up on that stuff about her own fear of marriage. I figured I had it all figured out. She put that part in about her own marriage even before she knew why because unconsciously her fear is that her own marriage could never work out because her parents' marriage did not. She did not pursue that, she said, because her paper is now not about that topic. And she is right. I have to quit writing another paper in my head. No, that is not right. I have to write many different papers. I have to make connections and I have to ask students, carefully, nondramatically, if my connections make sense to them. Of course this essay could go further, but I don't think Denise can right now. And I have to be grateful for what she has gotten out of this material, not regretful about what she has missed.

I believe that the associations of writing teachers have to play a crucial role in the writing conference. When I read Denise's line about the empty feeling, I sensed that it was the real center of her essay. Now I had several options: I could have kept my sense to myself, letting her find her own focus and questions; conversely, I could have told her directly that I wanted her to write her essay on that sentence and then offered my own interpretation of her feelings; or I could have taken a middle path, asking questions in which I was truly interested but trusting her to find her own meaning. Of course, in retrospect I am glad I took that middle path. By finding the sentence that contained the most (the only?) real tension in her essay, I played a role in the process. But in that role I was never trying to take over the essay; I was just trying to keep the ball in her court.

Evan

Conference 1

Evan's essay is about a fight he had with his best friend in high school. The fight began with a practical joke his friend had played on him. The friend had hidden Evan's car keys and would not tell Evan where they were. Evan "got back at the friend" the next day by placing several firecrackers in his friend's car. They created "a lot of noise and smoke but no damage or anything." The friend retaliated immediately by ripping the side mirror off Evan's car. The paper had no conclusion or analysis.

"I'm not really happy with this draft." That is how Evan starts the conference.

"Why not?"

"It has too many details . . . don't you think? And I didn't stick to my topic. My title is too general, too."

"You describe this fight clearly."

"Yeah, I think that's the strongest part."

"I do too. Do you think you will keep working on this one?"

"No."

"Why not?"

"It's too personal."

"Would writing help you gain perspective on it, understand it better?"

"I have perspective on it already. It's just personal."

"OK. That's fine. It is up to you to decide which essays you want to revise."

We then discuss some of his other essay ideas.

I'm frustrated in some ways. Evan's essay is ragged—many problems with mechanics—but it has potential. He seems very upset, clearly resistant to pursuing this topic—which naturally makes me more interested in it. I see the potential because I like essays that start with conflict, confusion, questions. No, that's not true; I like essays that start with order, a superficial order, and then unravel into conflict, confusion, questions, and then get put back together again in a new, better order. Evan cares about this fight but (or so) he cannot yet make sense of it. It is too painful to him to pursue. I felt dumb, embarrassed, asking him about gaining perspective through writing. He says he has it (I don't think he does) and that made me feel as if I were prying into his private life, made me feel a bit like a voyeur. Anyway, I think there is a paper in this experience, but unless he thinks there is a paper there, I have to let it go.

Conferences 2–5

Evan spends the next four conferences and drafts on another essay on volunteer firefighters. The essay has no real focus, no real voice. I question him. "Are you saying . . . ?" "Do you want to look at . . . ?" The drafts change a little, but still no real focus emerges.

I am worried that we are both growing frustrated and will soon lose all confidence in each other's abilities. I am disappointed that Evan chose to pursue this essay rather than the one about the fight. All I know now is that he needs some success soon or he will give up on himself and (I hate to admit this) I will give up on him.

Conference 6

To my great surprise, Evan brings in a revision of the essay about his friend. "Remember that paper I wrote about my fight with my friend? I decided to write another draft about it. I changed it a lot." He has dropped almost the entire narrative section about the details of the fight, leaving only a few sentences from the first essay.

Now he starts with a question: "Would a real friend do something terrible to another friend?" He goes on to argue that a real friend would not have torn off his car mirror. He explains again that the firecrackers were harmless. But then he says that the funny part is that when his parents asked him what happened to the car, he said, "It was vandalized." Evan concluded the draft this way: "I was still protecting my friend. I think inside he knows what he did was wrong."

"You have cut out a lot of details about the fight itself, haven't you?"

"Yeah. I didn't really need them. I wanted to explain more about how I feel."

"Are you happier with this one?"

"Yeah. It's more what I want to say, I think."

"How so?"

"I mean I explained about how I protected them. I told my parents the car was vandalized. That's weird in a way."

"But you say at the end your relationship will never be the same."

"Yeah. I can't forget about it."

"So it's forgive but not forget?"

"Yeah, I guess."

"Is that your central point?"

"I'm not sure."

"Isn't that it? You are going beyond the cliché—forgive and forget—to make an important distinction: that it is possible to forgive someone, at least to stop actively fighting with the person, without forgetting the pain of the experience."

No response for about twenty seconds. We both stare at the essay.

"Actually, you have already made this distinction. Look at this first page. It is all about forgiving him, about not telling your parents, about feeling bad about what happened. But then the second page is about how your friendship was never the same after that."

"Uh-huh."

Silence for about fifteen seconds.

"Could you start with the cliché, then introduce this idea—that the cliché does not really explain what often happens after an upsetting fight with a friend—and then make your point by explaining how forgiving and forgetting are two very different kind of actions?"

"Uh, yeah."

"And then what?"

There is a slight hesitation, and then I speak again: "Do you think you could revise it in that way? How does that sound?"

All in all I think that was a good conference. I know I talked too much. I know I took over towards the end, but what choice did I have at this point? At least he tried this topic again. The fact that it took him so long to come back to it and the fact that he is still clearly upset about this fight prove that he has finally found a topic that means something to him. And I am glad he moved away from straight narrative to some attempt at analysis, even if he doesn't know yet what he thinks about this stuff. I like the fact that he got into this forgive-and-forget stuff. That is qualitatively better than anything else he has come up with so far. It is about discrimination, questioning, not just describing. But I am afraid I am making it my essay. Evan seemed not able to recognize his own thesis, his own idea. To him, it was an offhand remark. He offered it almost metaphorically: "You know how people say, 'forgive and forget.' it's kind of like that, except I can forgive him but I can't really forget about it." So I jump on it and ask him about it and still he doesn't quite get it so I keep questioning him and finally I have to almost tell him, "Here is your main point." Could he have reached a different thesis—a better one—if I hadn't taken over? I think I made the right decision.

Conference 7

In our seventh conference Evan has "incorporated" the forgive-and-forget point by stapling a brief handwritten introduction and conclusion to his previous typed draft. Then he has indicated with arrows and numbers on his typed page that I should refer to those handwritten sections. "In the case of my friendship with my former best friend, the friendship had the quality to forgive but not to forget. Does that change a friendship? In this case it has." To the conclusion, he added: "People always say to forgive and forget is the best thing to retain a friendship. The forgiving part seems to be the easy part. It is the forgetting that's always the hardest. How can I look at him every time and not remember what he did to my car? I'll always remember. I think he knows as well as I do who was in the wrong."

At the end of the conference, Evan commented, "I think I am getting the hang of things now. The conferences help. I get to see what you want, what you think, and then I can make the changes. I am getting to know what you like."

"Is it what I like? Are *you* happy with the revision?"

"Oh, yeah. Definitely."

I am not happy with the revisions. The fact that they are just tacked on (literally) to the essay is an indication that they have not made an impression on Evan's thinking. But he is happy. He sensed correctly that I liked the forgive-and-forget idea, and now that he has added them he feels better and more confident. I feel conflicted. I am glad he is finally feeling good about something in writing, but he is feeling good about something I wrote. It is as if I lent something valuable to him and he is grateful and proud about it. And at first I feel good, too, that I have made him feel better and that I have helped our relationship. But now there is a problem: I was just lending him something to try out, to see if he wanted to get one of his own, but he has mistaken it for a gift. So now what do I do? Ask for it back? Give him credit for it? What the hell do I do now?

Conference 8

In Evan's next conference he brings in essentially the same essay, still not effectively integrating his ideas and mine.

His attitude is even more positive. "I am feeling much better about my writing now. I have a lot more ideas about how to organize stuff. I don't just throw it down on paper. At the beginning of the year I really didn't know what kind of writing you liked."

Now I know *I went too far by suggesting that forgive-and-forget thesis. He never made that point purely his own; but he believes that his writing is better, and that has certain advantages. I have tried to encourage him but also to push him to try to write and think on his own. The fact that he still keeps talking about what I want is discouraging, and I have contributed to it by telling him too much, by losing confidence in his ability. But again, what was my alternative?*

Perhaps the most interesting issue here is the role my tension played first in the conference itself and then in my post-conference comments. Although I admitted in my post-conference response that I "took over" Evan's conference "towards the end," I was not aware (until listening to tapes) that I distorted the conferences in my mind so that I could let myself believe I was not in complete control of Evan's essay. In retrospect I understand my motivation: I had seen several drafts and had several conferences with Evan, and I was growing increasingly worried that the "writing to learn" model was not well suited to his particular skills and needs, that he needed help that I was not providing, and that without intervention his essay would stagnate and our relationship would deteriorate. Given these fears, I began to worry that Evan would be unable to flourish within this approach and that I could at least give him some survival skills and some organizational strategies. It was as if I were saying, "Let's forget this meaning and voice stuff. Here is how you write a competent essay."

My perception that Evan was not making progress and that we were both ready to give up dictated my aggressive response. When I listened to the tapes, I found out that the first statement of the forgive-and-forget idea actually came from me and not from Evan. I made myself think that *he* suggested it because that helped me feel less anxious about taking over his essay. For me the key is what I thought after his second conference: *He needs some success soon or he will give up on himself and (I hate to admit this) I will give up on him.* To keep the process going, I needed to provide a great deal of structure, so much that I no longer viewed the draft as his. Once I felt compelled to offer Evan such direct advice about the thesis and organization of the essay, I was admitting unconsciously that the process had broken down. I was unwilling to let him (or me) continue to struggle, so I tried to cut my losses by giving Evan some sense of accomplishment and confidence in the hope that we would both do better on his next draft. The fact that I did not fully admit this to myself makes sense to me in retrospect: I was trying to control my own tension; I was trying to find a way to help both of us stay with the process.

I hope that these cases reflect some of the tension of real writing conferences and suggest the need for a decision-making process that goes beyond prescriptive rules. While it is convenient to identify a particular style of conference teaching as either "student based" or "teacher based," such neat categories fail to reflect the messily collaborative nature of conference teaching. I felt frustrated by the inadequacy of this either-or approach as soon as I started using conferences to teach writing, but I did not know that others felt the same frustration until I participated in a workshop a few years ago on the teacher's role in writing conferences. To demonstrate the different styles and strategies available to teachers, the workshop leaders gave us two packs of handouts. They were each transcripts of writing conferences. In the first one, the teachers interrupted, badgered, lectured, and trampled over their students, ending conferences by telling the student what to write for the next draft and how to write it. The second group of teachers asked questions, murmured "Mm-hmm" and "Yes, I see" at appropriate times, and encouraged enthusiastic students' plans for revision. The leaders then analyzed this good teacher/bad teacher exercise: "We can believe in freedom or authority; we can let our students write their own papers or we can take over their essays and make them our own."

But in the question-and-answer period, a teacher, looking and sounding exasperated, spoke up. "Of course I wouldn't treat my students like those first teachers did, but my conferences hardly ever turn out like the second ones either. For me the question is what I can do to help my students learn to write. I have a student who is taking comp for the third time because he keeps failing our college's proficiency exam and he comes to conferences trying to improve and I try to let him lead the way, to let him control our conferences. I keep waiting for him to figure out how to improve his own writing. But it is not happening. And when he is struggling with the organization of one of his essays, I can hardly stand it any longer. It takes all of my energy to keep myself from grabbing his pen and his paper out of his hand, writing down an outline, and yelling, 'Look, it goes *this* way!' I want to know how to deal with *that.*"

There must be teachers like the ones in the handouts, but I don't feel I have much in common with them. It is the teacher who spoke up who stays with me in writing conferences and in my research. I know what he is feeling. I've been there myself.

References

Brannon, Lil, and C. H. Knoblauch. 1982. "On Students' Rights to Their Own Texts: A Model of Teacher Response." *College Composition and Communication* 33 (May): 157–66.

Carnicelli, Thomas A. 1980. "The Writing Conference: A One-to-One Conversation." In *Eight Approaches to Teaching Composition*, ed. Timothy R. Donovan and Ben W. McClelland, 101–31. Urbana, Ill.: National Council of Teachers of English.

Dillard, Annie. 1985. "Sight into Insight." In *The Conscious Reader*. 3rd ed., ed. Caroline Shrodes, Harry Finestone, Michael Shugrue, 689–98. New York: Macmillan.

Garrison, Roger. 1974. "One-to-One: Tutorial Instruction in Freshman Composition." *New Directions for Community Colleges* 2: 55–84.

Graves, Donald. 1983. *Writing: Teachers and Children at Work.* Portsmouth, N.H.: Heinemann.

McKay, Ferguson. 1987. "Roles and Strategies in College Writing Conferences." In *Seeing for Ourselves: Case-Study Research by Teachers of Writing,* ed. Glenda Bissex and Richard Bullock. Portsmouth, N.H.: Heinemann.

Murray, Donald. 1985. *A Writer Teaches Writing.* 2nd ed. Boston: Houghton Mifflin.

Richards, Pamela. 1986. "Risk." In *Writing for Social Scientists: How to Start and Finish Your Thesis, Book, or Article* by Howard S. Becker with a chapter by Pamela Richards, 108–20. Chicago: University of Chicago Press.

10

Teaching the Other Self
The Writer's First Reader

Donald Murray
University of New Hampshire, Emeritus
Durham, New Hampshire

WE urge our students to write for others, but writers report they write for themselves. "I write for me," says Edward Albee. "The audience of me." Teachers of composition make a serious mistake if they consider such statements a matter of artistic ego alone.

The testimony of writers that they write for themselves opens a window on an important part of the writing process. If we look through that window we increase our understanding of the process and become more effective teachers of writing.

"I am my own first reader," says Issac Bashevis Singer. "Writers write for themselves and not for their readers," declares Rebecca West, "and that art has nothing to do with communication between person and person, only with communication between different parts of a person's mind." "I think the audience an artist imagines," states Vladimir Nabokov, "when he imagines that sort of thing, is a room filled with people wearing his own mask." Edmund Blunden adds, "I don't think I have ever written for anybody except the other in one's self."

The act of writing might be described as a conversation between two workmen muttering to each other at the workbench. The self speaks, the other self listens and responds. The self proposes, the other self considers. The self makes, the other self evaluates. The two selves collaborate: a problem is spotted, discussed, defined; solutions are proposed, rejected, suggested, attempted, tested, discarded, accepted.

This process is described in that fine German novel, *The German Lesson,* by Siegfried Lenz, when the narrator in the novel watches the painter, Nansen, at work. "And, as always when he was at work he was talking. He didn't talk to himself, he talked to someone by the name of Balthasar, who stood beside him, his Balthasar, who only he could see and hear, with whom he chatted and argued and whom he sometimes jabbed with his elbow, so hard that even we, who couldn't see any Balthasar, would suddenly hear the invisible bystander groan, or, if not groan, at least swear. The longer we stood there behind him, the more we began to believe in the existence of that Balthasar who made himself perceptible by a sharp intake of breath or a hiss of disappointment. And still the painter went on confiding in him, only to regret it a moment later."

Study this activity at the workbench within the skull and you might say that the self writes, the other self reads. But it is not reading as we usually consider it, the decoding of a completed text. It is a sophisticated reading that monitors writing before it is made, as it is made, and after it is made.

The term *monitor* is significant, for the reading during writing involves awareness on many levels and includes the opportunity for change. And when that change is made then everything must be read again to see how the change affects the reading.

The writer, as the text evolves, reads fragments of language as well as completed units of language, what isn't on the page as well as what is on the page, what should be left out as well as what should be put in. Even patterns and designs—sketches of possible relationships between pieces of information or fragments of rhetoric or language—that we do not usually consider language are read and discussed by the self and the other self.

It is time researchers in the discipline called English bridge the gulf between the reading researcher and the writing researcher. There are now many trained writing researchers who can collaborate with the trained researcher in reading, for the act of writing is inseparable from the act of reading. You can read without writing, but you can't write without reading. The reading skills required, however, to decode someone else's finished text may be quite different from the reading skills required to chase a wisp of thinking until it grows into a completed thought.

To follow thinking that has not yet become thought, the writer's other self has to be an explorer, a map maker. The other self scans the entire territory, forgetting, for the moment, questions of order or language. The writer/explorer looks for the draft's horizons. Once the writer has scanned the larger vision of the territory, it may be possible to trace a trail that will get the writer from here to there, from meaning identified to meaning clarified. Questions of order are now addressed, but questions of language still delayed. Finally, the writer/explorer studies the map in detail to spot the hazards that lie along the trail, the hidden swamps of syntax, the underbrush of verbiage, the voice found, lost, found again.

Map making and map reading are among man's most complex cognitive tasks. Eventually the other self learns to monitor the always changing relationship between where the writer is and where the writer intended to go. The writer/explorer stops, looks ahead, considers and reconsiders the trail and the ways to get around the obstacles that block that trail.

There is only one way the student can learn map reading—and that is in the field. Books and lectures may help, but only after the student writer has been out in the bush will the student understand the kind of reading essential for the exploration of thinking. The teacher has to be a guide who doesn't lead so much as stand behind the young explorer, pointing out alternatives only at the moment of panic. Once the writer/explorer has read one map and made the trip from meaning intended to meaning realized, will the young writer begin to trust the other self and have faith it will know how to read other trails through other territories.

The reading writer—map maker and map reader—reads the word, the line, the sentence, the paragraph, the page, the entire text. This constant back-and-forth reading monitors the multiple complex relationships between all the elements in writing. Recursive scanning—or reviewing and previewing—is beginning to be documented during revision by Sondra Perl, Nancy Sommers, and others. But further and more sophisticated investigation will, I believe, show that the experienced writer is able, through the writer's other self, to read what has gone before and what may come afterward during the writing that is done before there is a written text, and during the writing that produces an embryonic text.

I think we can predict some of the functions that are performed by the other self during the writing process.

- The other self tracks the activity that is taking place. Writing, in a sense, does not exist until it is read. The other self records the evolving text.
- The other self gives the self the distance that is essential for craft. This distance, the craftperson's step backwards, is a key element in that writing that is therapeutic for the writer.
- The other self provides an evolving context for the writer. As the writer adds, cuts, or records, the other self keeps track of how each change affects the draft.
- The other self articulates the process of writing, providing the writer with an engineering history of the developing text, a technical resource that records the problems faced and the solutions that were tried and rejected, not yet tried, and the one that is in place.
- The other self is the critic who is continually looking at the writing to see if, in the writer's phrase, "it works."
- The other self also is the supportive colleague to the writer, the chap who commiserates and encourages, listens sympathetically to the writer's complaints and reminds the writer of past success. The deeper we get into the writing process the more we may discover how affective concerns govern the cognitive, for writing is an intellectual activity carried on in an emotional environment, a precisely engineered sailboat trying to hold course in a vast and stormy Atlantic. The captain has to deal with fears as well as compass readings.

We shall have to wait for perceptive and innovative research by teams of reading and writing researchers to document the complex kind of reading that is done during the writing process. But fortunately, we do not have to wait for the results of such research to make use of the other self in the teaching of writing.

The other self can be made articulate. It has read the copy as it was being created and knows the decisions that were made to produce the draft. This does not mean that they were all conscious decisions in the sense that the writer articulated what was being done, but even instinctive or subconscious editorial decisions can be articulated retrospectively.

Many teachers of writing, especially those who are also teachers of literature, are deeply suspicious of the testimony of writers about their own writing. It may be that the critic feels that he or she knows more than the writer, that the testimony of writers is too simple to be of value. But I have found in my own work that what students and professional writers say about their own writing process is helpful and makes sense in relation to the text.

Writing is, after all, a rational act; the writing self was monitored by the reading self during the writing process. The affective may well control or stimulate or limit the cognitive, but writing is thinking, and a thinking act can, most of the time, be recreated in rational terms. The tennis pro may return a serve instinctively, but instinct is, in part, internalized consciousness, and if you ask the pro about that particular return the experienced player will be able to describe what was done and why. If the player thought consciously at the time of the serve, the ball would sail by. The return was a practiced, learned act made spontaneous by experience, and it can be described and explained after the fact.

This retroactive understanding of what was done makes it possible for the teacher not only to teach the other self but recruit the other self to assist in the teaching of writing. The teacher brings the other self into existence, and then works with that other self so that, after the student has graduated, the other self can take over the function of teacher.

When the student speaks and the student and teacher listen they are both informed about the nature of the writing process that produced the draft. This is the point at which the teacher knows what needs to be taught or reinforced one step at a time, and the point at which the student knows what needs to be done in the next draft.

Listening is not a normal composition teacher's skill. We tell and they listen. But to make effective use of the other self the teacher and the student must listen together.

This is done most efficiently in conference. But before the conference at the beginning of the course the teacher must explain to the class exactly why the student is to speak first. I tell my students that I'm going to do as little as possible to interfere with their learning. It is their job to read the text, to evaluate it, to decide how it can be improved so that they will be able to write when I am not there. I point out that the ways in which they write are different, their problems and solutions are different, and that I am a resource to help them find their own way. I will always attempt to underteach so that they can overlearn.

I may read the paper before the conference or during the conference, but the student will always speak first in the conference. I have developed a repertoire of questions—what surprised you? what's working best? what are you going to do next?—but I rarely use them. The writing conference is not a special occasion. The student comes to get my response to the work, and I give my response to the student's response. I am teaching the other self.

The more inexperienced the student and the less comprehensible the text, the more helpful the writer's comments. Again and again with remedial students I am handed a text that I simply cannot understand. I do not know what it is supposed to say. I cannot discover a pattern of organization. I cannot understand the language. But when the writer tells me what the writer was doing, when the other self is allowed to speak, I find that the text was produced rationally. The writer followed misunderstood instruction, inappropriate principles, or logical processes that did not work.

Most students, for example, feel that if you want to write for a large audience you should write in general terms, in large abstractions. They must be told that is logical; but it simply doesn't work. The larger the audience, the more universal we want our message to be, the more specific we must become. It was E. B. White who reminded us, "Don't write about Man, write about *a* man."

When the teacher listens to the student, the conference can be short. The student speaks about the process that produced the draft or about the draft itself. The teacher listens, knowing that the effective teacher must teach where the student is, not where the teacher wishes the student was, then scans or rescans the draft to confirm, adjust, or disagree with the student's comments.

One thing the responsible teacher, the teacher who listens to the student first then to the text, soon learns is that the affective usually controls the cognitive, and affective responses have to be dealt with first. I grew used to this with students, but during the past two years I have also worked with professionals on some of the best newspapers in the country, and I have found that it is even more true of published writers. Writers' feelings control the environment in which the mind functions. Unless the teacher knows this environment the teaching will be off target.

In conference, for example, the majority of men have been socialized to express a false confidence in their writing. The teacher who feels these men are truly confident will badly misread the writer's other self. The behavior of women in conference is changing, but not fast enough. Most women still express the false modesty about their accomplishments that society has said is appropriate for women. Again the teacher must recognize and support the other self that knows how good the work really is.

I am constantly astonished when I see drafts of equal accomplishment, but with writer evaluations that are miles apart. One student may say, "This is terrible. I can't write. I think I'd better drop the course." And right after that on a similar paper a student says, "I never had so much fun writing before. I think this is really a good paper. Do you think I should become a writer?"

Many students, of course, have to deal first with these feelings about the draft—or about writing itself. The conference teacher should listen to these comments, for they often provide important clues to why the student is writing—or avoiding writing—in a particular way.

The instructor who wishes to teach the other self must discuss the text with that other self in less despairing or elated tones. Too often the inexperienced conference teacher goes to the polar extreme and offers the despairing student absolute praise and the confident student harsh criticism. In practice, the effective conference teacher does not deal in praise or criticism. All texts can be improved, and the instructor discusses with the student what is working and can be made to work better, and what isn't working and how it might be made to work.

As the student gets by the student's feelings, the concerns become more cognitive. At first the students, and the ineffective writing teacher, focus on the superficial, the most obvious problems of language or manuscript preparation. But the teacher, through questioning, can reorient the student to the natural hierarchy of editorial concerns.

These questions over a series of conferences may evolve from "What's the single most important thing you have to say?" to "What questions is the reader going to ask you and when are they going to be asked?" to "Where do you hear the voice come through strongest?"

The students will discover, as the teacher models an ideal other self, that the largest questions of content, meaning, or focus have to be dealt with first. Until there is a clear meaning the writer cannot order the information that supports that meaning or leads towards it. And until the meaning and its supporting structure are clear the writer cannot make the decisions about voice and language that clarify and communicate that meaning. The other self has to monitor many activities and make sure that the writing self reads what is being monitored in an effective sequence.

Sometimes teachers who are introduced to teaching the other self feel that listening to this student first means they cannot intervene. That is not true. This is not a do-your-own thing kind of teaching. It is a demanding teaching, it is nothing less than the teaching of critical thinking.

Listening is, after all, an aggressive act. When the teacher insists that the student knows the subject and the writing process that produced the draft better than the teacher, and then has faith that the student has an other self that has monitored the producing of the draft, then the teacher puts enormous pressure on the student. Intelligent comments are expected, and when they are expected they are often received.

I have been impressed by how effectively primary students, those in the first three grades in school, have a speaking other self. Fortunately this other self that monitors the writing process has been documented on tape in a longitudinal study conducted in the Atkinson, New Hampshire, schools by Donald Graves, Lucy Calkins, and Susan Sowers at the University of New Hampshire. There the other self has been recorded and analyzed.

The most effective learning takes place when the other self articulates the writing that went well. Too much instruction is failure centered. It focuses on error and unintentionally reinforces error.

The successful writer does not so much correct error as discover what is working and extend that element in the writing. The writer looks for the voice, the order, the relationship of information that is working well, and concentrates on making the entire piece of writing have the effectiveness of the successful fragment. The responsive teacher is always attempting to get the student to bypass the global evaluations of failure—"I can't write about this," "It's an airball," "I don't have anything to say"—and move into an element that is working well. In the beginning of a piece of writing by a beginning student that first concern might well be the subject of the feeling that the student has toward the subject. The teacher may well say, "Okay. This draft isn't working, but what do you know about the subject that a reader needs to know?"

Again and again the teacher listens to what the student is saying—and not saying—to help the student hear that other self that has been monitoring what isn't yet on the page or what may be beginning to appear on the page.

This dialogue between the student's other self and the teacher occurs best in conference. But the conferences should be short and frequent.

"I dunno," the student says. "In reading this over I think maybe I'm more specific." The teacher scans the text and responds, "I agree. What are you going to work on next?" "I guess the ending. It sorta goes on." "Okay. Let me see it when it doesn't."

The important thing is that only one or two issues are dealt with in a conference. The conference isn't a psychiatric session. Think of the writer as an apprentice at the workbench with a master workman, a senior colleague, stopping by once in a while for a quick chat about the work.

We can also help the other self to become articulate by having the student write, after completing a draft, a brief statement about the draft. That statement can be attached on the front of the draft so the teacher can hear what the other self says and respond, after reading that statement and the draft, in writing. I have found this far less effective than the face-to-face conference, where the act of listening is personal, and where the teacher can hear the inflection and the pause as well as the statement and where the teacher can listen with the eye, reading the student's body language as well as the student's text.

The other self develops confidence through the experience of being heard in small and large group workshops. The same dynamics take place as have been modeled in the conference. The group leaders asks the writer, "How can we help you?" The other self speaks of the process or of the text. The workshop members listen and read the text with the words of the other self in their ears.

Then they respond, helping the other self become a more effective reader of the evolving text.

The papers that are published in workshops should be the best papers. The workshop members need to know how good writing is made, and then need to know how good writing can be improved. I always make clear that the papers being published in workshops are the best ones. As the other self speaks of how these good papers have been made and how they can be improved, the student being published has the student's most effective writing process reinforced. You can hear the other self becoming stronger and more confident as it speaks of what worked and as it proposes what may work next. The other workshop members hear an effective other self. They hear how a good writer reads an evolving draft. And during the workshop sessions their other selves start to speak, and they hear their own other selves participate in the helpful process of the workshop.

The teacher must always remember that the student, in the beginning of the course, does not know the other self exists. Its existence is an act of faith for the teacher. Sometimes that is a stupendous act of faith. Ronald, his nose running, his prose stalled, does not appear to have a self, and certainly not a critical, constructive other self. But even Ronald will hear that intelligent other self if the teacher listens well.

The teacher asks questions for which the student does not think there are answers: Why did you use such a strong word here? How did you cut this description and make it clearer? Why did you add so many specifics on Page 39? I think this ending really works, but what did you see that made you realize that old beginning was the new ending?

The student has the answers. And the student is surprised by the fact of answers as much as the answers themselves. The teacher addresses a self that the student didn't know exists, and the student listens with astonishment to what the other self is saying—"Hey, he's not so dumb." "That's pretty good, she knows what she's doing."

The teacher helps the student find the other self, get to know the other self, learn to work with the other self, and then the teacher walks away to deal with another Ronald in another course who does not know there is another self. The teacher's faith is building experience. If Ronald has another self, then there is hope for faith.

What happens in the writing conference and the workshop in which the other self is allowed to become articulate is best expressed in the play *The Elephant Man,* by Bernard Pomerance, when Merrick, the freak, who has been listened to for the first time in his life, says, "Before I spoke with people, I did not think of all those things because there was no one to think them for. Now things come out of my mouth which are true."

11

Writer-Based Prose

A Cognitive Basis for Problems in Writing

Linda Flower
Carnegie-Mellon University
Pittsburgh, Pennsylvania

IF writing is simply the act of "expressing what you think" or "saying what you mean," why is writing often such a difficult thing to do? And why do papers that do express what the writer meant (to his or her own satisfaction) often fail to communicate the same meaning to a reader? Although we often equate writing with the straightforward act of "saying what we mean," the mental struggles writers go through and the misinterpretations readers still make suggest that we need a better model of this process. Modern communication theory and practical experience agree: writing prose that actually communicates what we mean to another person demands more than a simple act of self-expression. What communication theory does not tell us is how writers do it.

An alternative to the "think it/say it" model is to say that effective writers do not simply *express* thought but *transform* it in certain complex but describable ways for the needs of a reader. Conversely, we may find that ineffective writers are indeed merely "expressing" themselves by offering up an unretouched and underprocessed version of their own thought. Writer-Based prose, the subject of this paper, is a description of this undertransformed mode of verbal expression.

As both a style of writing and a style of thought, Writer-Based prose is natural and adequate for a writer writing to himself or herself. However, it is the source of some of the most common and pervasive problems in academic and professional writing. The symptoms can range from a mere missing referent or an underdeveloped idea to an unfocused and apparently pointless discussion. The symptoms are diverse but the source can often be traced to the writer's underlying strategy for composing and to his or her failure to transform private thought into a public, reader-based expression.

In *function,* Writer-Based prose is a verbal expression written by a writer to himself and for himself. It is the record and the working of his own verbal thought. In its *structure,* Writer-Based prose reflects the associate, narrative path of the writer's own confrontation with her subject. In its *language,* it reveals her use of privately loaded terms and shifting but unexpressed contexts for her statements.

In contrast, Reader-Based prose is a deliberate attempt to communicate something to a reader. To do that it creates a shared language and shared context between writer and reader. It also offers the reader an issue-centered rhetorical structure rather than a replay of the writer's discovery process. In its language and structure, Reader-Based prose reflects the *purpose* of the writer's thought; Writer-Based prose tends to reflect its *process.* Good writing, therefore, is often the cognitively demanding transformation of the natural but private expressions of Writer-Based thought into a structure and style adapted to a reader.

This analysis of Writer-Based prose style and the transformations that create Reader-Based prose will explore two hypotheses:

1. Writer-Based prose represents a major and familiar mode of expression which we all use from time to time. While no piece of writing is a pure example, Writer-Based prose can be identified by features of structure, function, and style. Furthermore, it shares many of these features with the modes of inner and egocentric speech described by Vygotsky and Piaget. This paper will explore that relationship and look at newer research in an effort to describe

Writer-Based prose as a verbal style which in turn reflects an underlying cognitive process.

2. Writer-Based prose is a workable concept which can help us teach writing. As a way to intervene in the thinking process, it taps intuitive communication strategies writers already have, but are not adequately using. As a teaching technique, the notion of transforming one's own Writer-Based style has proved to be a powerful idea with a built-in method. It helps writers attack this demanding cognitive task with some of the thoroughness and confidence that comes from an increased and self-conscious control of the process.

My plan for this paper is to explore Writer-Based prose from a number of perspectives. Therefore, the next section, which considers the psychological theory of egocentrism and inner speech, is followed by a case study of Writer-Based prose. I will then pull these practical and theoretical issues together to define the critical features of Writer-Based prose. The final section will look ahead to the implications of this description of Writer-Based prose for writers and teachers.

Inner Speech and Egocentrism

In studying the developing thought of the child, Jean Piaget and Lev Vygotsky both observed a mode of speech which seemed to have little social or communicative function. Absorbed in play, children would carry on spirited elliptical monologues which they seemed to assume others understood, but which in fact made no concessions to the needs of the listener. According to Piaget, in Vygotsky's (1962) synopsis, "In egocentric speech, the child talks only to himself, takes no interest in his interlocutor, does not try to communicate, expects no answers, and often does not even care whether anyone listens to him. It is similar to a monologue in a play: The child is thinking aloud, keeping up a running accompaniment, as it were, to whatever he may be doing" (15). In the seven-year olds Piaget (1932) studied, nearly fifty percent of their recorded talk was egocentric in nature (49). According to Piaget, the child's "non-communicative" or egocentric speech is a reflection, not of selfishness, but of the child's limited ability to "assume the point of view of the listener: [the child] talks of himself, to himself, and by himself" (Ginsberg and Opper 1969, 89). In a sense, the child's cognitive capacity has locked her in her own monologue.

When Vygotsky (1962) observed a similar phenomenon in children he called it "inner speech" because he saw it as a forerunner of the private verbal thought adults carry on. Furthermore, Vygotsky argued, this speech is not simply a by-product of play, it is the tool children use to plan, organize, and control their activities. He put the case quite strongly: "We have seen that egocentric speech is not suspended in a void but is directly related to the child's practical dealings with the real world . . . it enters as a constituent part into the process of a rational activity" (22).

The egocentric talk of the child and the mental, inner speech of the adult share three important features in common. First, they are highly elliptical. In talking to oneself the psychological subject of discourse (the old information to which we are adding new predicates) is always known. Therefore, explicit subjects and referents disappear. Five people straining to glimpse the bus need only say, "Coming!" Secondly, inner speech frequently deals in the sense of words, not their more specific or limited public meanings. Words become "saturated with sense" in much the way a key word in a poem can come to represent its entire, complex web of meaning. But unlike the word in the poem, the accrued sense of the word in inner speech may be quite personal, even idiosyncratic; it is, as Vygotsky (1962) writes, "the sum of all the psychological events aroused in our consciousness by the word" (146).

Finally, a third feature of egocentric/inner speech is the absence of logical and causal relations. In experiments with children's use of logical-causal connectives such as *because, therefore,* and *although,* Piaget (1926) found that children have difficulty managing such relationships and in spontaneous speech will substitute a non-logical, non-causal connective such as *then.* Piaget described this strategy for relating things as *juxtaposition:* "the cognitive tendency simply to link (juxtapose) one thought element to another, rather than to tie them together by some causal or logical relation" (Flavell 1963, 275).

One way to diagnose this problem with sophisticated relationships is to say, as Vygotsky (1962) did, that young children often think in *complexes* instead of concepts (75; see also Woditsch, which places this question in the context of curriculum design). When people think in complexes they unite objects into families that really do share common bonds, but the bonds are concrete and factual rather than abstract or logical. For example, the notion of "college student" would be a complex if it were based, for the thinker, on facts such as college students live in dorms, go to classes, and do homework.

Complexes are very functional formations, and it may be that many people do most of their day-to-day thinking without feeling the need to form more demanding complex concepts. *Complexes* collect related objects; *concepts,* however, must express abstract, logical relations. And it is just this sort of abstract, synthetic thinking that writing typically demands. In a child's early years the ability to form complex concepts may depend mostly on developing cognitive capacity. In adults this ability appears also to be a skill developed by training and a tendency fostered by one's background and intellectual experience. But whatever its source, the ability to move from the complexes of egocentric speech to the more formal relations of conceptual thought is critical to most expository writing.

Piaget and Vygotsky disagreed on the source, exact function, and teleology of egocentric speech, but they did agree on the features of this distinctive phenomenon, which they felt revealed the underlying logic of the child's thought. For our case, that may be enough. The hypothesis on which this paper rests is not a developmental one. Egocentric speech, or rather its adult written analogue, Writer-Based prose, is not necessarily a stage through which a writer must develop or one at which some writers are arrested. But for adults it does represent an available mode of expression on which to fall back. If Vygotsky is right, it may even be closely related to normal verbal thought. It is clearly a natural, less cognitively demanding mode of thought and one which explains why people, who can express themselves in complex and highly intelligible modes, are often obscure. Egocentric expression happens to the best of us; it comes naturally.

The work of Piaget and Vygotsky, then, suggests a source for the cognitive patterns that underlie Writer-Based prose, and it points to some of the major features such a prose style would possess. Let us now turn to a more detailed analysis of such writing as a verbal style inadequately suited for the needs of the reader.

Writer-Based Prose: A Case Study of a Transformation

As an introduction to the main features of Writer-Based prose and its transformations, let us look at two drafts of a progress report written by students in an organizational psychology class. Working as consulting analysts to a local organization, the writers needed to show progress to their instructor and to present an analysis with causes and conclusions to the client. Both readers—academic and professional—were less concerned with what the students did or saw than with *why* they did it and *what* they made of their observations.

To gauge the Reader-Based effectiveness of this report, skim quickly over Draft 1 and imagine the response of the instructor of the course, who needed to answer these questions: As analysts, what assumptions and decisions did my student make? Why did they make them? At what stage in the project are they now? Or, play the role of the client-reader who wants to know: How did they define my problem, and what did they conclude? As either reader, can you quickly extract the information the report should be giving you? Next, try the same test on Draft 2.

Draft 1: Group Report

(1) Work began on our project with the initial group decision to evaluate the Oskaloosa Brewing Company. Oskaloosa Brewing Company is a regionally located brewery manufacturing several different types of beer, notably River City and Brough Cream Ale. This beer is marketed under various names in Pennsylvania and other neighboring states. As a group, we decided to analyze this organization because two of our group members had had frequent customer contact with the sales department. Also, we were aware that Oskaloosa Brewing had been losing money for the past five years and we felt we might be able to find some obvious problems in their organizational structure.

(2) Our first meeting, held February 17th, was with the head of the sales department, Jim Tucker. Generally, he gave us an outline of the organization from president to worker, and discussed the various departments that we might ultimately decide to analyze. The two that seemed the most promising and most applicable to the project were the sales and production departments. After a few group meetings and discussions with the personnel manager, Susan Harris, and our advisor Professor Charns, we felt it best suited our needs and the Oskaloosa Brewing's to evaluate their bottling department.

(3) During the next week we had a discussion with the superintendent of production, Henry Holt, and made plans for interviewing the supervisors and line workers. Also, we had a tour of the bottling department which gave us a first hand look into the production process. Before beginning our interviewing, our group met several times to formulate appropriate questions to use in interviewing, for both the supervisors and workers. We also had a meeting with Professor Charns to discuss this matter.

(3a) The next step was the actual interviewing process. During the weeks of March 14–18 and March 21–25, our group met several times at Oskaloosa Brewing and interviewed ten supervisors and twelve workers. Finally during this past week, we have had several group meetings to discuss our findings and the potential problem areas within the bottling department. Also, we have spent time organizing the writing of our progress report.

(4) The bottling and packaging division is located in a separate building adjacent to the brewery, where the beer is actually manufactured. From the brewery the beer is piped into one of five lines (four bottling lines and one canning line), in the bottling house where the bottles are filled, crowned, pasteurized, labeled, packaged in cases, and either shipped out or stored in the warehouse. The head of this operation, and others, is production manager, Phil Smith. Next in line under him in direct control of the bottling house is the superintendent of bottling and packaging, Henry Holt. In addition, there are a total of ten supervisors who report directly to Henry Holt and who oversee the daily operations and coordinate and direct the twenty to thirty union workers who operate the lines.

(5) During production, each supervisor fills out a data sheet to explain what was actually produced during each hour. This form also includes the exact time when a breakdown occurred, what it was caused by, and when production was resumed. Some supervisors' positions are production staff oriented. One takes care of supplying raw material (bottles, caps, labels, and boxes) for production. Another is responsible for the union workers' assignment each day.

These workers are not all permanently assigned to a production line position. Men called "floaters" are used filling in for a sick worker, or helping out after a breakdown.

(6) The union employees are generally older than 35, some in their late fifties. Most have been with the company many years and are accustomed to having more workers per a slower moving line. They are resentful to what they declare "unnecessary" production changes. Oskaloosa Brewery also employs mechanics who normally work on the production line, and assume a mechanics

job only when a breakdown occurs. Most of these men are not skilled.

Draft 2: Memorandum

TO: Professor Martin Charns

FROM: Nancy Lowenberg, Todd Scott, Rosemary Nisson, Larry Vollen

DATE: March 31, 1977

RE: *Progress Report: The Oskaloosa Brewing Company*

Why Oskaloosa Brewing?

(1) Oskaloosa Brewing Company is a regionally located brewery manufacturing several different types of beer, notably River City and Brough Cream Ale. As a group, we decided to analyze this organization because two of our group members have frequent contact with the sales department. Also, we were aware that Oskaloosa Brewing had been losing money for the past five years and we felt we might be able to find some obvious problems in their organizational structure.

Initial Steps: Where to Concentrate?

(2) Through several interviews with top management and group discussion, we felt it best suited our needs, and Oskaloosa Brewing's, to evaluate the production department. Our first meeting, held February 17, was with the head of the sales department, Jim Tucker. He gave us an outline of the organization and described the two major departments, sales and production. He indicated that there were more obvious problems in the production department, a belief also implied by Susan Harris, personnel manager.

Next Step

(3) The next step involved a familiarization of the plant and its employees. First, we toured the plant to gain an understanding of the brewing and bottling process. Next, during the weeks of March 14–18 and March 21–25, we interviewed ten supervisors and twelve workers. Finally, during the past week we had group meetings to exchange information and discuss potential problems.

The Production Process

(4) Knowledge of the actual production process is imperative in understanding the effects of various problems on efficient production; therefore, we have included a brief summary of this process.

The bottling and packaging division is located in a separate building, adjacent to the brewery, where the beer is actually manufactured. From the brewery the beer is piped into one of five lines (four bottling lines and one canning line) in the bottling house where the bottles are filled, crowned, pasteurized, labeled, packaged in cases, and either shipped out or stored in the warehouse.

People Behind the Process

(5) The head of this operation is the production manager, Phil Smith. Next in line under him in direct control of the bottling house is the superintendent of bottling and packaging, Henry Holt. He has authority over ten supervisors who each have two major responsibilities: (1) to fill out production data sheets that show the amount produced/hour, and information about any breakdown—time, cause, etc., and (2) to oversee the daily operations and coordinate and direct the twenty to thirty union workers who operate the lines. These workers are not all permanently assigned to a production line position. Men called "floaters" are used to fill in for a sick worker or to help out after a breakdown.

(6) The union employees are a highly diversified group in both age and experience. They are generally older than 35, some in their late fifties. Most have been with the company many years and are accustomed to having more workers per a slower moving line. They are resentful to what they feel are unnecessary production changes. Oskaloosa Brewing also employs mechanics who normally work on the production line, and assume a mechanics job only when a breakdown occurs. Most of these men are not skilled.

Problems

Through extensive interviews with supervisors and union employees, we have recognized four apparent problems within the bottle house operations. First, the employees' goals do not match those of the company. This is especially apparent in the union employees whose loyalty lies with the union instead of the company. This attitude is well-founded as the union ensures them of job security and benefits. . . .

In its tedious misdirection, Draft 1 is typical of Writer-Based prose in student papers and professional reports. The reader is forced to do most of the thinking, sorting the wheat from the chaff and drawing ideas out of details. And yet, although this presentation fails to fulfill our needs, it does have an inner logic of its own. The logic which organizes Writer-Based prose often rests on two principles: its underlying focus is egocentric, and it uses either a narrative framework or a survey form to order ideas.

The *narrative framework* of this discussion is established by the opening announcement: "Work began. . . . " In paragraphs 1–3 facts and ideas are presented in terms of when they were discovered, rather than in terms of their implications or logical connections.

The writers recount what happened when; the reader, on the other hand, asks, "Why?" and "So what?" Whether he or she likes it or not the reader is in for a blow-by-blow account of the writers' discovery process.

Although a rudimentary chronology is reasonable for a progress report, a narrative framework is often a substitute for analytic thinking. By burying ideas within the events that precipitated them, a narrative obscures the more important logical and hierarchical relations between ideas. Of course, such a narrative could read like an intellectual detective story, because, like other forms of drama, it creates interest by withholding closure. Unfortunately, most academic and professional readers seem unwilling to sit through these home movies of the writer's mind at work. Narratives can also operate as a cognitive "frame" which itself generates ideas (Minsky 1973; Kuipers 1975). The temporal pattern, once invoked, opens up a series of empty slots waiting to be filled with the details of what happened next, even though those details may be irrelevant. As the revision of Draft 2 shows, our writers' initial narrative framework led them to generate a shaggy project story, instead of a streamlined logical analysis.

The second salient feature of this prose is its focus on the discovery process of the writers: the "I did/I thought/I felt" focus. Of the fourteen sentences in the first three paragraphs, ten are grammatically focused on the writers' thoughts and actions rather than on issues: "Work began," "We decided," "Also, we were aware . . . and we felt. . . . "

In the fourth paragraph the writers shift attention from their discovery process to the facts discovered. In doing so they illustrate a third feature of Writer-Based prose: its idea structure simply copies the structure of the perceived information. A problem arises when the internal structure of the data is not already adapted to the needs of the reader or the intentions of the writers. Paragraph five, for example, appears to be a free-floating description of "What happens during production." Yet the client-reader already knows this and the instructor probably does not care. Lured by the fascination of facts, these writer-based writers recite a litany of perceived information under the illusion they have produced a rhetorical structure. The resulting structure could as well be a neat hierarchy as a list. The point is that the writers' organizing principle is dictated by their information, not by their intention.

The second version of this report is not so much a "rewrite" (i.e., a new report) as it is a transformation of the old one. The writers had to step back from their experience and information in order to turn facts into concepts. Pinpointing the telling details was not enough: they had to articulate the meaning they saw in the data. Secondly, the writers had to build a rhetorical structure which acknowledged the function these ideas had for their reader. In the second version, the headings, topic sentences, and even some of the subjects and verbs reflect a new functional structure focused on Process, People, and Problems. The report offers a hierarchical organization of the facts in which the hierarchy itself is based on issues both writer and reader agree are important. I think it likely that such transformations frequently go on in the early stages of the composing process for skilled writers. But for some writers the under-transformed Writer-Based prose of Draft 1 is also the final product and the starting point for our work as teachers.

In the remainder of this paper I will look at the features of Writer-Based prose and the ways it functions for the writer. Clearly, we need to know about Reader-Based prose in order to teach it. But it is also clear that writers already possess a great deal of intuitive knowledge about writing for audiences when they are stimulated to use it. As the case study shows, the concept of trying to transform Writer-Based prose for a reader is by itself a powerful tool. It helps writers identify the lineaments of a problem many can start to solve once they recognize it as a definable problem.

Writer-Based Prose: Function, Structure, and Style

While Writer-Based prose may be inadequately structured for a reader, it does possess a logic and structure of its own. Furthermore, that structure serves some important functions for the writer in his or her effort to think about a subject. It represents a practical strategy for dealing with information. If we could see Writer-Based prose as a *functional system*—not a set of random errors known only to English teachers—we would be better able to teach writing as a part of any discipline that asks people to express complex ideas.

According to Vygotsky (1962), "the inner speech of the adult represents his 'thinking for himself' rather than social adaptation [communication to others]: i.e., it has the same function that egocentric speech has in the child" (18). It helps him solve problems. Vygotsky found that when a child who is trying to draw encounters an obstacle (no pencils) or a problem (what shall I call it?), the incidence of egocentric speech can double.

If we look at an analogous situation—an adult caught up in the complex mental process of composing—we can see that much of the adult's output is not well adapted for public consumption either. In studies of cognitive processes of writers as they composed, J. R. Hayes and I observed much of the writer's verbal output to be an attempt to manipulate stored information into some acceptable pattern of meaning (Flower and Hayes 1982). To do that, the writer generates a variety of alternative relationships and trial formulations of the information she has in mind. Many of these trial networks will be discarded; most will be significantly altered through recombination and elaboration during the composing process. In those cases in which the writer's first pass at articulating knowledge was also the final draft—when she wrote it just as she thought it—the result was often a series of semi-independent, juxtaposed networks, each with its own focus.

Whether such expression occurs in an experimental protocol or a written draft, it reflects the working of the writer's mind upon his material. Because dealing with one's material is a formidable enough task in itself, a writer may allow himself to ignore the additional problem of accommodating a reader. Writer-Based prose, then, functions as a medium for thinking. It offers the writer the luxury of one less constraint. As we shall see, its typical structure and style are simply paths left by the movement of the writer's mind.

The *structure* of Writer-Based prose reflects an economical strategy we have for coping with information. Readers generally expect writers to produce complex concepts—to collect data and details under larger guiding ideas and place those ideas in an integrated network. But as both Vygotsky and Piaget observed, forming such complex concepts is a demanding cognitive task; if no one minds, it is a lot easier to just list the parts. Nor is it surprising that in children two of the hallmarks of egocentric speech are the absence of expressed causal relations and the tendency to express ideas without proof or development. Adults too avoid the task of building complex concepts buttressed by development and proof, by structuring their information in two distinctive ways: as a narrative of their own discovery process or as a survey of the data before them.

As we saw in the Oskaloosa Brewing Case Study, a *narrative* structured around one's own discovery process may seem the most natural way to write. For this reason it can sometimes be the best way as well, if a writer is trying to express a complex network of information but is not yet sure of how all the parts are related. For example, my notes show that early fragments of this paper started out with a narrative, list-like structure focused on my own experience: "Writer-Based prose is a working hypothesis because it works in the classroom. In fact, when I first started teaching the concept. . . . In fact, it was my students' intuitive recognition of the difference between Writer-Based and Reader-Based style in their own thought and writing. . . . It was their ability to use even a sketchy version of the distinction to transform their own writing that led me to pursue the idea more thoroughly."

The final version of this sketch keeps the reference to teaching experience, but subordinates it to the more central issue of why the concept works. This transformation illustrates how a writer's major propositions can, on first appearance, emerge embedded in a narrative of the events or thoughts which spawned the proposition. In this example, the Writer-Based early version recorded the raw material of observations; the final draft formed them into concepts and conclusions.

This transformation process may take place regularly when a writer is trying to express complicated information which is not yet fully conceptualized. Although much of this mental work normally precedes actual writing, a first draft may simply reflect the writer's current place in the process. When this happens rewriting and editing are vital operations. Far from being a simple matter of correcting errors, editing a first draft is often the act of transforming a narrative network of information into a more fully hierarchical set of propositions.

A second source of pre-fabricated structure for writers is the internal structure of the information itself. Writers use a *survey* strategy to compose because it is a powerful procedure for retrieving and organizing information. Unfortunately, the original organization of the data itself (e.g., the production process at Oskaloosa Brewing) rarely fits the most effective plan for any given piece of focused analytical writing.

The prose that results from such a survey can, of course, take as many forms as the data. It can range from a highly structured piece of discourse (the writer repeats a textbook exposition) to an unfocused printout of the writer's memories and thoughts on the subject. The form is merely a symptom, because the governing force is the writer's mental strategy: namely, to compose by surveying the available contents of memory without adapting them to a current purpose. The internal structure of the data dictates the rhetorical structure of the discourse, much as the proceedings of Congress organize the *Congressional Record.* As an information processor, the writer is performing what computer scientists would call a "memory dump": dutifully printing out memory in exactly the form in which it is stored.

A survey strategy offers the writer a useful way into the composing process in two ways. First, it eliminates many of the constraints normally imposed by a speech act, particularly the contract between reader and writer for mutually useful discourse. Secondly, a survey of one's own stored knowledge, marching along like a textbook or flowing with the tide of association, is far easier to write than a fresh or refocused conceptualization would be.

But clearly most of the advantages here accrue to the writer. One of the tacit assumptions of the Writer-Based writer is that, once the relevant information is presented, the reader will then do the work of abstracting the essential features, building a conceptual hierarchy, and transforming the whole discussion into a functional network of ideas.

Although Writer-Based prose often fails for readers and tends to preclude further concept formation, it may be a useful road into the creative process for some writers. The structures which fail to work for readers may be powerful strategies for retrieving information from memory and for exploring one's own knowledge network. This is illustrated in Linde and Labov's (1975) well-known New York apartment tour experiment. Interested in the strategies people use for retrieving information from memory and planning a discourse, Linde and Labov asked one hundred New Yorkers to "tell me the layout of your apartment" as a part of a "sociological survey." Only 3% of the subject responded with a map which gave an overview and then filled in the details; for example, "I'd say it's laid out in a huge square pattern, broken down into 4 units." The overwhelming majority (97%) all solved the problem by describing a tour: "You walk in the front door. There was a narrow hallway. To the left, etc." Furthermore, they had a common set of rules for how to conduct the tour (e.g., you don't "walk into" a small room with no outlet, such as a pantry; you just say, "on the left is . . . "). Clearly the tour structure is so widely used because it is a remarkably efficient strategy for recovering all of the relevant information about one's apartment, yet without repeating any of it. For example, one rule for "touring" is that when you dead-end after walking through two rooms, you don't "walk" back but suddenly appear back in the hall.

For us, the revealing sidenote to this experiment is that although the tour strategy was intuitively selected by the overwhelming majority of the speakers, the resulting description was generally very difficult for the listener to follow and almost impossible to reproduce. The tour strategy—like the narrative and textbook structure in prose—is a masterful method for searching memory but a dud for communicating that information to anyone else.

Finally, the *style* of Writer-Based prose also has its own logic. Its two main stylistic features grow out of the private nature of interior monologue, that is, of writing which is primarily a record or expression of the writer's flow of thought. The first feature is that in such monologues the organization of sentences and paragraphs reflects the shifting focus of the writer's attention. However, the psychological subject on which the writer is focused may not be reflected in the grammatical subject of the sentence or made explicit in the discussion at all. Secondly, the writer may depend on code words to carry his or her meaning. That is, the language may be "saturated with sense" and able to evoke—for the writer—a complex but unexpressed context.

Writers of formal written discourse have two goals for style which we can usefully distinguish from one another. One goal might be described as stylistic control, that is, the ability to choose a more embedded or more elegant transformation from variations which are roughly equivalent in meaning. The second goal is to create a completely autonomous text, that is, a text that does not need context, gestures, or audible effects to convey its meaning.

It is easy to see how the limits of short-term memory can affect a writer's stylistic control. For an inexperienced writer, the complex transformation of a periodic sentence—which would require remembering and relating a variety of elements and optional structures such as this sentence contains—can be a difficult juggling act. After all, the ability to form parallel constructions is not innate. Yet with practice many of these skills can become more automatic and require less conscious attention.

The second goal of formal written discourse—the complete autonomy of the text—leads to even more complex problems. According to David Olson (1977) the history of written language has been the progressive creation of an instrument which could convey complete and explicit meanings in a text. The history of writing is the transformation of language from utterance to text—from oral meaning created within a shared context of a speaker and listener to a written meaning fully represented in an autonomous text.

In contrast to this goal of autonomy, Writer-Based prose is writing whose meaning is still to an important degree in the writer's head. The culprit here is often the unstated psychological subject. The work of the "remedial" student is a good place to examine the phenomenon because it often reveals first thoughts more clearly than the reworked prose of a more experienced writer who edits as he or she writes. In the most imaginative, comprehensive, and practical book to be written on the basic writer, Mina Shaughnessy (1977) has studied the linguistic strategies which lie behind the "errors" of many otherwise able young adults who have failed to master the written code. As we might predict, the ambiguous referent is ubiquitous in basic writing: *he*'s, *she*'s and *it*'s are sprinkled through the prose without visible means of support. *It* frequently works as a code word for the subject the writer had in mind but not on the page. As Professor Shaughnessy says, *it* "frequently becomes a free-floating substitute for thoughts that the writer neglects to articulate and that the reader must usually strain to reach if he can"(69).

> With all the jobs available, he will have to know more of *it* because there is a great demand for *it*.

For the writer of the above sentence, the pronoun was probably not ambiguous at all; *it* no doubt referred to the psychological subject of his sentence. Psychologically, the subject of an utterance is the old information, the object you are looking at, the idea on which your attention has been focused. The predicate is the new information you are adding. This means that the psychological subject and grammatical subject of a sentence may not be the same at all.

In our example, "college knowledge" was the writer's psychological subject—the topic he had been thinking about. The sentence itself is simply a psychological predicate. The pronoun *it* refers quite reasonably to the unstated but obvious subject in the writer's mind.

The subject is even more likely to be missing when a sentence refers to the writer herself or to "one" in her position. In the following examples, again from *Errors and Expectations,* the "unnecessary" subject is a person (like the writer) who has a chance to go to college.

> Even if a person graduated from high school who is going on to college to obtain a specific position in his career [   ] should first know how much in demand his possible future job really is.
>
> [he]
>
> If he doesn't because the U.S. Labor Department say's their wouldn't be enough jobs opened, [   ] is a waste to society and a "cop-out" to humanity.
>
> [he]

Unstated subjects can produce a variety of minor problems from ambiguous referents to amusing dangling modifiers (e.g., "driving around the mountain, a bear came into view"). Although prescriptive stylists are quite hard on such "errors," they are often cleared up by context or common sense. However, the controlling but unstated presence of a psychological subject can lead to some stylistic "errors" that do seriously disrupt communication. Sentence fragments are a good example.

One feature of an explicit, fully autonomous text is that the grammatical subject is usually a precise entity, often a word. By contrast, the psychological subject to which a writer wished to refer may be a complex event or entire network of information. Here written language is often rather intransigent; it is hard to refer to an entire clause or discussion unless one can produce a summary noun. Grammar, for example, normally forces us to select a specific referent for a pronoun or modifier: it wants referents and relations spelled out. ("Pronouns like *this, that, which,* and *it* should not vaguely refer to an entire sentence or clause" and "make a pronoun refer clearly to one antecedent, not uncertainly to two"—Watkins et al. 1974, 30.) This specificity is, of course, its strength as a vehicle for precise reasoning and abstract thought. Errors arise when a writer uses one clause to announce his topic or psychological subject and a second clause to record a psychological predicate, a response to that old information. For example:

> The jobs that are listed in the paper, I feel you need a college degree.
>
> The job that my mother has, I know I could never be satisfied with it.

The preceding sentences are in error because they have failed to specify the grammatical relationship between their two elements. However, for anyone from the Bronx, each statement would be perfectly effective because it fits a familiar formula. It is an example of topicalization or Y-movement and fits a conventionalized, Yiddish influenced, intonation pattern much like the one in "Spinach—you can have it!" The sentences depend heavily on certain conventions of oral speech, and insofar as they invoke those patterns for the reader, they communicate effectively.*

However, most fragments do not succeed for the reader. And they fail, ironically enough, for the same reason—they too invoke intonation patterns in the reader which turn out to be misleading. The lack of punctuation gives off incorrect cues about how to segment the sentence. Set off on an incorrect intonation pattern, the thwarted reader must stop, reread and reinterpret the sentence. The following examples are from Maxine Hairston's *A Contemporary Rhetoric* (1974, 322):

> The authorities did not approve of their acts. These acts being considered detrimental to society. (society, they . . .)
>
> Young people need to be on their own. To show their parents that they are reliable. (reliable, young people . . .)

Fragments are easy to avoid; they require only minimal tinkering to correct. Then why is the error so persistent? One possible reason is that for the writer the fragment is a fresh predicate intended to modify the entire preceding psychological subject. The writer wants to carry out a verbal trick easily managed in speech. For the reader, however, this minor grammatical oversight is significant. It sets up and violates both intonation patterns and strong structural expectations, such as those in the last example where we expect a pause

*I am greatly indebted here to Thomas Huckin for his insightful comments on style and to his work in linguistics on how intonation patterns affect writers and readers.

and a noun phrase to follow "reliable." The fragment, which actually refers backward, is posing as an introductory clause.

The problem with fragments is that they are perfectly adequate for the writer. In speech they may even be an effective way to express a new idea which is predicated on the entire preceding unit thought. But in a written text, fragments are errors because they do not take the needs of the reader into consideration. Looked at this way, the "goodness" of a stylistic technique or grammatical rule such as parallelism, clear antecedents, or agreement is that it is geared to the habits, expectations, and needs of the reader as well as to the demands of textual autonomy.

Vygotsky noticed how the language of children and inner speech was often "saturated with sense." Similarly, the words a writer chooses can also operate as code words, condensing a wealth of meaning in an apparently innocuous word. The following examples come from an exercise which asks writers to identify and transform some of their own pieces of mental shorthand.

The students were asked to circle any code words or loaded expressions they found in their first drafts of a summer internship application. That is, they tried to identify those expressions that might convey only a general or vague meaning to a reader, but which represented a large body of facts, experiences, or ideas for them. They then treated this code word as one would any intuition—pushing it for its buried connections and turning those into a communicable idea. The results are not unlike those brilliant explications one often hears from students who tell you what their paper really meant. This example also shows how much detailed and perceptive thought can be lying behind a vague and conventional word:

First Draft

By having these two jobs, I was able to see the business in an entirely (different perspective.) [Circle indicates a loaded expression marked by the writer.]

Second Draft (with explanation of what she actually had in mind in using the circled phrase)

By having these two jobs, I was able to see the true relationship and relative importance of the various departments in the company. I could see their mutual dependence and how an event in one part of the firm can have an important effect on another.

The tendency to think in code words is a fact of life for the writer. Yet the following example shows how much work can go into exploring our own saturated language. Like any intuition, such language is only a source of potential meanings, much as Aristotle's topics are places for finding potential arguments. In this intended example, the writer first explores her expression itself, laying out all the thoughts which were loosely connected under its name. This process of pushing our own language to give up its buried meanings forces us to make these loose connections explicit and, in the process, allows us to examine them critically. For the writer in our example, pushing her own key words leads to an important set of new ideas in the paper.

Excerpt from an Application for the National Institute of Health Internship Program

First Draft

I want a career that will help other people while at the same time be challenging scientifically. I had the opportunity to do a biochemical assay for a neuropsychophamocologist at X-Clinic in Chicago. Besides learning the scientific procedures and techniques that are used, I realized some of the organizational, financial and people problems which are encountered in research. This internship program would let me pursue further my interest in research, while concurrently exposing me to relevant and diverse areas of bioengineering.

Excerpts from Writer's Notes Working on the Circled Phrases

Brainstorm

How did research of Sleep Center tie into overall program of X-Clinic? Not everyone within dept. knew what the others were doing, could not see overall picture of efforts.

Dr. O.—dept. head—trained for lab yet did 38–40 hrs. paperwork. Couldn't set up test assay in Sleep Center because needed equip. from biochem.

Difficulties in Getting Equipment

1. Politics between administrators
   Photometer at U. of ——— even though Clinic had bought it.
2. Ordering time, not sufficient inventory, had to hunt through boxes for chemicals.
3. Had to schedule use by personal contact on borrowing equipment—done at time of use and no previous planning.

No definite guidelines had been given to biochem. people as to what was "going on" with assay. Partner who was supposed to learn assay was on vacation. Two people were learning, one was on vac.

No money from state for equipment or research grants.
Departments stealing from each other.
Lobbying, politics, included.

My supervisor from India, felt prejudices on job. Couldn't advance, told me life story and difficulties in obtaining jobs at Univ. Not interested in research at Clinic per se, looking for better opportunities, studying for Vet boards.

Revision (Additions in Italics)

As a biomedical researcher, I would fulfill my goal of a career that will help other people while at the same time be challenging scientifically. I had exposure to research while doing a biochemical assay for a neuropsychopharmocologist at X-Clinic in Chicago. Besides learning the scientific procedures and techniques that are used, I realized some of the organizational, financial and people problems which are encountered in research. *These problems included a lack of funds and equipment, disagreements among research staff, and the extensive amounts of time, paperwork and steps required for testing a hypothesis which was only one very small but necessary part of the overall project. But besides knowing some of the frustrations, I also know that many medical advancements, such as the cardiac pacemaker, artificial limbs and cures for diseases, exist and benefit many people because of the efforts of researchers.* Therefore I would like to pursue my interest in research by participating in the NIH Internship Program. The exposure to many *diverse projects, designed to better understand and improve the body's functioning, would help me to decide which areas of biomedical engineering to pursue.*

We could sum up this analysis of style by noting two points. At times a Writer-Based prose style is simply an interior monologue in which some necessary information (such as intonation pattern or a psychological subject) is not expressed in the text. The solution to the reader's problem is relatively trivial in that it involves adding information that the writer already possesses. At other times, a style may be Writer-Based because the writer is thinking in code words at the level of intuited but unarticulated connections. Turning such saturated language into communicable ideas can require the writer to bring the entire composing process into play.

Implications for Writers and Teachers

From an educational perspective, Writer-Based prose is one of the "problems" composition courses are designed to correct. It is a major cause of that notorious "breakdown" of communication between writer and reader. However, if we step back and look at it in the broader context of cognitive operations involved, we see that it represents a major, functional stage in the composing process and a powerful strategy well fitted to a part of the job of writing.

In the best of all possible worlds, good writers strive for Reader-Based prose from the very beginning: they retrieve and organize information within the framework of a reader/writer contract. Their top goal or initial question is not, "What do I know about physics, and in particular the physics of wind resistance?" but, "What does a model plan builder need to know?" Many times a writer can do this. For a physics teacher this particular writing problem would be a trivial one. However, for a person ten years out of Physics 101, simply retrieving any relevant information would be a full-time processing job. The reader would simply have to wait. For the inexperienced writer, trying to put complex thought into written language may also be task enough. In that case, the reader is an extra constraint that must wait its turn. A Reader-Based strategy which includes the reader in the entire thinking process is clearly the best way to write, but it is not always possible. When it is very difficult or impossible to write for a reader from the beginning, writing and then transforming Writer-Based prose is a practical alternative which breaks this complex process down into manageable parts. When transforming is a practiced skill, it enters naturally into the pulse of the composing process as a writer's constant, steady effort to test and adapt his or her thought to a reader's needs. Transforming Writer-Based prose is, then, not only a necessary procedure for all writers at times, but a useful place to start teaching intellectually significant writing skills.

In this final section I will try to account for the peculiar virtues of Writer-Based prose and suggest ways that teachers of writing—in any field—can take advantage of them. Seen in the context of memory retrieval, Writer-Based thinking appears to be a tapline to the rich sources of episodic memory. In the context of the composing process, Writer-Based prose is a way to deal with the overload that writing often imposes on short term memory. By teaching writers to use this transformation process we can foster the peculiar strengths of writer-based thought and still alert writers to the next transformation that many may simply fail to attempt.

One way to account for why Writer-Based prose seems to "come naturally" to most of us from time to time is to recognize its ties to our episodic as opposed to semantic memory. As Tulving (1972) describes it, "episodic memory is a more or less faithful record of a person's experiences." A statement drawn from episodic memory "refers to a personal experience that is remembered in its temporal-spatial relation to other such experiences. The remembered episodes are . . . autobiographical events, describable in terms of their perceptible dimension or attributes" (387).

Semantic memory, by contrast, "is the memory necessary for the use of language. It is a mental thesaurus, organized knowledge a person possesses about words and other verbal symbols, their meaning and referents, about relations among them, and about rules, formulas, and algorithms for the manipulation of these symbols, concepts, and relations." Although we know that table salt is NaCl and that motivation is a mental state, we probably do not remember learning the fact or the first time we thought of that concept. In semantic memory facts and concepts stand as the nexus for other words and symbols, but shorn of their temporal and autobiographical roots. If we explored the notion of "writing" in the semantic memory of someone we might produce a network such as this:

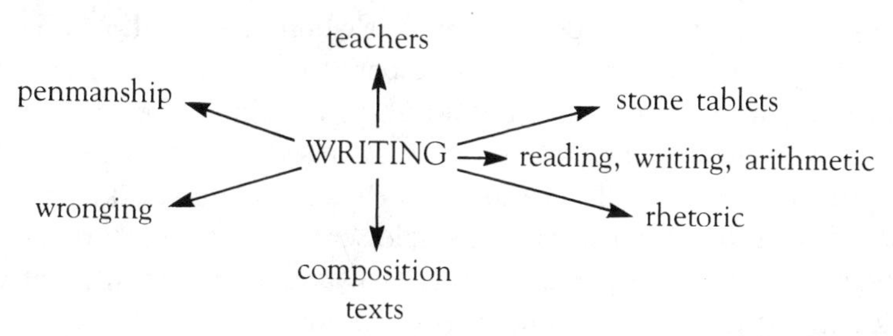

In an effort to retrieve what she or he knew about stone tablets, for example, this same person might turn to episode memory: "I once heard a lecture on the Rosetta stone, over in Maynard Hall. The woman, as I recall, said that . . . and I remember wondering if. . . ."

Writers obviously use both kinds of memory. The problem only arises when they confuse a fertile source of ideas in episodic memory with a final product. In fact, a study by Russo and Wisher (1976) argues that we sometimes store our ideas or images (the symbols of thought) with the mental operations we performed to produce these symbols. Furthermore, it is easier to recall the symbols (that fleeting idea, perhaps) when we bring back the original operation. In other words, our own thinking acts can serve as memory cues, and the easiest way to recover some item from memory may be to *reprocess* it, to reconstruct the original thought process in which it appeared. Much Writer-Based prose appears to be doing just this—reprocessing an earlier thinking experience as a way to recover what one knows.

Writing is one of those activities that places an enormous burden on short-term or working memory. As George Miller (1967) put it, "The most glaring result [of numerous experiments] has been to highlight man's inadequacy as a communication channel. As the amount of input information is increased, the amount of information that the man transmits increases at first but then runs into a ceiling. . . . That ceiling is always very low. Indeed, it is an act of charity to call man a channel at all. Compared to telephone or television channels, man is better characterized as a bottleneck" (48).

The short-term memory is the active central processor of the mind, that is, it is the sum of all the information we can hold in conscious attention at one time. We notice its capacity most acutely when we try to learn a new task, such as driving a car or playing bridge. Its limited capacity means that when faced with a complex problem—such as writing a college paper—we can hold and compare only a few alternative relationships in mind at once.

Trying to evaluate, elaborate, and relate all that we know on a given topic can easily overload the capacity of our working memory. Trying to compose even a single sentence can have the same effect, as we try to juggle grammatical and syntactic alternatives plus all the possibilities of tone, nuance, and rhythm even a simple sentence offers. Composing, then, is a cognitive activity that constantly threatens to overload short-term memory. For two reasons Writer-Based prose is a highly effective strategy for dealing with this problem.

1. Because the characteristic structure of Writer-Based prose is often a list (either of mental events or the features of the topic) it temporarily suspends the additional problem of forming complex concepts. If that task is suspended indefinitely, the result will fail to be good analytical writing or serious thought, but as a first stage in the process the list-structure has real value. It allows the writer freedom to generate a breadth of information and a variety of alternative relationships before locking himself or herself into a premature formulation. Furthermore, by allowing the writer to temporarily separate the two complex but somewhat different tasks of generating information and forming networks, each task may be performed more consciously and effectively.

2. Taking the perspective of another mind is also a demanding cognitive operation. It means holding not only your own knowledge network but someone else's in conscious attention and comparing them. Young children simply can't do it (Scardamalia 1982). Adults choose not to do it when their central processing is already overloaded with the effort to generate and structure their own ideas. Writer-Based prose simply eliminates this constraint by temporarily dropping the reader out of the writer's deliberations (Flower and Hayes 1979).

My own research suggests that good writers take advantage of these strategies in their composing process. They use scenarios, generate lists, and ignore the reader, but only for a while. Their composing process, unlike that of less effective writers, is marked by constant re-examination of their growing product and an attempt to refine, elaborate, or test its relationships, plus an attempt to anticipate the response of a reader. Everyone uses the strategies of Writer-Based prose; good writers go a step further to transform the writing these strategies produce.

But what about the writers who fail to make this transformation or (like all of us) fail to do it adequately in places? This is the problem faced by all teachers who assign papers. I think this study has two main and quite happy implications for us as teachers and writers.

The first is that Writer-Based prose is not a composite of errors or a mistake that should be scrapped. Instead, it is a half-way place for many writers and often represents the results of an extensive search and selection process. As a stage in the composing process it may be a rich compilation of significant thoughts which cohere *for the writer* into a network she or he has not yet fully articulated.

Writer-Based prose is the writer's homework, and so long as the writer is also the audience, it may even be a well-thought-out communication.

The second happy implication is that writing Reader-Based prose is often simply the task of transforming the groundwork laid in the first stage of the process. (For a study of heuristics and teaching techniques for this transformation process see Flower and Hayes 1977.) Good analytical writing is not different in kind from the writer-based thought that seems to come naturally. It is an extension of our communication with ourselves transformed in certain predictable ways to meet the needs of the reader. The most general transformation is simply to try to take into account the reader's purpose in reading. Most people have well-developed strategies for doing this when they talk. For a variety of reasons—from cognitive effort to the illusion of the omniscient teacher/reader—many people simply do not consider the reader when they write.

More specifically, the transformations that produce Reader-Based writing include these:

Selecting a focus of mutual interest to both reader and writer (e.g., moving from the writer-based focus of "How did I go about my research or reading of the assignment and what did I see?" to a focus on "What significant conclusions can be drawn and why?").

Moving from facts, scenarios, and details to concepts.

Transforming a narrative or textbook structure into a rhetorical structure built on the logical and hierarchical relationships between ideas and organized around the purpose for writing, rather than the writer's process.

Teaching writers to recognize their own Writer-Based writing and transform it has a number of advantages. It places a strong positive value on writing that represents an effort and achievement for the writer even though it fails to communicate to the reader. This legitimate recognition of the uncommunicated content of Writer-Based prose can give anyone, but especially inexperienced writers, the confidence and motivation to go on. By defining writing as a multistage process (instead of a holistic act of "expression") we provide a rationale for editing and alert many writers to a problem they could handle once it is set apart from other problems and they deliberately set out to tackle it. By recognizing transformation as a special skill and task, we give writers a greater degree of self-conscious control over the abilities they already have and a more precise introduction to some skills they may yet develop.

References

Flavell, John. 1963. *The Developmental Psychology of Jean Piaget.* New York: D. Van Nostrand.

Flower, Linda, and John L. Hayes. 1977. "Problem-Solving Strategies and the Writing Process." *College English* 39: 449–61.

———. 1979. "The Dynamics of Composing: Making Plans and Juggling Constraints." In *Cognitive Processes in Writing: An Interdisciplinary Approach,* ed. Lee Gregg and Irwin Steinberg. Hillsdale, N.J.: Lawrence Erlbaum.

———. 1982. "Plans That Guide the Composition Process." In *Writing: The Nature, Development and Teaching of Written Communication,* ed. C. Frederikson, M. Whiteman, and J. Dominic. Hillsdale, N.J.: Lawrence Erlbaum.

Ginsberg, Herbert, and Sylvia Opper. 1969. *Piaget's Theory of Intellectual Development.* Englewood Cliffs, N.J.: Prentice-Hall.

Hairston, Maxine. 1974. *A Contemporary Rhetoric.* Boston: Houghton Mifflin.

Kuipers, B. 1975. "A Frame for Frames." In *Representation and Understanding: Studies in Cognitive Science,* ed. D. Bowbow and A. Collins, 151–84. New York: Academic Press.

Linde, C., and W. Labov. 1975. "Spatial Networks as a Site for the Study of Language and Thought." *Language* 51: 934–39.

Miller, George. 1967. *The Psychology of Communication.* New York: Basic Books.

Minsky, M. 1973. "A Framework for Representing Knowledge." In *The Psychology of Computer Vision,* ed. P. Winston. New York: McGraw Hill.

Olson, David R. 1977. "From Utterance to Text: The Bias of Language in Speech and Writing." *Harvard Educational Review* 47: 257–81.

Piaget, Jean. 1926. *Language and Thought of the Child* and *Judgment and Reasoning in the Child,* trans. M. Warden, last chapter. New York: Harcourt, Brace.

———. 1932. *The Language and Thought of the Child,* trans. Marjorie Gabin. New York: Harcourt, Brace.

Russo, J., and R. Wisher. 1976. "Reprocessing as a Recognition Cue." *Memory and Cognition* 4: 683–89.

Scardamalia, Marlene. 1982. "How Children Cope with the Cognitive Demands of Writing." In *Writing: The Nature, Development and Teaching of Written Communication*, ed. C. Frederikson, M. Whiteman, and J. Dominic. Hillsdale, N.J.: Lawrence Erlbaum.

Shaughnessy, Mina. 1977. *Errors and Expectations*. New York: Oxford University Press.

Tulving, Edel. 1972. "Episodic and Semantic Memory." In *Organization of Memory*, ed. Edel Tulving and Wayne Donaldson. New York: Academic Press.

Vygotsky, Lev. 1962. *Thought and Language*, ed. and trans. Eugenia Hanfmann and Gertrude Vakar. Cambridge: MIT Press.

Watkins, Floyd, et al. 1974. *Practical English Handbook*. Boston: Houghton Mifflin.

Woditsch, Gary. n.d. "Developing Generic Skills: A Model for a Competency-Based General Education." Paper available from CUE Center, Bowling Green State University.

Time for Questions

What is a writing conference?

A writing conference is a *conversation* between teacher and student. It may be only a few seconds long—merely checking in with a student—or it may be an extended conversation that runs for several minutes. A major purpose of the writing conference is to encourage the students to examine and evaluate their own writing, to re-*see* it. For this reason, it is useful to ask questions like:

1. What do you like best about this draft? What do you like least?
2. What gave you the most trouble in writing this?
3. What kind of reaction do you want your readers to have—amusement, anger, increased understanding?
4. What surprised you when you wrote this? What came out different from what you expected?
5. What is the most important thing you learned about your topic in writing this?

Some teachers ask students to fill out cover sheets for their papers on which they are to answer questions like those above. Such a procedure forces a student to reflect on the process of writing and the quality of the writing *before* the teacher comments. Then, as Don Murray has suggested, the teacher responds to the student's response. I do a modified version of this approach. I ask students to draw a double line in the margin to mark a paragraph or section that they find most effective. They also draw a single line in the margin alongside a passage that they didn't like. In this way, I can read the student's paper in light of the student's own evaluation.

The classic danger in a writing conference is that the teacher talks too much. We all regularly violate the Shaker maxim—"Never miss an opportunity to keep your mouth shut." As students talk about their writing, they often discover connections, examples, and incidents that can strengthen their writing. Talking helps them "know what they know"; it gives them access to information that often didn't make it onto the page.

But doesn't the teacher have the responsibility of making suggestions and giving her reaction?

Yes. I see the conference as a kind of trade—the teacher and student share reactions to the paper. But it is crucially important *how* the teacher shares a reaction. Suppose the teacher feels that a description of a bully in a student paper needs more detail. The teacher can say, "You need to add more information about the bully," or, "I was interested in the bully when he entered the room, but I have trouble picturing him. What did he look like?" Aside from being more diplomatic, the second response continues a conversation; it allows the student to talk his way to a clearer visualization of the bully.

How do I find time to meet with my students individually?

Most high school teachers meet too many students. One would hope that if school districts want writing taught, they might designate "writing-intensive courses" and keep the number in these courses to a reasonable number—no more than twenty. But until that day comes there are things that can be done.

First, something very simple. It helps if the teacher moves around the classroom, spends part of the writing period conducting "roving conferences." If the teacher is on the move, conferences are generally shorter than one-on-one conferences at the teacher's desk. I've watched teachers talk to as many as twelve to fifteen students in a fifty-minute class period when they move from desk to desk.

Teachers can be brief in their conferences if they don't try to do everything on a particular paper; a conference generally focuses on one aspect of the paper that is working and one that needs improvement. A teacher working, for example, on developing a fuller description of the bully should ignore spelling mistakes in the draft. In an early draft of a paper the teacher might read with these questions in mind:

1. What is the paper really about? Is the true subject embedded in another topic?
2. Does the paper need more detail or documentation?
3. Is the paper sufficiently complex? Are important alternatives explored, important questions answered?
4. Is the paper focused? Does it seem to make one point or general impression?
5. Is the information ordered? Does one part move into the next?
6. Are there parts that can be cut because they're off the subject or uninteresting? (Beginnings, for example, can often be cut.)

These are some of the questions that can focus a first reading. As Donald Murray has noted, the experienced composition teacher "encourages the student to see that on most pieces of writing there is one fundamental problem that must be dealt with before the next problem can be spotted and then solved."

When the larger issues of information, focus, and order are resolved, the teacher can focus on questions of style and language conventions. A different set of questions can then focus the reading:

1. Which errors are proofreading errors and which indicate that the student does not know certain usage rules?
2. Is there any pattern to the errors the writer makes? (Mina Shaughnessy's *Errors and Expectations* is an invaluable aid here.)
3. Are there sentences that can be combined? broken into two sentences?

I've found that when teachers discipline their responses to papers, when they deal with one issue at a time and are not shuttling between trying to elicit more information and dealing with the semicolon, they are more effective and a conference is briefer. Conferences that lack this discipline can be long, aimless, and ineffective.

How can I get students to be more effective in responding to the papers of their classmates?

Many teachers worry that when students get together to comment on each other's writing they might be too harsh and negative. In my experience students err on the side of blandness; comments are very general—"this is interesting," "I can relate to this," and so forth. Peter Elbow, in his books *Writing Without Teachers* and *Writing with Power,* offers a number of strategies for responding more specifically. One of the most basic is "pointing," which he describes as follows:

> Start by simply pointing to words and phrases which successfully penetrated your skull: perhaps they seemed loud and full of voice; or they seemed to have a lot of energy; or they somehow rang true, or they carried special conviction.

Students should also be encouraged to ask the writer questions that can help expand or clarify what has been written. Again we're talking about *questions* that allow the writer to expand and clarify orally, not *judgments* passed on to the writer.

It is often easier to begin peer response by having students pair up; there is generally no hesitancy to confer in pairs. Once groups of four or five are formed they should remain constant for at least several weeks.

I have to grade my students. How can I assign grades and still maintain a workshop approach to writing?

It's best not to grade every piece of writing. Students should be encouraged to select their best writing from their writing folders to be evaluated for a grade. By grading only the best work, the system provides a real incentive for revising because it is often in the student's interest to revise a promising piece than to continually start a new one.

At the end of a marking period a student might be evaluated as follows. All students who complete a satisfactory volume of writing—those who worked regularly and met deadlines—should get a base grade, perhaps a C+. This base grade can go up if the student has made major improvement on a skill identified at the beginning of the marking term or if the quality of the selected pieces of writing is superior.

This system rewards productivity; a student who writes several thousand words in a marking term does not, in my opinion, deserve a D, even if there are substantial difficulties in that writing. The system also rewards quality; excellent writing gets an excellent grade. The system penalizes sloth—and that's the way it should be.

Suggestions for Further Reading

Atwell, Nancie. 1988. "Making the Grade: Evaluating Writing in Conference." In *Understanding Writing: Ways of Observing, Learning, and Teaching,* 2nd ed., ed. Thomas Newkirk and Nancie Atwell. Portsmouth, N.H.: Heinemann.

Berkenkotter, Carol. 1984. "Student Writers and Their Sense of Authority over Texts." *College Composition and Communication* 35:312–19.

Carnicelli, Thomas. 1980. "The Writing Conference: A One-to-One Conversation." In *Eight Approaches to Teaching Composition,* ed. Timothy Donovan and Benjamin McClelland. Urbana, Ill.: National Council of Teachers of English.

Cooper, Charles, and Lee Odell. 1977. *Evaluating Writing: Describing, Measuring, and Judging.* Urbana, Ill.: National Council of Teachers of English.

Elbow, Peter. 1973. *Writing Without Teachers.* New York: Oxford University Press.

———. 1981. *Writing with Power: Techniques for Mastering the Writing Process.* New York: Oxford University Press. See especially his chapters on "reader-based" and "criterion-based" feedback.

Freedman, Sarah W., and Melanie Sperling. 1985. "Written Language Acquisition: The Role of Response and the Writing Conference." In *The Acquisition of Written Language: Response and Revision,* ed. Sarah Freedman. Norwood, N.J.: ABLEX.

Halley, Hasse. 1988. "The Bundle." In *Understanding Writing: Ways of Observing, Learning, and Teaching,* 2nd ed., ed. Thomas Newkirk and Nancie Atwell. Portsmouth, N.H.: Heinemann.

Harris, Muriel. 1986. *Teaching Writing: One-to-One.* Urbana, Ill.: National Council of Teachers of English.

Kirby, Dan, and Tom Liner. 1980. "Revision: Yes, They Do It." *English Journal* 69 (March):41–45.

Knoblauch, C.H., and Lil Brannon. 1984. *Rhetorical Traditions and the Teaching of Writing.* Portsmouth, N.H.: Boynton/Cook, 1984. See especially the chapter "Responding to Texts."

Murray, Donald. 1979. "The Listening Eye: Reflections on the Writing Conference." *College English* 41:13–18.

———. 1985. *A Writer Teaches Writing,* rev. 2nd ed. Boston: Houghton Mifflin. This is essentially a different book from the first edition, with far more information on responding to writing.

Newkirk, Thomas. 1984. "Direction and Misdirection in the Peer Response." *College Composition and Communication* 35 (October):300–311.

Reigstad, Thomas, and Donald A. McAndrew. 1984. *Training Tutors for Writing Conferences.* Urbana, Ill.: ERIC Clearing House on Reading and Communication Skills and the National Council of Teachers of English.

Shaughnessy, Mina. 1977. *Errors and Expectations.* New York: Oxford University Press.

Sommers, Nancie. 1982. "Responding to Student Writing." *College Composition and Communication* 33 (May):148–56.

Stanford, Gene, ed. 1979. *How to Handle the Paper Load: Classroom Practices in Teaching English, 1979–1980.* Urbana, Ill.: National Council of Teachers of English.

White, Edward. 1985. *Teaching and Assessing Writing: Recent Advances in Understanding, Evaluating, and Improving Students' Performance.* San Francisco: Jossey Bass.

Writing and Literature

12

Dialogue with a Text

Robert E. Probst
Georgia State University
Atlanta, Georgia

A Story

I was observing a class in a suburban junior high school, one that drew many of its students from comfortable homes with parents in successful professional roles, parents who expected a great deal of their children, and of the school. The entire class, but especially one girl sitting directly in front of me, was intrigued by the story. It was C. D. B. Bryan's "So Much Unfairness of Things," and the unfairness of which it spoke seemed to trouble and awaken the students (342–67). They stirred, noticeably uncomfortable and disturbed when the time came to discuss the reading.

The story is that of a young man, a student at a tough preparatory school in Virginia, who found himself in difficulty with his Latin course and succumbed to the temptation to cheat on an examination. He regretted the lapse immediately, and painfully, but too late. He was reported, his father was called, and the story ended as he was driven away from the campus.

Many of the students reading the story must have been painfully aware of the complexity of the situation Bryan had created. P. S., as the student was called, had no intention of cheating. It wasn't planned or premeditated. He hadn't even considered the possibility. Not until well into the examination did he realize that the translation of the test passage was in his desk—he hadn't brought it to the exam planning to use it—and even then he fought the temptation. But he *was* in desperate straits, having failed the exam the year before. He needed to pass it to graduate, and he didn't want to stay at the school another year. Things were not going well on the exam, he was obviously in bad shape, and the notes were there in his desk. The temptation was just too great. He slid the sheet out, copied the translation, and went off to his room in terror.

He was not habitually dishonest and corrupt. If somewhat too casual about his work, too easily distracted from his studies, he was nonetheless a pleasant, good-natured, likable fellow, and not the sort of character whose punishment the readers could watch with equanimity. It must have been easy for the students to imagine themselves in a similar situation.

On the other hand, those readers could not permit themselves the satisfaction of railing against the teacher and the headmaster who expelled P. S. Both the Latin teacher, Dr. Fairfax, and the headmaster, Mr. Seaton, appeared to be kind men, nearly as upset and unhappy with the situation as P. S. was. Bound by the school's strict honor code, they had little choice but to abide by its demands. Even the student who reported P. S. was a good fellow, whose motivations were respectable. There was no villain to blame and thus relieve the reader of his problem.

Before the teacher could begin the discussion, the girl sitting in front of me raised her hand, and without waiting for the teacher to call on her, began to talk. "I know exactly how he felt," she said, obviously troubled. "My parents expect me to become a doctor, and if I were going to fail I'd *have* to cheat."

Her remark provoked a flurry of comment, some students confirming the point, almost sadly and shamefully, as if revealing an unhappy truth about their lives. Some were casually amoral. "Everyone cheats," one student said, "that's the way it works." And some spoke almost belligerently, as if expecting the teacher to reprimand them for asserting that they would, if they thought it necessary, cheat to succeed in school. But the teacher didn't reprimand them. She tolerated the outpouring for a few moments, then waved the class into relative quiet and asked, "What techniques does the author use to reveal character in this story?"

The girl in front of me waved her hand this time, waited until the teacher acknowledged her, and said, "My father has warned me what medical school is going to be like, and I'm not sure I can get through it—I'm not even sure I want to be a doctor . . . ," which was understandable, since she was at the moment in the eighth grade.

The teacher acknowledged that, replying, "Yes, Jane, you have plenty of time to make up your mind. Now, there are three ways an author reveals character—can you tell me what they are?"

Jane slumped a bit in her seat, in a gesture that often reveals ignorance, but that in this case seemed an expression of indifference, and another student joined in, "The kid who turned him in for cheating is a character, all right—he ought to be shot. Nobody turns you in for cheating."

Another flurry of argument followed that remark, with several students agreeing but with several objecting that there were good reasons not to tolerate cheating, even if it did mean turning in a friend. One youngster argued that there were reasons for having rules against this kind of behavior, and others responded that no circumstances justified turning in a friend. A few of them tried to defend the concept of a code of ethics, while others spoke for unconditional loyalty among friends. They were searching for their arguments when the teacher again interrupted.

Bending slightly to the path the discussion insisted on taking, against her will, she asked, "All right, how does the author reveal the character of the student who turns P. S. in?"

The students stared blankly, apparently unable to turn their thoughts away from the moral complexities of the story toward the teacher's questions, and the room was, for the first time, silent. One boy, introspectively, as if speaking to himself, muttered quietly, "I *did* cheat once, on a test, and I was scared to death, but no one turned me in."

"What techniques," the teacher repeated, sternly now, "does the author use to reveal character in this story? We've had them before, you studied them last year, you know what they are, there are only three—now what are they?"

The class was subdued.

"Well, the author can just tell you about somebody's character," one student responded.

"He can show how the character acts," said another.

And the girl in front of me, still preoccupied with other thoughts, offered distractedly, "He can show other characters reacting to him or talking about him."

"Good," said the teacher, breathing a sigh of relief, "now let's go on. . . ."

But I forget what she went on to. She had to move on, she explained later. There were other stories to cover, other skills and techniques to learn, and there was to be a test that Friday. They had to be ready for that test. It had to do with techniques of characterization, and it was important. Those kids, that girl, would be under a great deal of pressure to pass it, one way or another. . . .

The Argument

I'm sure that all of the pressures the teacher felt were real, almost as real as those her students felt and wanted to talk about, and the discussion might have served her as it might have served them, but her vision of literature and its function led her to other matters. She saw her job as the teaching of skills and terms and techniques. The students wanted to address the moral dilemmas presented in the story. Their instincts and inclinations led them to talk about the intense pressure to succeed that comes to bear upon some of them, about the temptation to cheat that confronts them all, about the weight of parents' expectations, about the conflicting values of friendship and honesty, about the burdens of a demanding honor code that is supposed to be valued even above friendship. But their teacher wanted to conduct a recitation on the three techniques of characterization.

Louise Rosenblatt (1985) would argue that the students in that class had the clearer, more vital conception of literature:

> Surely, of all the arts, literature is most immediately implicated with life itself. The very medium through which the author shapes the text—language—is grounded in the shared lives of human beings. Language is the bloodstream of a common culture, a common history. What might otherwise be mere vibrations in the air or black marks on a page can point to all that has been thought or imagined—in Henry James' phrases, to "all life, all feeling, all observation, all vision." (65)

Had the teacher viewed literature that way, she might have considered the students' questions and interests more significant—they came, after all, from the life, the feeling, the observation, the vision of the students. They were focused clearly and intently upon the connecting links between the text and their own lives. The story was, for them, implicated with life itself, and they wanted to consider those implications. To have done so would have been to invite the students into the literature in the most powerful and effective way, allowing it to be, not an exercise or a drill, but a shaping experience, one out of which students could make meaning. They could have, if the teacher had allowed it, participated in the making of meaning about their own lives as well as about the text, engaging in real thought rather than in simple recall of terms and definitions.

Rosenblatt (1983) has suggested some principles for that sort of teaching (66, 69, 71, 74):

> First, the students must be free to deal with their own reactions.

These students clearly were not free to deal with their own reactions, which were strong and clear. They were instead constrained to ignore them in favor of the teacher's exercise.

> Second, there must be an opportunity for "an initial crystallization of a personal sense of the work."

The personal sense of the work *was* crystallizing quickly for these students. They had begun to articulate the personal implications of the story even before the teacher was able to start her lesson, and it took some effort for her to interrupt it so that she could proceed with her work on characterization.

> Third, the teacher should attempt to find the points of contact among the opinions of students.

These students were finding the connections easily. Some said "cheating cannot be tolerated"; others, "you can't betray your friends." They had begun to notice and discuss their different perspectives upon cheating, upon the honor code, upon the issue of loyalty. There was great potential in that discussion, because there *was* conflict, in their lives and in the story, between two codes of behavior. An opportunity to talk about those matters would have been very valuable to them.

> Fourth, the teacher's influence should be "an elaboration of the vital influence inherent in literature itself."

In this incident, the teacher was working—struggling—*against* the influence inherent in the literature, rather than allowing the students to pursue it.

None of Rosenblatt's principles eliminate careful, reasoned analysis in the study of literature, but they suggest that the basis for intelligent and productive reading is in the unique, individual, perhaps idiosyncratic, connection between readers and the text. Rosenblatt has demonstrated that the meaning made of a literary text depends upon the readers as well as upon the text itself. Meaning is the product of a transaction between active minds and the words on the page—it does not reside in the ink, to be ferreted out, unearthed, uncovered. Rather, it is created, formed, shaped, by readers in the act of reading, and thus it is *their* meaning.

That doesn't, however, necessarily condemn us to total intellectual isolation. Language has both idiosyncratic and social dimensions, and meanings can, to an extent, be shared. Even widely accepted conceptions are the result of such sharing and negotiating among individuals. What we understand by such terms as "love," "justice," "good" is the result of our immersion in a culture that has dealt with these issues in its art and literature and law, continually refining and modifying its understandings in the light of new experiences. All of these crucial concepts have their roots in concrete human experience and emerge from continual reinvestigation of that experience—it is the role of literature to present and explore those roots.

Instruction in literature should enable readers to find the connections between their experience and the literary work. If it does so, it may enable them to use the literature, to employ it in making sense of their lives.

The Dialogue

If we were to devise instruction consistent with Rosenblatt's principles, what shape might that instruction take? If students are to be "free to deal with [their] own reactions," her first principle, they must be working in a comfortable setting, freed, at least for the moment, of some of the customary burdens of classroom discourse—the obligation to prove all assertions, the pervasive concern with accuracy and correctness, and the competitiveness that often rules the talk. Further, they must be invited to attend to matters that are often considered extraneous and irrelevant in classrooms—their feelings, perceptions, memories.

They must be given time to articulate all of those thoughts and help in finding the links—the "points of contact"—between their various reactions that will reward talk. They may need assistance in identifying the elements in the text that have contributed most powerfully to shaping their responses and help in figuring out how they have worked. And they are likely to need a great deal of assistance in learning the difficult process of talking with others.

Finally, they need an opportunity to shape the discussion, pursuing it toward their own goals. They need to sense the "influence inherent" in the literary work and attempt, in the discussion and writing, to articulate it, define it, explore it.

The questions following below are intended to lead students to the sort of literary experience implicit in Rosenblatt's principles, giving them some assistance along the way. The activity is an effort to demonstrate some of the potential satisfactions in beginning a consideration of a literary work with the reader's response. It asks you—and your students—to read a short literary work, probably a poem, although a short story—Bryan's, for instance—might work as well, and then to discuss it by responding to a series of questions designed and arranged to encourage reflection on several aspects of the act of reading. The questions are an attempt to transform Rosenblatt's guiding principles into a pattern for discussion, one that is necessarily loose and flexible, but that respects the ways in which response to literature might vary.

The talk can be guided gently, without too much interference from the teacher, by providing a selection from these questions—perhaps five to ten, depending on the time available and the maturity of the group—reworded to be suitable for the group, of course, and prepared without the sidenote (the column labeled "Focus"). Placing each question to be used on a separate small page (4″ × 5″) stapled into a small book provides a place to jot down notes and encourages the readers to address each question more thoroughly before going onto the others. The first page of the booklet might give such instructions as those following, again, reworded appropriately for the group:

> Please read the text, and take a moment or two to reflect on it. Then turn to the next page and begin. Take a few minutes—as

much as you need or want—with each question. Please reflect on each question for a moment, or two, perhaps jotting down brief notes, before discussing it. Some may be more productive than others for you, and you may wish to give those more time. There is no rush, no need to finish them all. Please don't glance ahead in the booklet.

The discussion might be conducted in pairs, or in small groups of perhaps four or five students. Each arrangement has its virtues and its problems. In pairs, if the students are compatible, the talk may be more intimate, more personal, and more likely to lead to discoveries about the self. The small groups, however, are sometimes better able to sustain the discussion because they have more minds at work on each question. Decide how you wish to arrange the talk, give the students a copy of the text and the booklet, and explain the activity. If you've chosen a poem, read it aloud, and then let them begin. . . .

Focus	Questions
First reaction	What is your first reaction or response to the text? Describe or explain it briefly.
Feelings	What feelings did the text awaken in you? What emotions did you feel as you read the text?
Perceptions	What did you see happening in the text? Paraphrase it—retell the major events briefly.
Visual images	What image was called to mind by the text? Describe it briefly.
Associations	What memory does the text call to mind—of people, places, events, sights, smells, or even of something more ambiguous, perhaps feelings or attitudes?
Thoughts, ideas	What idea or thought was suggested by the text? Explain it briefly.
Selection of textual elements	Upon what, in the text, did you focus most intently as you read—what word, phrase, image, idea?
Judgments of importance	What is the most important word in the text? What is the most important phrase in the text? What is the most important aspect of the text?

Dialogue with a Text

Focus	Questions
Identification of problems	What is the most difficult word in the text? What is there in the text or in your reading that you have the most trouble understanding?
Author	What sort of person do you imagine the author of this text to be?
Patterns of response	How did you respond to the text—emotionally or intellectually? Did you feel involved with the text, or distant from it?
Other readings	How did your reading of the text differ from that of your discussion partner (or the others in your group)? In what ways were they similar?
Evolution of your reading	How did your understanding of the text or your feelings about it change as you talked?
Evaluations	Do you think the text is a good one—why, or why not?
Literary associations	Does this text call to mind any other literary work (poem, play, film, story—any genre)? If it does, what is the work and what is the connection you see between the two?
Writing	If you were to be asked to write about your reading of this text, upon what would you focus? Would you write about some association or memory, some aspect of the text itself, about the author, or about some other matter?
Other readers	What did you observe about your discussion partner (or the others in your group) as the talk progressed?

Discussion

The questions guiding the discussion of the text reflect a concern for the variability of response, and for the possibility of moving from response into analysis without denying the validity of initial responses, of unique personal reactions and associations. They are, you may have noticed, generic questions, tied not to a particular text, but rather to a conception of the reading process. They invite the students to attend to themselves, to their own experience with the work; to identify aspects of the text that seem, to them, significant; to consider their reading in the light of other readings by other students; and finally, to reflect on what they have observed, about themselves and their classmates, in the process.

After the pairs, or the groups, have finished with the booklet and reconvened, consider reactions to the activity. In particular, you might raise questions such as these:

- Do you have any first reactions to the discussion, any thoughts or observations about its results for you or for the group?
- Did differences in readings of the text emerge as you talked? Did those differences reveal the possibility of other legitimate experiences with the text? Did the talk lead to any insights into the text, or yourself, or others at the table?
- Did the discussion occasionally drive you back to the text to find examples, evidence, sources of ideas? Did you find yourselves engaging in analysis, either of the text or of your interpretations and associations?
- How did your understanding of the text or your feelings about it change as you talked? Do you view the text differently now that you have discussed it extensively with others?

Conclusions

If the activity works, and the discussion seems productive, it should suggest that the teaching of a literary work might begin with the reader's response, whether that response is emotional, visceral, aesthetic, or intellectual. The teacher might then encourage students to examine that response, looking at themselves, the text, other readers, and other texts. That discussion might lead to several possible outcomes. Students might find that their initial impressions or interpretations are reinforced and confirmed, that they are refuted, or, most likely, that they are modified in the course of discussion and writing. This is not, however, necessarily a matter of right and wrong, of dispelling error, but rather a process of refining and clarifying. The confirmation, modification, or refutation resulting from the discussion indicates not simply that mistakes have been corrected, though of course that may have happened, but rather that there has been some growth in understanding, some change in perspective. To see the changes simply as rejection of error is to suggest once again that there is a single correct interpretation.

Discussion beginning with response might then extend to biography, history, criticism, culture, and intellectual history. Beginning with the personal and unique does not necessitate a purely egocentric study that denies the validity of other information, other lines of inquiry; it simply asserts that the fundamental literary experience is intimate, personal, and dependent upon the nature of the individual. It is, in fact, quite likely that these discussions of personal readings will lead the students into close analysis of the texts, and that other questions—biographical, historical, and the like—will emerge as students attempt to understand and reconcile their different readings.

For this sort of instruction to succeed, the tone in the classroom must be cooperative; debate is an inappropriate model. Discussions must build, must have an organic nature, pursuing questions that arise from encounters with the text. The questions suggested for this activity are an attempt to simulate that natural development of the talk, suggesting the possibilities for it. It would probably be desirable to abandon even such gentle, open questions as these if, and when, students learn to identify and pursue the potential in the literature on their own initiative.

Because the reading of literature is in many ways an exploration, it is suitable for teachers not to read in advance some of the works they intend to teach. Coming to them cold, as their students do, enables teachers to think matters through with their classes, modeling for them the process of speculating and probing, examining memories and finding associations, tentatively proposing interpretations or assessments and then revising them. Too often students have the impression that teachers simply know. Students don't know how they know, nor see the process that leads to that knowing, only that teachers know and students don't. Reading along with the students, approaching a text as something new, allows teachers to think with the students, showing them the processes they are to learn.

A few cooperative colleagues might agree to provide each other, once every other week or two, with sufficient copies of a poem or story. Opening the package along with the students, not knowing before they do what it contains, may suggest to them that teacher and student are in something together, colleagues in the task of making sense out of literary encounters rather than adversaries. The first few attempts to teach a text you haven't seen before may be unsettling, but the practice can have the benefit of focusing attention upon response and upon the strategies for making sense of literary experience.

There may be a problem with transition for students, too. Not used to an approach that emphasizes working with responses to texts, they may not like it and may even fight it. If they have learned well to play according to other rules—predicting the interests and interpretations of the teacher, for instance, or memorizing details, or whatever other pattern may prevail—they may not be happy with a sudden change in the game.

Although it may seem to them, as it does to many teachers, permissive and indulgent, this sort of reading—and teaching—can be rigorous and demanding. It requires the reader to consider not just the text, but also one's self and the readings of others. Readers must analyze and think, producing their own understandings, not simply remembering information provided by teacher or textbook. This exploration of responses can be either fascinating or exhausting or both. It may reveal much about the individual who engages in it. It is easy to resist, however, since teachers cannot spell out precisely what they expect. There are no absolutes in such a classroom; all readers individually must make their own sense of things. Still, it is possible to be foolish and wrong about texts or about statements of others, and possible also to be deceitful or confused about one's own perceptions. The exploration of responses can be hard work.

Teachers trying to elicit and work with response to literary texts may find it useful to try predicting students' reactions, at least some of the time, but the predictions can become boundaries. There can be tension between the need to prepare for possibilities and the desire to allow for developments. Teachers need to sense the direction the discussion seems naturally to take rather than decide in advance exactly what will be covered. They need to be open to the possibilities that arise in the thirty different responses—and thus the thirty different poems—that they have before them. Without abandoning that flexibility, it is desirable for teachers to have in mind some possible direction for follow-up, that is, some idea of the issues that may arise and the literary works or writing activities that might develop them (see LaConte). Being prepared with at least some of the possibilities gives teachers some sense of stability and security. Again, though, they must remain open to the possibility that something unexpected will arise in the talk and be prepared to capitalize on it.

That uncertainty may be nerve-wracking, but it has its rewards. It keeps the class alive, allowing a vital exchange of ideas rather than the working out of a script. Both students and teachers need to develop a tolerance for ambiguity in such a classroom. There may rarely be a satisfying consensus at the close of the lesson. Individuals are responsible for their own conclusions and summations.

If we accept the idea that literature ought to be significant, that readers have to assimilate it and work with it, that transforming it into knowledge is more significant than memorizing the definitions of technical terms, then we need to find some ways of bringing readers and text together, and of forcing upon readers the responsibility for making meaning of text. First efforts are very likely doomed to fail for obvious reasons: the students aren't used to it and don't trust it; we aren't used to it and haven't figured out all of its complications; it places tremendous responsibility on everyone involved, not the teacher alone; it requires that we deal with thirty evolving poems at a time rather than just one stable text; it requires that students accept a new and frightening notion of what knowledge is; and it demands a tolerance for ambiguity and digression. But if meaning is a human act rather than a footlocker full of dusty facts, then we must focus attention on the act of making meaning rather than simply on the accumulation of data.

References

Bryan, C. D. B. 1979. "So Much Unfairness of Things." *Literature and Life*, ed. Helen McDonnell and others. Glenview, IL: Scott-Foresman.

LaConte, Ronald. 1980. "A Literary Heritage Paradigm for Secondary English." *Three Language Arts Curriculum Models*, ed. Barrett John Mandel. Urbana: NCTE.

13

Watching Sarah Think

A Journal in Retrospect

Maureen Barbieri
Laurel School
Shaker Heights, Ohio

IN the play *Camelot* (Lerner and Loewe 1961) when Merlyn the magician realizes he is going to die, leaving his young student Arthur to fend for himself, he has misgivings.

> All his life I've tried to teach him to think. . . . Wait! Have I told him everything he should know? Did I tell him of Lancelot? But Lancelot and Guenevere! And Mordred? It's all gone. My magic is all gone. . . . Wart! Remember to think! (19)

Each year when June came and my eighth graders would prepare to leave me and go on to high school, I used to feel like Merlyn. Had we read enough Shakespeare? What of Steinbeck, O'Connor, Frost? Would they be able to write analytic essays? Did they understand metaphor?

But now, saying good-bye to my students once again, I feel sad but not concerned. I will miss them, certainly, but I know they will thrive. They have demonstrated to me and, more importantly, to themselves that they are readers and writers who certainly do think. It's clear in their writing folders, it's clear in their class discussions. But most of all, I believe, it's clear in their journals. I sit now in an empty classroom that still rings with the shouts of party plans, still sighs with sad farewells to those leaving for the summer or forever, and I feel a familiar lump in my throat. The year, like all the other years, has flown by too fast. I open Sarah's journal to figure out where it all went. . . .

The pink cover of the spiral notebook is marked with a tiny unicorn and her name is etched in calligraphy. It's a lot like Sarah herself—dignified and earnest. The cover's edges are not frayed, in the manner of some of her classmates', assuring me that this journal has been well cared for over the past year. I smile, recalling the Sarah I met back in September. Shy and unsure of herself, she did not seem particularly eager to be in this class of twenty-four. A tall girl with huge brown eyes and long blonde hair, she appeared to want to go unnoticed in the classroom. It was not to be.

I'd looked forward to getting to know all of them better; I had read Toby Fulwiler's *Teaching with Writing* (1987) over the summer and felt ready for something new. For the previous three years my students had written letters to me and to one another about the novels they were reading, as suggested by Nancie Atwell in *In the Middle* (1987) and elsewhere. I'd been surprised and pleased with the depth of their involvement with their books, and I wanted to try nudging them towards examining other literature in much the same way. And so it was that during Sarah's eighth-grade year we added journals to our program.

In the beginning, I chose poems, stories, and essays, trying always to keep the kids and their interests in mind. (Eventually they would choose poems and stories themselves, just as they did their novels.) In order to help them focus on the content of what we were about to read, I'd sometimes ask them to do a quick journal entry on a topic related to the piece, a prereading write. I was careful to keep my suggestions general, so as not to impose my own reading of the poem on them.

For example, in September I asked the class to write about their thoughts on the changing seasons, in preparation for reading Stanley Kunitz's poem "End of Summer" (1983). Sarah wrote:

> Time to go back to school. No more free days when you can just do whatever comes to mind. Seeing friends five days a week and usually more. No more staying up until you collapse and getting up when you want. It means playing field hockey, no more mow-

> ing the lawn, saying goodbye to all summer flowers and to summer friends.

It was a free-writing kind of entry, her own associations on the time of year we were in. Sarah was a rambler, I could tell from the start, and I knew that was a good sign—she seemed comfortable writing.

We all read the Kunitz poem and, before discussing it, wrote reactions in our journals. I wanted to leave lots of room for diversity, so my only instructions to the students were, "Respond to the poem any way you like. Tell about your opinion, ask questions, make connections—or anything else you'd like to do with it."

"Should we say what we think it means?" someone asked.

"If you like," I replied, "but it will mean something different to everyone in the room. Write about what it says to you."

My goal was to have my students understand that a poem is experienced differently by everyone who reads it, that the personal connection is a valid and important aspect of reading poetry or any literature. I didn't say all this to them; I wanted them to come to the realization on their own through lots of reading and sharing reactions to poetry. I believed journal writing would be an integral part of the process.

Journal writing allowed them to focus as individuals on any aspect of the poem they chose before hearing other people's views. They weren't able to be passive, as the writing encouraged them to really examine their own thoughts. Sarah wrote:

> This poem made me feel as if the man was alone, or almost alone, because it seemed as though the air and the light were alive in that they had human emotions. The blue part made me think of two different colors of blue dripping into one another. I got the idea that the change of seasons reminded him of his age.

It was a good beginning. I could tell Sarah was not intimidated at all by the poet. She saw images in her mind, and she speculated on the seasons' changing as a metaphor for aging. I was encouraged by her response and eager to explore more poetry with her in the future.

Once everyone had written, we'd usually talk. Students would volunteer to read their journal entries, sometimes I'd read mine, and then a discussion would ensue. We were always careful to listen to each other and to respect any personal associations people made.

I believe the journal entries made our talks much livelier than in other years, simply because everyone had already invested time and energy in thinking about the poem, and thus had something to bring to the group. Hearing one another's entries helped students avoid perfunctory comments or summaries, since we soon realized we appreciated specific observations or personal associations more than glib critiques.

Sarah was generous and open in all her journal entries. When I asked the class to write about what it meant to be alone, Sarah wrote:

> It's dark and very quiet. No one is around. It's very lonely. It's cold and the wind is blowing. It's not outside or inside. It's nowhere, it's nothing.
>
> It's loud. Many are rushing by, but no one stops to notice. It's everywhere, it's everything.
>
> I sometimes feel more alone with many people than I do when no one is around me.
>
> I feel alone when I have a problem that seems so important to me and I feel as if it should be important to everyone but no one seems to notice.
>
> I sometimes feel alone when I see someone who has no family or friends.
>
> Alone isn't always so bad.
>
> I love be by myself. It gives me a chance to get to know myself and sort out problems. The chance to be alone doesn't come that often. You have to take it when you can.

We read "Alone" by Jonathan Holden (1983), and Sarah commented in her journal:

> I'm curious to see how Holden related being alone to eating clouds and the sky. I don't really see the connection. I love the idea of eating clouds and I love the poem, but I don't like the way it was used in "Alone."
>
> This piece is totally opposite to the first part of my reaction to the word alone. It is even totally different to the second part of my piece. But, from the line, "alone is luscious," I can see he thinks alone is a good thing, at least some of the time. And so do I.

When I read Sarah's first entry about being alone, I was amazed at her fluency. She seemed to write quickly and easily, making excellent points as she went along. Best of all, she was able to change her mind about being alone as she wrote! "Alone isn't always so bad." When she read Holden's poem, she was confident enough to question his use of an image, and eager for class discussion, knowing someone else would have ideas on Holden's poem and being alone.

And, of course, Sarah was right. Ideas seemed to come fast and furious. Was this a poem about overeating? Was the speaker a glutton or a stargazer? Were the clouds meant to represent books, perhaps, or were they really just clouds? Differences of opinion were accepted in class, as long as students could support whatever they said by referring to the text. After much talk, we agreed on one thing: alone can sometimes be a very good state of being. My kids were beginning to understand how much fun sharing reactions to poetry could be. Forget the "secret meaning," we agreed; a poem is better when we can bring our own associations to it, making meaning rather than finding it.

Naturally, the question of grading the journals came up fairly early in the year. I'd encouraged lots of freedom in the entries, insisting, "There's no wrong way to respond." But, being schooled for years in a rigorous system of evaluation, students soon demanded to know if the journals would "count." It was a dilemma for me, since my highest priority was that the kids be relaxed and fluent enough to make their own meanings of the poems and stories through writing about them. How would this happen if they were paralyzed with concern for assessment?

We talked it out together. They wanted me to read their journals frequently, since we never really had time for everyone to read the entries aloud in class. They wanted me to keep a record of whose journal was up to date and whose was not, because we were all members of this class, and fair was fair. They also wanted me to respond to their entries, either by writing in their journals or by bringing their issues up in class.

I agreed to do all these things. I would read their journals at least every other week, more often when necessary (such as after a particularly difficult or troubling poem) and write encouraging, nonjudgmental comments in response to what they had said.

We designed our own system of self-evaluation for the overall English grade and determined to meet in conference at the end of each marking period to talk about goals and possible obstacles to meeting them. At these conferences, I'd ask how the journals were working out; did they help the students understand literature? I would then ask them to give themselves a journal grade, based on how seriously they were working towards full engagement with what we read. My students were as honest in evaluating their commitment to journals as they were in all other areas of the course. We had no problem agreeing on grades.

I wanted my students to feel excited and curious, challenged and capable in any genre they encountered. I wanted them to be hungry for more and more poetry. I wanted them to know what a joy it can be to really experience a story. Making personal connections was the beginning; but, of course, there was more to it than that.

In *Response and Analysis: Teaching Literature in Junior and Senior High School* (1988), Robert Probst states:

> The teacher must establish an atmosphere in which students feel secure enough to respond openly, but must not deceive them into believing that initial responses are sufficient. (25)

One of the obvious ways Sarah moved beyond personal response was to focus on language in poetry. In November I gave everyone six poems to take home, asking them to choose just one to respond to in the journals. Sarah chose "Night" by Patricia Hubbell (1986).

> I love the adjectives [Sarah wrote]. It seems like what she wrote is what I have always been wanting to write. The theme of this is spiders, and it's great the way the words themselves suggest spiders and webs and all. I really couldn't think of a spider as this many things myself. I get a silvery, shimmery, sparkly, glistening feeling when I read it—like just in the morning after the dew.

Appreciating the language of literature was something Sarah would continue to do throughout the year, although her primary concern seemed to be the emotional implications of any given piece. She was also willing, as were most of her classmates, to allow her writing to change her ideas.

After we had read Eudora Welty's story "A Worn Path" (1980), Sarah wrote:

> The woman described sounds like she's blind and she reminds me of Sophia in *The Color Purple.* As she walks it seems she's walked there before. I guess she isn't blind. I don't understand the part with the boy and the cake. The woman knows every little detail of the path she's taking—she does take that trip often. I wonder what happened to her grandson's parents.
>
> This story is so sad. I love the way Welty writes with every little detail coming out.

> I bet when you get old you start to think about things like dying and leaving it all behind. Did the woman in the story do that?

I encouraged my kids to write about anything that puzzled them, to wonder and to speculate in their journals. As the year progressed, Sarah did more and more of this. She was able to admit that she was sometimes confused, but usually her journal writing led her to find tentative answers to her questions. Her confidence grew.

We read "Heyday of the Blood" by Dorothy Canfield Fisher (1984), and Sarah commented:

> I thought the beginning of the story was very odd. I didn't understand why the professor told the younger man this story. Was he telling him that he should get out of his slump and live his life?
>
> I like the great-grandfather's motto—it's true, if you're half alive, then you're half dead. I liked the grandfather—he's the rebellious type. He seemed kinda like a child except with more memory and experience in life.

Throughout the year my kids reacted to the values of characters we met in stories. I don't remember asking them to do this; they did it on their own. Probst says this is a natural function of adolescence.

> Students read literature to know themselves, and—insofar as they each are a composite of their ideas, attitudes, beliefs, and emotions—to create themselves, for reading will enable them to refine and sharpen their conceptions of the world and the people in it. It is those conceptions that make them who they are. (5)

I could see Sarah defining herself in her journal. In reflecting on the great-grandfather's values, she was trying them on for herself.

After Christmas break, another serious issue came up. After reading "Romeo and Juliet" together, Sarah's classmate Bryan wrote a paper on whether or not Romeo really had the right to commit suicide. Knowing his ideas would provoke some serious discussion, I asked the class to write for ten minutes one day on the subject of taking one's own life.

Sarah wrote:

> What do I think about suicide? Well, at this point in my life, nothing so awful has happened to me that I would take my own life. I think it would be a very selfish thing to do because you would be putting those who love you through so much pain. I

> was always told that suicide is selfish because in a way your life isn't only yours. So many other people have things invested in you. That bothered me also. I feel that my life, if nothing else, is something I have control over.

About the poem "Suicide" by Joyce Carol Oates (1983), Sarah had this to say:

> Listening to this poem made me feel the confusion of the poet when a loved one committed suicide. I guess if a loved one of mine died, I would wonder if they really appreciated my love and care.

I had not planned an in-depth look at suicide, but the subject was weighing on my students' minds, and they seemed to need to talk about it and write about it. My function was to provide a literary framework for such reflection, to use both Shakespeare's play and Oates' poem as the bases for our talk. Once again, examining works of literature led to examining our own attitudes, beliefs, and values.

The year rolled along, and we moved into more free choice in both poetry and short story reading. In February, I brought in a collection of black poetry and fiction anthologies, and Sarah chose Owen Dobson's poem "Sorrow Is the Only Faithful One" (1968) to examine in her journal.

> It seems when I first read it that the only thing that this black person can think about is his sorrow. The only thing he or she talks about is sorrow. I guess maybe that is true for a lot of people. When I read it again, I see that the speaker feels sorrow is everywhere, with high mountains, the sun and even inside him. He can't get away from it, and it's taking over his life. I think maybe other people let him down. Maybe he has had a lot of tragedies.
>
> I think one of the most powerful lines is where it says, "Sorrow has a song like a leech." It sounds to me like the sorrow has sucked all the pleasure and life from the person. Imagine the only thing being dependable to you is sorrow!

I could see that Sarah was working harder. She'd read the poem several times, looking at individual lines and their relevance to the whole poem. Her entry showed her own sorrow in the face of such despair, and her other responses to the black poetry she chose were among her most sensitive.

> In "Hokku: in the Falling Snow" by Richard Wright [1968] it's amazing how so few words can mean so much! When I first read

> it, I saw how the boy was out in the snow. I associated that with being out in the cold, and being unfortunate. But if he's laughing, he must be happy. Maybe he's happy because he is hiding his color in the snow. Maybe he sees this as a way to make him better. One reason I love the snow is because it covers up so much ugliness, but I never applied it to people.

By April Sarah and her classmates were doing so well with their journals that I decided to "raise the bar," our own way of saying "make things more challenging." We read two poems, "Forecast" by Dan Jaffe (1968) and "Dreams" by Langston Hughes (1968) and we compared voices and attitudes in each.

> The speaker in "Forecast" seems sorry that we are not as in touch with outdoors as we once were. And it's not just outdoors, it's other people. We tend to keep to ourselves. It's like we're too wrapped up in ourselves. We don't even see what's going on in the world. Someone on television will tell us, and we'll take that person's word for it.
>
> This poem makes me feel sorry and rather ashamed. It's true. We do spend too much time isolated from other people. Everything we need is right inside our own houses, food, clothing, water. . . . I want to find out what's going on myself, not have to take someone else's word for it!
>
> Hughes' poem is different. The dreams in this poem must be our ambitions or our hope, not our thoughts wandering at night. Without hope, we are grounded for life, like a bird that cannot fly. Without something to drive us on in life, we will remain immobile. Without dreams we will be as numb and as cold as a frozen field. This poem makes me feel as if my dreams are the most important thing. I think how awful it would be to have those dreams shattered, like so many people's dreams have been.
>
> Not all people are like the ones in "Forecast." There are still a few that are not full of despair, a few that can say that they have found out for themselves what it is like to have your own dream.

Her examination of these poems, along with her previous study of several black writers, led Sarah to write a piece of fiction about a homeless person. It was evident to me that she was connecting with her literature in significant ways. I felt she and the others were ready for a truly challenging poem, and I chose "After Grief" by Mekeel McBride (1988). As always, we read the poem aloud several times, and then dove into our journals. I remember how they squirmed and frowned, but also how they soon settled down.

Sarah used her strategy of looking at the poem in segments first:

> When I read the first 11 lines of this piece, I thought about the shells on the waves as the good things in life, people, objects or anything that help a person through. But all these were gone! All that was left was a blue pool, which I saw as grief or sadness. The whole stones were problems.
>
> Then the anenome opens "like an invalid's heart." I saw this as a person in the sadness, first beginning to except it and be able to find the light, the hope and the good things about the situation.
>
> When I read the part about the man walking w/out any of these things, I thought about a person without anything in life except himself.
>
> I think that the day moon is good, full of autumn and salt. Maybe it will bring some relief. Maybe the salt is tears. I think his own body is salty from tears.
>
> I think that the man will be happy or at least content dealing with his life now.

We ran out of time that day—they'd written for so long. I took all their journals home with me. I was thrilled with all Sarah had done with the poem. She saw so many metaphors, making her own sense of some very sophisticated and complex imagery. I responded with a question I'd had after reading the poem myself: "Does life hold more than grief?"

The next day in class I asked the kids to write again on an aspect of poetry that was new to them—the poet's intention. Why had McBride written this? What did she intend her readers to see here? Again, they were wary but willing.

I remember watching Sarah grimace as she wrote, and I wondered whether she'd address the question I'd posed in her journal. Sarah noted:

> It's impossible for me to say exactly what the poet is trying to get across with this poem. I can, however, say the message I got from it.
>
> The poet has written such a descriptive and strong piece that I can only guess that she is getting over a great loss. I don't know how else she could pinpoint these feelings.
>
> I think maybe this poet is actually trying to help herself cope with loss. Maybe she is trying to convince herself that she must go on and let herself grow from circumstances like these.
>
> The message that I get is that life is a school and all experiences are lessons. I think maybe some are actually tests of our strength and courage. I get the message from this poem that we

> should allow ourselves to learn and grow from these disappointments because that is what life brings, but that is not all that life brings.

It's an old cliché that we teachers learn from our students, but never was it truer for me than on the day Sarah shared that entry with our class. I knew she had the perception and the perserverance to examine whole new worlds of literature with her writing.

We wanted to wrap up the year with something really special, so I brought in Mary Oliver's poem "May" (1978). At first, it was elusive to Sarah:

> I have a hard time getting an understanding of this poem. I like the blossoms storming out of the darkness. That's what it seems like, all of a sudden, the flowers just burst out.
>
> The bees seem to be looking for more that just honey. They're looking for something spiritual. So is the speaker. That's like when we search in places for spiritual feelings.

In the face of difficulty, Sarah used a sensible approach; she looked at specific images to make some meaning of the poem. We shared journal entries aloud, and then, since many were still struggling, I asked them to write again.

Sarah wrote:

> When I read this the first time, I tried to overcomplicate it. I made the flowers out to be more than just flowers, but actually places that we search for goodness. I didn't just let them be flowers.
>
> Now, when I read this, I see that the flowers really are wonderful and are places that we search for spiritual food, and that they let us know that even though you are small and insignificant, you are as good as any poem or prayer.
>
> And flowers with their color, sweet smells and delicate beauty, can brighten any place, no matter how dark and can lift your spirits, no matter how low.

Sarah had come to the realization that poems can work on several levels, both literal and figurative. She had shown the ability to think in metaphor and to back off and look again at other aspects of the piece.

The lump in my throat is dissipating, but I'm wishing I could follow Sarah and her classmates on to high school, to continue listening to what they have to write and say in the years ahead. They have been such stalwart companions this year, stretching their minds, making me stretch my own. Surely there will never be another class like this one. . . .

I've come now to Sarah's last entry:

Dear Mrs. B.,

This year I changed from an almost non-reader to a person who is eager to read, eager to see what else is out there. I've learned to pay attention to every word and to allow myself to be drawn into a book or a piece of writing because I know how much I can get out of it.

This whole year in English has been a learning experience. The things that I've learned in this class apply to all other aspects of my life.

Thanks for all you did. Thank you for the poems.

Love,
Sarah

References

Atwell, Nancie. 1987. *In the Middle: Writing, Reading, and Learning with Adolescents.* Portsmouth, N.H.: Boynton/Cook.

Dobson, Owen. 1968. "Sorrow is the Only Faithful One." In *I Am the Darker Brother: An Anthology of Poems by Black Americans,* ed. Arnold Adoff. New York: Macmillan.

Fisher, Dorothy Canfield. 1984. "Heyday of the Blood." In *Twenty Grand: Great American Short Stories from Scholastic Magazine,* ed. Ernestine Taggard. New York: Bantam Books.

Fulwiler, Toby. 1987. *Teaching with Writing.* Portsmouth, N.H.: Boynton/Cook.

Holden, Jonathan. 1983. "Alone." In *Poetspeak: In Their Work, About Their Work,* collected by Paul B. Janeczko. Scarsdale, N.Y.: Bradbury Press.

Hubbell, Patricia. 1986. "Night." in *Piping Down the Valleys Wild,* ed. Nancy Larrick. New York: Dell.

Hughes, Langston. 1968. "Dreams." In *Reflections on a Gift of Watermelon Pickle . . . and Other Modern Verses,* ed. Stephen Dunning, Edward Lueders, and Hugh Smith. New York: Scholastic.

Jaffe, Dan. 1968. "Forecast." In *Reflections on a Gift of Watermelon Pickle . . . and Other Modern Verses,* ed. Stephen Dunning, Edward Lueders, and Hugh Smith. New York: Scholastic.

Kunitz, Stanley. 1983. "End of Summer." In *Poetspeak: In Their Work, About Their Work,* collected by Paul B. Janeczko. Scarsdale, N.Y.: Bradbury Press.

Lerner, Alan Jay, and Frederick Loewe. 1961. *Camelot.* New York: Random House.

McBride, Mekeel. 1988. "After Grief." In *Red Letter Days.* Pittsburgh, Pa.: Carnegie-Mellon University Press.

Oates, Joyce Carol. 1983. "Suicide." In *Poetspeak: In Their Work, About Their Work,* collected by Paul B. Janeczko. Scarsdale, N.Y.: Bradbury Press.

Oliver, Mary. 1978. "May." In *American Primitive.* Boston: Atlantic–Little, Brown.

Probst, Robert E. 1988. *Response and Analysis: Teaching Literature in Junior and Senior High School.* Portsmouth, N.H.: Boynton/Cook.

Welty, Eudora. 1980. "A Worn Path." In *The Collected Stories of Eudora Welty.* New York: Harcourt Brace Jovanovich.

Wright, Richard. 1968. "Hokku: In the Falling Snow." In *I Am the Darker Brother: An Anthology of Poems by Black Americans,* ed. Arnold Adoff. New York: Macmillan.

14

Making Time

Nancie Atwell
Southport, Maine

My education was the liberty I had to read indiscriminately and all the time, with my eyes hanging out.

Dylan Thomas

MY sister called with good news: their offer was accepted. She, her husband, and my nephew Eric were about to move to a new house, one with actual closets, a two-car garage, a big yard with shade trees—and an above-ground pool. Bonnie called to break the good news, and to warn me. "Please," she asked, "whatever you do when you visit us, promise you won't let on to Eric that Atwells don't swim."

My sister wants us Atwells to pretend that learning to swim is not a big deal. Specifically, she wants to be able to dress Eric in life preservers and introduce him to their pool without any adult relatives betraying our longstanding panic about deep water. Bonnie remembers the swimming lessons of our youth—how our parents conveyed their own unease in the water, how their eyes worried, and how we kids kept our feet firmly planted, touching bottom,

Nancie Atwell wrote "Making Time" while a teacher at Boothbay Region Elementary School. Currently she directs a literacy project for the Bread Loaf School of English.

and refused to put our faces in the water. We were no fools. We believed our parents when they showed us that learning to swim was going to be difficult and dangerous.

My sister knows that her smart little boy, like all humans, learns at least as much from the implicit as the explicit. In defining conditions necessary for learning to take place, Frank Smith (1982) refers to incidents of teaching, implicit and explicit, as "demonstrations." We humans are surrounded by demonstrations; everything anyone does "demonstrates not only what can be done and how it can be done, but what the person doing it feels about the act" (171–72). We learn by engaging with particular demonstrations, as I learned more by engaging with my parents' inadvertent demonstrations concerning deep water than from all of their good, explicit advice about stroking, kicking, and breathing.

In our classrooms each day, we explicitly teach and students learn; this is a fact, Janet Emig writes, that "no one will deny. But," she continues, "to believe that children learn *because* teachers teach and only what teachers explicitly teach is to engage in magical thinking . . . " (1983, 135). It is magical thinking for me to believe I convey to the students in my classroom only my good, explicit advice about writing and reading. The information that comes out of my mouth when I talk is at least equaled by implicit data. Every minute that they observe me I'm providing demonstrations with which eighth graders may or may not engage. I can never account for what each learns through the ways I teach.

As the ways my parents approached deep water taught me tacit lessons about swimming, so the ways we approach writing and reading in the secondary English classroom convey inadvertent messages to our students about writing and reading. Recent studies of language arts instruction in U.S. schools, particularly Applebee (1982) and Goodlad (1984), give us a pretty clear picture of exactly how we are approaching writing and reading. We know:

- Our students spend little of their time in U.S. classrooms actually reading: on average, 6 percent at elementary, 3 percent at junior high, and, at high school, just 2 percent of a typical student's school day is devoted to reading.
- Our students spend little of their time in U.S. classrooms actually writing. Only 3 percent of the writing our students do in school is composing of at least paragraph length.

- Our students spend most of their time in English classes listening to their teachers talk about writing and reading. Between 70 and 90 percent of English class time is devoted to teacher talk, either lectures or directions.

- When our students are asked to what extent they participate in choosing what they'll do in class, 55 percent of elementary school kids report having no say. *Two-thirds* of students in grades seven through twelve, students who might reasonably be expected to take on greater individual responsibility, report they do not participate in any way in deciding what they'll do in class.

Teachers mostly decide what students will do in language arts classes. We choose and assign texts, generally one chapter or chunk at a time to be read by the whole class as homework then discussed or formally tested in the following day's session, at the end of which another part of the text is assigned. We present lectures on literary topics and require our students to study and memorize various bits of literary information—characteristics of the New Criticism, the chronology of Shakespeare's plays, lists of Latin roots, literary definitions—followed by exams where students report back what we said and assigned them to memorize. They also complete worksheets and textbook exercises concerned with punctuation, capitalization, sentence structure, paragraph organization, word analysis, and parts of speech. Finally, on occasion their homework consists of a writing exercise where the subject of the writing is an idea of the teacher's.

We talk about the importance of writing clearly and gracefully and reading well and widely, but we seldom make class time for students to write and read, seldom accommodate students' knowledge or choices, and seldom do our students see us writing or reading, see their teachers entering or captivated by the world of written language. Our students are learning from us. The question is, what exactly are they learning? What inadvertent messages do we transmit via this standard approach to the teaching of English? I've begun to try to make explicit the tacit lessons I learned as a student, as well as those I conveyed to my own students for too many years:

- Reading and writing are difficult, serious business.

- Reading and writing are performances for an audience of one: the teacher.

- There is one interpretation of a text or topic: the teacher's.
- "Errors" in comprehension or interpretation will not be tolerated.
- Student readers and writers are not smart or trustworthy enough to choose their own texts and topics.
- Intensive, repetitive drill and preparation are necessary before you can read and write independently.
- Reading and writing require memorization and mastery of information, conventions, rules, definitions, and theories.
- Reading and writing somehow involve drawing lines, filling in blanks, circling, and coloring in.
- Readers break whole texts into separate pieces to be read and dissected one fragment at a time. Writers compose whole texts one fragment at a time (punctuation marks, spelling, grammatical constructions, topic sentences, paragraphs, and so on).
- Reading is always followed by a test, and writing mostly serves to test reading (book reports, critical papers, essays, and multiple choice/fill-in-the-blank/short answer exams).
- Reading and writing are solitary activities that you perform as a member of a group. Readers and writers in a group may not collaborate, as this is cheating.
- You learn about literature and composition by listening to teachers talk about them.
- Teachers talk a lot about literature and composition, but teachers don't read or write.
- Reading and writing are a waste of the school's time.
- You can fail English yet still succeed at reading and writing.

I know these demonstrations from the inside, as an avid reader and writer who read and wrote only dreaded, assigned texts during my high school years. And I know these demonstrations as a junior high English teacher who spent years teaching the junior high English curriculum, alternately spoon-feeding and force-feeding one text or assignment after another to my students, dosing them with my English teacher notions of basic skills, appropriate topics for writing, and Great Works of Literature.

Some of this was the same Great Literature I'd been dosed with too, but had eventually come around to loving in college. I was incredulous when I read *Pride and Prejudice* at age twenty, convinced it could not be the same novel I'd suffered through my sophomore year in high school. It took me longer than that to give Willa Cather a second chance. I finally gathered my courage last summer and reread *My Antonia,* eighteen years after barely passing a multiple-choice test on the novel. My list of reconsidered readings goes on and on: *Anna Karenina, The Scarlet Letter, Crime and Punishment, The Mill on the Floss, Hamlet, Moby Dick,* and *The Canterbury Tales* (which, I discovered, when I finally got hold of a copy minus the standard high school ellipses, were bawdy).

I was a good reader as a teenager but a different reader—and person—than today. When I was ready for complicated and complex themes and language, those books were there, waiting for me to enter and enjoy. It took me a very long time to consider the implications of my experience as a developing reader for the students who struggled through my courses. My only models for teaching literature were university English education courses that perpetuated lit-crit methodologies, and those high school English teachers whose classes I'd endured in my teens. Glenda Bissex (1980) observes, "The logic by which we teach is not always the logic by which children learn." My assumptions about my role as English teacher blinded me to the illogic of my teaching.

I teach reading and English, as two separate, daily courses, to all of Boothbay Harbor's eighth graders. A few years ago, on the heels of research showing that sustained silent reading boosted students' reading comprehension, I began letting reading class students choose their own books one period each week, and they began driving me crazy. Daily at least one eighth grader would ask, "Are we having reading today?" We had reading every day—or at least that was my impression. Once again I bypassed an implication for teaching, clinging to each week's four days of curriculum and one day of reading.

My breakthrough in reading finally came by way of writing. Drawing on the work of Donald Murray (1985), Donald Graves (1983), Lucy Calkins (1983), and Mary Ellen Giacobbe (1983), as well as our own classroom research, teachers at my school transformed our daily English classes into writing workshops. I'm going to define a writing workshop as a place where writers have what writers need. Writers need Mary Ellen Giacobbe's three basics of time, ownership, and response (1983).

Writers need regular time set aside *in school* for them to write—time to think, write, confer, write, read, write, change their minds, and write some more. Writers need time they can count on, so even when they aren't writing they're anticipating the time they will be. Writers need time to write well, to see what they think, shape what they know, and get help where and when they need it. Good writers and writing don't take less time; they take more.

Writers need choices. They need to take responsibility for their writing: their own materials, subjects, audiences, genres, pacing, purposes, number of drafts, and kinds of changes to be made, if any. When we invite student writers to choose, they write for all the reasons literate people anywhere engage as writers—to recreate happy times, work through sad times, discover what they know about a subject and learn more, convey and request information, apply for jobs, parody, petition, play, argue, apologize, advise, make money.

Finally, writers need help discovering what they'll choose to do with the time at their disposal. They need response, not at the end when it's too late for our advice to do them any good, but while the words are churning out, in the midst of the messy, tentative act of drafting meaning. In school, this help comes in the form of conferences with the teacher and other students. In writing conferences, students read or describe their writing. Responders begin with information. They listen hard to the content of the draft, then tell what they hear, ask questions about things they don't understand or want to know more about, and invite writers to reflect on what they have done and might do next (Graves 1983).

When I allow time, ownership, and response, I'm expecting that students will participate in written language as writers do, that they'll use the writers' workshop to tell their stories. And they do, writing every day for forty-five minutes, an average of twenty finished pieces each year. My whole-group instruction is limited to a mini-lesson of five or ten minutes at the beginning of class on an issue they or I have identified in their writing (Calkins 1986). Mini-lesson topics include skills issues, such as methods for punctuating dialogue and checking for consistent voice or tense, and process issues: how to brainstorm to find a title, showing rather than telling, deleting and adding information, narrowing the focus of one's content, lead writing.

After the mini-lesson I find out what each writer will do that day, recording my students' plans, and for the remainder of the period writers write. They discover topics, confer with other writers and with me as I move among them, draft, revise, and, when they've made their best meanings, edit and publish. All the while I offer questions and options. Mary Ellen Giacobbe calls this "nudging"—that gentle guidance designed to move students beyond where they are to where they might be. In all of this, the key is time—regular, sustained time to craft texts, seek help, and plan. Habitual writing makes students writers.

Habitual reading makes students readers. The same qualities that characterize writing workshop have come to characterize my reading course, now a daily reading workshop. I had help here, too, this time from my eighth graders. As they assumed responsibility for their writing, they showed me how their participation in written language could be enriched and extended through reading. The powerful connections that they made between their writing and reading dismantled brick by brick the walls I had erected separating writing and literature. In reading workshop, students have what writers *and readers* need: time, ownership, and response.

Readers need regular time set aside *in school* for them to read—time to think, read, confer, read, reflect, reread, and read some more. Readers need time they can count on, so that even when they aren't reading they're anticipating the time they will be. Readers need time to lose track of as they become absolutely caught up in the world of written language. Readers need time to grow.

Readers grow when they assume responsibility for deciding what and how and why they will read: their own materials, subjects, audiences, genres, pacing, purposes, number of readings and rereadings. When we invite student readers to choose, they read for all the reasons that literate people anywhere engage as readers—to live other lives, learn about their own, see how other writers have written, acquire others' knowledge, escape, ponder, travel, laugh, cry.

Finally, readers too need help discovering what they'll choose to do with the time at their disposal. They need response. People who read naturally talk with others as an extension of our lives as readers, sharing opinions, surprises, insights, questions, speculations, and appreciations. Readers don't need lesson plans, study guides, or teachers' manuals. Readers need a text and a listening friend.

Writers and readers need some kind of personal meaning. They need written language to make sense, to give shape to and challenge their worlds. Both writers and readers need to engage naturally and purposefully in the *processes* of written language.

Writers and readers *rehearse*, planning and predicting:

- What will I write?
- What will it be like?
- How will it be shaped by my prior experiences as a writer?

- What will I read?
- What will it be like?
- How will it be shaped by my prior experiences as a reader?

Writers and readers *draft*, discovering meaning:

- Where will these words I am writing take me?

- Where will these words I am reading take me?

- What surprises, disappointments, problems, questions, and insights will I encounter along the way?

Writers and readers *revise*, reseeing and reseeking meaning:

- Is this what I expected, what I hoped for?
- What do I think of those words on the page?
- What new thoughts do I think because of those words on the page?
- What makes sense? What needs to be changed so sense can be made?

Making time for students to read in school invites this engagement. I make time every day for a forty-five-minute reading workshop; last year's eighth graders, including eight special education students, read an average of thirty-five full-length works. Reading workshop, too, begins with a mini-lesson. We spend five or ten minutes talking about an author—Richard Wright, Robert Frost, Lois Duncan, S. E. Hinton—or genre. We read and discuss a poem or a short story by cummings, Updike, Wilbur, London, or one of the kids in the class, peeling away layers of the text and coming to meaning together. We focus on reading and writing processes, how we read and reread the text and how authors might have come to write as they did.

The rest of the period is devoted to independent reading. Students choose their own books, settle back, and dive in. I move among them for the first ten minutes or so, finding out if anyone needs my immediate assistance, and then I sit down and read too, my books and their books. I expect that they will read and discover books they love. But I also help, in conferences about their reading.

Most of my talk with eighth graders about literature is written down. We write because writing allows deeper, richer responses than speech, but we write in a special way. For the past two years, eighth graders and I have conferred about literature in letters, thousands of letters back and forth about books, authors, reading, and writing. In our correspondence we nudge each others' thinking. We confirm, challenge, extend, and suggest. And we engage in some serious, and not so serious, literary gossip.

For example, this is an exchange with Jennipher. We're calling each other "Robert" here because one week we happened to read or talk about four works by various authors named Robert; Jenn decided that we would substantially increase our chances of becoming published authors if we were white males named Robert, so she changed our names.

5/2

Ms. A. Robert,

Just to see what Anne Frank was going through was miserable. Her "growing up" with the same people everyday. I think she got to know them a lot better than she would have if they weren't in hiding, her mother especially. That sudden change, going into hiding, must have been hard.

It amazed me how much more they went downstairs in the book. [Jennipher had also read the Broadway stage play script of *The Diary of Anne Frank.*] And it seems so much bigger in the book. It also told a lot more of her feelings, right up until the end. It must have come suddenly—to see police come in and arrest them.

I'm going to read some Robert Frost poetry now.

J. J. Robert

P. S. I think she would have been a writer.

5/3

Dear J. J. R.,

I don't have any doubt—if she'd survived, she would have been a writer all her life. Her prose style is so lively, and her insights are so deep. And she loved to write.

We've talked about how movies alter (often for the worse) the books on which they're based. Plays can't help but do the same. All that inner stuff—reflections, dreams, thoughts and feelings—doesn't easily translate into stage action, although Hackett and Goodman tried with Anne's between-act voice-overs.

If you're hungry for more information on Anne, please borrow my copy of Ernst Schnabel's *Anne Frank: Portrait in Courage* when Tom Apollonio returns it to me.

Ms. A. Robert

5/10

Ms. A. Robert,

We missed you! You get used to peoples' voice. The switch is hard for me.

Robert Frost's poems are really good. "The Witch of Coos" seemed to me somewhere between Stephen King and Ray Bradbury. Kind of wierd, huh? I heard someone quote (kind of!) one of his poems. It was on "People's Court," (Dumb Show) and there was a fight about a fence. In the end the guy came out of the courtroom and was talking to the reporter. He said something like, "This goes to show—good fences don't make good neighbors." I almost freaked out.

Back to the books.

J. J. Robert

5/10

Dear J. J. R.,

They quoted Frost on "People's Court"? (You *watched* "People's Court"?)

I need an aspirin.

N. A. R.

For half of last year, in addition to conferring with me in letters, readers conferred in letters to each other. One day in January, Jane and Arelitsa were passing notes in the back of my classroom. I asked, "What are you two doing?" and Jane said, "Oh, you'll be interested in this." She was right. Their notes were about Frost's "Nothing Gold Can Stay" and what it meant to them, two exuberant thirteen-year-olds gossiping about poetry, forging meaning together. So Jane and Arlee put their letters on overheads, shared them with my classes, and opened the door to students' exchanges about literature.

Suzy was one of my students that year. She started the year as a lip reader. She used only class time to read and said, "I guess reading is a pretty good thing to do, but sometimes I read and I don't know what I read." By May, Suzy had read nineteen novels. She said, "I really enjoy reading for pleasure. But I hate having books assigned. I can't get into them as much."

Through her own choice of books, time to read, and a place to reflect on her reading, Suzy got into books. She wrote the letter below, to her classmate Hilary, at home. It concerns *Mr. and Mrs. Bo Jo Jones,* a novel that Hilary loaned Suzy about a teenage shotgun marriage. In getting into her book, Suzy critiqued the lead and conclusion, connected the novel to her own life, predicted while she was reading what would happen, and made plans to reread.

> Hilary,
>
> It's about 12:00 (midnight). I just finished *Mr. and Mrs. Bo Jo Jones.* It was the best book I've ever read in my life.
>
> The book was a slow start and got to be a little boring at times. But the end was fast and different. I loved it! I cried so much. Did you? (I hope so, 'cause I'll feel quite embarrassed about what I'm going to say!)
>
> I didn't cry until right when the doctor and Bo Jo came in to say the baby was dead. It was strange?! I felt so sorry for her (even though it's fiction) for having that happen. Then at the Coffee Pot, when they said it was quits, I was so mad! I knew they were just getting to be very much in love, but thought it probably would be best. I knew for some reason that something good was going to happen when they met at the apartment.
>
> When they sat down and talked and realized they wanted each other but couldn't face it until their decision, it was great. I cryed there too 'cause I was so happy for them! It was great how they went ahead three years and said how it was going. The book was great! I'd recommend it to anyone.
>
> I almost forgot. Did you stop to think if that was you or someone you knew? I did and it seemed so terrible. I thought what if that happened, if I'd do the same. That's not how I wanted to say it, but good enough.
>
> I might want to reread that in the fourth quarter, if you don't mind?
>
> Well, that's all! Finally. I had to right this right now because it was so fresh and I just can't get over how good this book was.
>
> Suzy
>
> P. S. I hope you don't think I'm some sort of freak writing this!!!

Suzy,

Don't worry; you're not a freak!

I'm so glad you liked the book. I know I sure did. I loved all the same parts that you did. I cried too; boy did I.

The book *What About Me?* must be funny. You've been laughing a lot while reading it. What's it about?

Gotta go.

Hilary

Last year, Suzy and her classmates averaged at the seventy-second percentile on standardized reading tests, up from an average at the fifty-fourth percentile when fully 21 percent scored in the bottom quartile; last year, that figure was just two percent. In June of last year, 92 percent of my students indicated that they regularly read at home for pleasure, and when I asked how many books they owned, the average figure they gave was ninety-eight, up from September's fifty-four. This is the kind of evidence that convinces administrators. I am more convinced by some nonstatistical results.

My students discover that they love to read. Even the least able, most reluctant readers eventually find the one great book that absolutely impels them, and they are changed readers. For Tim, who never read at home and had never found a book he wanted to reread, the one great book was Jay Bennett's *The Dangling Witness.* Every day for two weeks he came into class, waved his copy of the mystery, and announced in an awed voice, "This is a good book. I mean, this is a *really good* book." Until Jay Bennett, Tim hadn't trusted that there was such a thing as a good book.

Eighth graders discover authors who write well for them. They learn names of writers whose books they can look for in bookstores and libraries: Frank Bonham, Lois Lowry, Madeleine L'Engle, Cynthia Voigt, Anne Tyler, Jack London, Susan Beth Pfeffer, Todd Strasser, Robert Lipsyte, Robert Cormier, Nat Hentoff, Farley Mowat, even, for those ready and willing, Shakespeare. Patrice was ready and willing.

5/17

Dear Ms. Atwell,

I finished *Macbeth* today. The reason I decided to read *Macbeth* was because a girl at Skyway Middle School, who I am friends with, read it and really loved it.

I found that the three witches were my favorite characters. Many movies have used take-offs of these characters. *The Beast*

Master, a movie I saw on cable, did. They used them differently, but they were used to tell the future.

macbeth himself was, overall, a very confused guy. His wife made him kill the king, and he was hearing voices that told him to "sleep no more." Putting one of Shakespeare's plays into movie form could almost be as bad as Steven King, because of all the killing and walking around with people's heads.

I truly enjoyed *The Comedy of Errors.* I enjoyed the way the two characters called Dromio spoke. Every time they opened their mouths they spoke in riddles. The overall idea was very good and funny. The reunions were like this: 2 father-son, 3 husband-wife, 2 brother, and 2 owner-slave. There is one wedding. Some of the reunions are *very* technical.

Patrice

Eighth graders discover their own theories about literature. Patrice's remark about technical reunions has its roots in a discussion that had taken place about a month before. We were talking about Hardy's poem "The Man He Killed" and Mike said, "Ms. Atwell, I really don't like this poem. I mean, why couldn't he just say it in regular language?"

Mike had been reading Frost and Wilbur. He loved e e cummings. He wasn't asking for colloquial prose when he said "regular language."

I said, "Show me what you mean, Mike," and he read the line "We should have set us down to wet right many a nipperkin"—a word I'd had to look up the night before and could find only in our *O.E.D.*

I'd made a dumb assumption. I thought my kids knew language changed over time, that English wasn't just American and contemporary. So we talked. Over the next weeks kids began collecting and bringing to class examples of prose and poetry from other times. When they hit Shakespeare, I made copies of speeches from five of the plays and we looked at how the language differed within the plays, how Romeo and Juliet spoke one way, Macbeth another, and why. We began to puzzle out what makes a tragedy a tragedy and a comedy a comedy. They decided that just about everyone dies in a tragedy and a new order begins; in a comedy, almost everyone gets married, reinstated, or reunited. John said, "Yeah, just like on Love Boat." And from there we talked about basic plot conventions through all of literature, and how and where Shakespeare had borrowed his plots. Then they found and read to each other stories from Greek and Roman mythology.

They and I were collaborating as theorists, discovering, testing, and acting on literary principles. As readers, eighth graders discovered that literature is accessible; that literature is reading, and reading is sensible, interesting, and fun.

As writers, eighth graders discovered they could draw on their experiences as readers, trying out the themes, styles, and modes they read and finding their own voices in collaboration with the voices they love to read. Dede and Billy loved Robert Frost. They collaborated with him by borrowing the theme from "Nothing Gold Can Stay," Frost's poem about the inevitability of change:

Dawn

The lake sparkled
in the light of the moon.
Dawn was near—
it would be soon.
The clouds gave off a goldish light
and broke the silence of the night.

Now the dawn has come to be noon,
just like grown-up life—all too soon.

Billy Snow

Beyond the Light

The sunset is so lovely,
with its warm colors and bright glow.
I could sit and stare for hours
at the elegant sight.
Then I shiver
as a cold breeze blows—
to warn me of the darkness
and to warn me of the night.

Dede Reed

Luanne collaborated with John Updike. Her poem arrived at my house in the mail during April vacation, when Luanne was in the middle of basketball tournaments. She borrowed her subject, learning from Updike that basketball was a suitable poetic topic, and she borrowed a simile from his description of the "Ex-Basketball Player" whose hands were "like wild birds":

The Turnover

I was going for a lay-up
as I remember it;

the brown leathered ball
under my hands,
through half-court
and down toward the middle.

When suddenly the rhythm

stopped.

A hand came down
in place of mine—
like a bird doing
a wild dive:

Just empty space
between my hands
and the floor.

I stood there
wondering where I'd gone wrong,

when I looked up to see
two more points
added to the other side's score.

Luanne Bradley

I've made some discoveries too. I've learned that by giving students more time to learn reading, I've given myself more time to teach reading. I have much less homework than in the old days of lesson plans, lectures, ditto masters, and essay tests. Reading workshop is a workshop for me, too, as I quietly confer with readers, answer letters, and read.

I've learned about adolescent literature, a genre virtually nonexistent twenty years ago when I was an eighth grader. My students introduced me to authors of juvenile fiction who write as well for adolescents as my favorite contemporary novelists—Atwood, Tyler, Heller, Updike—write for me.

I've learned to fill my classroom with books—novels, and also short stories, biographies, histories, and poetry, as many paperbacks as I can buy or budget.

I've learned that good, rich discussion of literature happens naturally when real readers are talking together, as opposed to the sterile, grudging responses given by too few students to my old, lesson plan questions. I've learned that the context of students' self-selected texts is ripe for high-level literary talk about such traditional teacher's manual issues as theme, genre, and technique, and that it's entirely possible to go beyond these to consider reading process, professional authors' processes, relationships between reading and writing, between one text or author and others, between literature and real life.

My students taught me that they loved to read. They showed me that in-school reading, like in-school writing, could actually do something for them, that the ability to read for pleasure and personal meaning, like writing ability, is not a gift or a talent. It comes with the freedom to choose and with time to exercise that freedom. I learned that freedom to choose and time to read in school are not luxuries. They are not complements to a good literature curriculum. They are the wellspring of student literacy and literary appreciation.

If my class schedule were more typical—that is, forty-five minutes a day for English, including literature—I'd continue to give over class time to reading and writing. But I'd teach writing on three regular, consecutive days, so students would experience that sense of routine and continuity writers need, and follow it with two days of reading workshop, encouraging kids to take home over the weekend those books they read in class on Thursday and Friday. And I would continue to nudge, pointing students toward new topics, modes, styles, authors, techniques, books, and genres.

The most recent National Assessment of Educational Progress reports that American thirteen- and seventeen-year-olds do less reading, especially of fiction, than our nine-year-olds. In a feature in the *New York Times* about Americans' reading habits (Fiske 1983), Jan Marsten of the University of Chicago suggested that "there seem to be periods in the life-span during which reading tends to drop off, including adolescence. It would hardly be surprising if people did less reading during periods of such upheaval in their lives" (1).

Secondary teachers know about upheaval in adolescents' lives. First jobs, first cars, first boyfriends and girlfriends are hallmarks of adolescence. So are a preoccupation with peers and participation in junior and senior highs' extracurricular activities. Reading necessarily takes a back seat as teenagers' worlds become impossibly full. A former student of mine anticipated April vacation of her freshman year by saying, "Ms. Atwell, I'm going to read six books this week. All of them are books I've been dying to read since

Christmas. I just look at them and feel depressed. There's always something else I've got to do." When reading doesn't happen at school, it's unlikely to happen away from school, which means it's unlikely to happen at all.

English teachers can help. We help by giving reading—and writing—our highest priority; we do so when we make time for them to happen in our classrooms. What single, more powerful demonstration can we provide our students of the value we place on these activities? Encircling this are other compelling demonstrations—of the uses of literacy, of writing and reading as whole, sense-making activities, of the ways an adult finds meaning and pleasure in her own and others' written expression, of *all* students' rights as literate human beings.

Genuine, independent reading and writing are not the icing on the cake, the reward we proffer gifted twelfth graders who have survived the curriculum. Reading and writing are the cake. Given what we know about adolescents' lives and priorities, can we afford to continue to sacrifice literate school environments for skills environments? For multiple-choice and essay-question environments? For spoon-fed and force-fed environments? I say we can't. Making time makes readers and writers, and readers and writers can remake their worlds, using language to see and shape their lives as Jennipher did in her final letter to me.

6/8

Dear Ms. A. Robert,

I finished *Autumn Street.* It was excellent how she told it from her childhood view of things, her feelings and then how she was back in the present in the end.

Sunday morning was special. The cats were under my bed at 4:15 doing something, I don't know how they got upstairs. I took them down and looked out the window. Low and behold, sunrise! But no, it did not rise. All I could see was a golden strip across the sky. I pulled up a chair and put my feet up. I said "Nothing Gold Can Stay" in my mind without stumbling and found how Ponyboy could have felt in *The Outsiders.* After fifteen minutes when the sun didn't appear I went back to bed feeling new.

We're really going to miss you.

See you sometime.

J. J. Robert

References

Applebee, Arthur. 1982. *Writing in the Secondary School: English and the Content Areas.* Urbana, Ill.: National Council of Teachers of English.

Bissex, Glenda. 1980. *GNYS AT WORK: A Child Learns to Write and Read.* Cambridge: Harvard University Press.

Calkins, Lucy. 1983. *Lessons from a Child.* Portsmouth, N.H.: Heinemann.

———. 1986. *The Art of Teaching Writing.* Portsmouth, N.H.: Heinemann.

Emig, Janet. 1983. "Non-Magical Thinking: Presenting Writing Developmentally in Schools." In *The Web of Meaning: Essays on Writing, Teaching, Learning and Thinking,* ed. Dixie Goswami and Maureen Butler. Portsmouth, N.H.: Boynton/Cook.

Fiske, Edward B. 1983. "Americans in Electronic Era Are Reading as Much as Ever." *The New York Times.* September 8.

Giacobbe, Mary Ellen. 1983. Classroom presentation to the Northeastern University Summer Writing Institute, Martha's Vineyard, Massachusetts (July).

Goodlad, John. 1984. *A Place Called School.* New York: McGraw Hill.

Graves, Donald H. 1983. *Writing: Teachers and Children at Work.* Portsmouth, N.H.: Heinemann.

Murray, Donald. 1985. *A Writer Teaches Writing: A Practical Method of Teaching Composition.* 2nd ed. Boston: Houghton Mifflin.

Smith, Frank. 1982. *Writing and the Writer.* New York: Holt, Rinehart and Winston.

15

Looking for Trouble
A Way to Unmask Our Readings

Thomas Newkirk
University of New Hampshire
Durham, New Hampshire

THE past decade has seen an attack on the myth of the inspired writer. Linda Flower (1981) has traced this myth to Coleridge's account of the creation of "Kubla Khan" (41–43). According to Coleridge the idea for the poem came without conscious effort; it came fully assembled; it did not require time-consuming choices; and, because it was a gift from the gods, the process of achieving the poem could not be repeated. While Flower does not deny the existence of these Eureka moments, she does argue that this myth breeds passivity on the part of the student, who then wants to wait by an open window for inspiration to strike. Fortunately, the testimonies of published writers and the protocols that researchers like Flower have elicited have done much to dispel such myths. Textbooks now go to great lengths to suggest that writing involves a range of choices under conscious control.

Less attention has been given to myths of "inspired reading." Students frequently speak of the "hidden meanings" of poetry, and by that expression they usually mean hidden from them but open to another class of readers—professional readers, teachers. So long as the process of interpretation is unrevealed, myths of inspiration can persist; students will claim that they cannot read poetry because they are not good at getting hidden meanings. The poem comes to be viewed as a Tarot card.

Traditional practices of teaching literature in introductory courses promote the view of "inspired reading" because they obscure the process of forming an interpretation. In the traditional classroom the instructor rarely reveals what happens in his or her initial contact with a poem. I recently asked a group of senior English majors whether they had ever seen a literature professor read something for the first time. None had. Indeed it could be argued that many would have resented a professor assigning a poem he or she had not read, coming to class without having read it, and then winging through it, fumbling as we all fumble on any first encounter. Our evaluation forms tell us that we should come to class prepared. But preparation can be a mask hiding the very process we expect students to master. Our prepared certainty belies the uncertainty of the earlier part of our reading, and by withholding our fumbling from students we can misrepresent the process we claim to teach. If students never see instructors confused, never see them puzzled by a particular usage, never see how an interpretation is revised in subsequent readings, it is logical for the students to conclude that reading is inspired in the same way that Coleridge's composition of "Kubla Khan" was inspired.

There is also little room for uncertainty in the writing required in the traditional introductory course. The mainstay, of course, is the critical analysis paper. Because this type of writing does not exist outside the academic community, its justification presumably is that it helps the student engage with the text. But the constraints of this form seem to preclude the muddling that occurs when readers confront difficult texts for the first time. Most critical analysis papers are supposed to contain a thesis, stated early in the paper; this thesis is subdivided, and each subdivided point must be supported with evidence from the text. The purpose of such writing is to demonstrate a coherent reading, not to explore the possibilities of the incoherencies in a reading. The tone frequently is that of a lawyer, not a reader.

The standard complaint about these papers is that the student fails to probe a response, that the generalizations, while supported, do not take the student very far into the work. David Bartholomae (1983) suggests that the tyranny of the thesis may inhibit inquiry:

> When, for example, we ask students to write about texts, the tyranny of the thesis often invalidates the very act of analysis we hope to invoke. Hence, in assignment after assignment, we find students asked to reduce a novel, a poem or their own experience into a single sentence, and then to use the act of writing in order to defend or "support" that single sentence. Writing is used to close a subject down rather than to open it up, to put an end to discourse rather than to open up a project. (311)

Like Bartholomae I feel that the traditional critical analysis paper may discourage students from dealing with reactions that are not easily resolved into a thesis, that it may discourage the student from dealing with the more puzzling (and very likely more complex) issues of meaning and language, that, in sum, they encourage the student to play it safe.

In a recent summer school freshman English course I experimented with a different approach to writing about literature that dealt directly with the issue of certainty in reading. Once a week for five weeks the class and the instructor (a graduate assistant) read and wrote about a poem that I selected.* I passed around a photocopy of each poem with the name of the poet removed. Both instructor and students then marked words, phrases, lines, whatever gave them difficulty. On each reading they changed their instrument for marking to help indicate the progression of the reading. After the readers had resolved the difficulties (or had worked as hard toward resolving them as they wanted to), they each wrote a narrative account of the reading, using the markings to cue their memory. Once the accounts were written, students and instructor shared the stories of their reading.

This procedure was designed, first of all, to put the instructor and the students on roughly the same footing. All were reading the poem for the first time; the instructor could not meet the student with a prepared reading. Secondly, the method suggested to the student that the reading of poems involved difficulties and that rereading the poem was one way of working through the difficulties. Finally, the students and the instructor were able to write about

*The poems used were: Robert Hedin, "Tornado," *Poetry* 140 (1982), 28; Theodore Roethke, "Moss-Gathering," in *Words for the Wind* (Bloomington: Indiana University Press, 1961), 43; William Stafford, "Traveling Through the Dark," in *Traveling Through the Dark* (New York: Harper & Row, 1962), 11; Seamus Heaney, "Death of a Naturalist," in *Poems 1965–1975* (New York: Farrar, Straus and Giroux, 1980), 5–6; Maxine Kumin, "The Grace of Geldings in Ripe Pastures," in *The Retrieval System* (New York: Viking Press, 1978), 67.

difficulties that went unresolved in their readings. As might be expected, many of these unresolved difficulties were evidence of their deepest probes into the poem.

I have grouped the identified difficulties into four very rough categories. The first kind is not so much identified as exhibited; it involves what Martin Minsky calls dealing in "attitudes" (Bernstein 1981). Though writing about the use of the computer, Minsky makes telling comments about any act of thinking:

> [T]hinking is a process, and if your thinking does something you don't want it to you should be able to say something microscopic and analytic about it, and not something enveloping and evaluating about yourself as a learner. The important thing in refining your thought is to try to depersonalize your interior; it may be all right to deal with other people in a vague global way—by having "attitudes" toward them, but it is devastating if this is the way you deal with yourself. (122)

Rike & minnows

Minsky's phrase "depersonalize the interior" may at first seem antithetical to the act of reading poetry; clearly the act calls for the engagement of feeling and prior experience. But Minsky correctly identifies the debilitating effect of assigning blame when confronted with difficulty. This blame can be assigned either to the creator of the difficulty, in this project to the willful obscurity of the poet, or more frequently, to the reader.

Both types of blame-laying were evident in the student responses. Some took the Poem-as-Tarot-card view and simply confessed an inability to deal with such mysteries:

> If there was some hidden meaning [to "Death of a Naturalist"] I missed it. Just as most of the poems we have done thus far, the author's hints to the meanings behind the poem slipped me. After I finished the first reading I went back and read it again, but still there was nothing. . . . At the end of most of these poems the depth still leaves me unknowing. I usually look for the title to help. *I guess I just haven't got a great or even good poetic mind.* (italics added)

Another reader, one who turned out to be perhaps the most perceptive respondent in the class, interspersed her first protocol with admissions of inadequacy:

> Admittedly, I get easily confused and frustrated. Always have and always will hate poetry. . . . My only comment is that I do not like PUZZLES, MYSTERIES, OR POETRY. All are frustrating; none worth the effort.

Other responses shifted the anger to the poet or poem. One student wrote the following concluding statement:

> Bull. While many of the images are nice, the general choppiness should have been smoothed over. Also some of the key words need to be expanded or explained in greater detail.

Whether the blame is placed on the poet or on the reader, the result is the same: the inquiry stops. The students have withheld what Michael Polanyi (1958) calls their "personal allegiance"; in order to grant this allegiance the learner must "believe before he can know." The belief is twofold. There is belief in the learner's own ability, and there is a confidence in others that manifests itself in "anticipation that what he tried to understand is in fact reasonable." Granting allegiance, then, becomes "an act of heuristic conjecture—a passionate pouring of oneself into untried forms of existence" (208).

The other difficulties involve the attempt to "grant allegiance" to the act of reading. As might be expected, many of the comments about the initial readings centered on difficult vocabulary, particularly in "Death of a Naturalist" and "The Grace of Geldings in Ripe Pastures."

> In reading this poem through for the first time, I got stuck in a few places—I'm not sure what "bluebottles" means or refers to. And "jampotfuls of jellied specks"? Why would he want them displayed at home? But when I gave up there and read on to the next two lines, I realized he meant a jarful of frogspawn that he was watching hatch into tadpoles. So that section pretty much explained itself.

> For starters, I was reading the words [in "The Grace of Geldings in Ripe Pastures"] wrong. "Timothy" was read as a person's name. I was misreading it in the beginning.

Students generally used one of three strategies for deciphering problem words: looking them up; guessing their meaning from context; or "satisficing," assigning a general plausible meaning to the word and going on.

The instructor frequently shared her struggles with the basic sense of the poems. She (and several students) found the opening line of "Tornado" problematic: "Four farms over it looked like a braid of black hemp." To make sense of the line one must pause as if for a comma before "it." For example, one student wrote: "At the outset I was unsure what was happening because I didn't know what the farms looked on." The teacher had the same difficulty and specified the nature of the problem:

> It was not until the third reading that I finally figured out that the "four farms" *were not* "over it" but rather that the beginning was a naming of location. "It" was confusing up until then—was "it" the tornado—no, syntactically that didn't work.

During the class discussion following the exercise, almost all of the students agreed that they had had precisely the same problem.

A third type of difficulty is one George Steiner (1978) calls "contingent difficulties." Here the poem "articulates a stance toward human conditions which we find essentially inaccessible or alien. The tone, the manifest subject of the poem is such that we fail to see a justification for poetic form, that the root occasion of the poem's composition eludes or repels our internalized sense of what poetry should or should not be about" (28). For many students this type of difficulty occurred in reading "The Grace of Geldings in Ripe Pastures." The conclusion of the poem describes the geldings as they "one by one let down / their immense indolent penises / to drench the everlasting grass / with the rich nitrogen / that repeats them." The students balked:

> I found the poem rather interesting. The climax, however, was a disappointment and seemed in bad taste. . . . The last stanza was a let down because I expected something wild, beautiful and splendid, and instead I got a bunch of horses going to the bathroom.

Another student on her copy of the poem circled the last line and wrote, "Disgusting. Visually repugnant. Eating piss-covered grass is what makes them so graceful? Oh Joy!" These responses differ from the first category, dealing in attitudes, in that both readers had worked through the poem, and, at least provisionally, they had given their personal allegiance to the act of reading it. Yet it so violated their sense of appropriate matter for poetry that they were unable to take the role cast for them by the poet.

A fourth and more complex problem had to do with the relationship of images. Many of the instructor's comments were in this category. She commented, for example, on the difficulty with two lines in "Tornado": "and the sky is about to step down / On one leg." She writes:

> [This line] still poses problems for me. I like the feel of it, the way it sounds, the possibility of action but I can't quite see it no matter how hard I try to conjure it up in my mind—I keep trying to have clouds "step down / on one leg."

Sometimes these difficulties were with sets of images. In "Tornado" there are two sets of images that to many of the students had no direct connection: the images of the tornado and the images "of the bulls my father slaughtered every August / How he would pull out of that rank sea / A pair of collapsed lungs, stomach, / Eight bushels of gleaming rope he called intestines." One student worked at reconciling these images as follows:

> The first time through the poem it seemed to make no coherent sense except for the lines of the first stanza reminded me of the tornados I'd seen and lived through in Nebraska. During the second reading I realized that . . . the rest of the poem seemed disjointed from any experience I had ever had with tornados. The third time through was no more enlightening about what the second and third stanzas were trying to put across to the reader. My fourth time through was when it all came to light after just a little thinking and reflection; it dawned on me that he is comparing his father and the slaughter of bulls to the tornado and its devastating properties of retching things right from the ground.

In one response to "Moss-Gathering" a student laboriously worked his way through the transitions in the poem that he found difficult, only to encounter a new problem in his third reading. It suddenly occurs to him that there is a conflict between his image of moss gathering and the ominous set of words that the poet uses to describe this activity: "afterwards I always felt mean, . . . / By pulling off flesh from the living planet; / As if I had committed, against the whole scheme of life, a desecration."

> This is really far-fetched, but I get the feeling of impending doom as I read this. "Cemetary," "old-fashioned," "hollow," "underside," "old," "natural order of things," "pulling off the flesh," "desecration," and "went out" all bring to mind scenes of death/destruction. Lord, I don't get it. He's talking about moss-gathering, etc. Why should he be interested in how/why things die? . . . I don't see the connection. All of the transitions are fairly clear now so long as I don't hang up on the "evil" words.
>
> Concluding statement: What the hell is going on?

The writer of this response may feel that after considerable work he still doesn't know what the hell is going on, but his response suggests otherwise. In this and many other responses, the ability to clearly define a reading difficulty suggests considerable insight into the poem.

This specification of difficulty often fits the model of problem-solving developed by John Dewey in *How We Think* (1933). In this model, problem solving begins with an interruption of activity. Our ordinary course of action will not work, or two or more competing possibilities confront us, and we must maintain a state of suspense in order to inquire further. In the second stage, which Dewey calls intellectualization, the perplexity of the first stage is pinpointed:

> Our uneasiness, the shock of the disturbed activity, gets started in some degree on the basis of observed conditions, of objects. The width of the ditch, the slipperiness of the bank, not the mere presence of the ditch, is the trouble. The difficulty is getting located and defined; it is becoming a true problem, something intellectual, not just an annoyance. (108–9)

In the response to "Tornado" quoted above we see this movement. The difficulty begins with a sense of incoherence, in what Dewey calls an "emotional quality" that pervades the experience. On subsequent readings this general sense is given conscious definition; the reader discovers that the root of the sensed incoherence is in the relationship of the first stanza to the rest of the poem. The reader then proceeds to generate a hypothesis to account for the relationship. In the response to "Moss-Gathering" we see a move to intellectualization; the reader notices a sense of "uneasiness" and then goes on to specify the "observed conditions" that can explain his uneasiness.

Thus far I have included excerpts from student and instructor responses to illustrate types of difficulties encountered. As a final example I include a complete response written to Seamus Heaney's poem "Death of a Naturalist," which more clearly illustrates the movement that can occur over several readings. This response was written by the student who originally claimed that she was "easily confused" and would "always hate poetry."

First reading:

> In reading this poem through for the first time, I got stuck in a few places—I'm not sure what "bluebottles" means or refers to. And "jampotfuls of jellied specks"? What jellied specks? Why would he want them displayed at home? But when I gave up there and read on to the next two lines, I realized he meant a

jarful of frogspawn that he was watching hatch into tadpoles. So that section pretty much explained itself.

The second stanza seemed full of fear—"invading angry frogs," "mud grenades," "obscene threats," "slime kings," "gathered for vengeance." Makes it sound like the author is frightened by these masses of grown frogs. Sounds like he is afraid these big frogs will punish him for removing frogspawn to take home in the first place; like a big guilt complex.

Don't understand how the title ties into the poem yet—I assume the author is a naturalist, but he's not DEAD. . . .

Second reading:

I get the impression the second time through that the author was describing his first year in the location of the poem. "I had not heard before"—but it's a seasonal occurrence—in the reproductive cycle of frogs. But then he did mention "every spring" that he was collecting frogspawn—maybe this was the first time he'd seen the summer phenomena and didn't expect so many frogs (power in numbers he thinks?). I think I understand the title now, though the author describes about learning about frogs in school and watching them hatch—ties them into nature by frogs turning color with the weather. Makes it sound like he was so fascinated by watching them hatch that maybe he was thinking about becoming a naturalist when he grew up or maybe "naturalist" was just his interest in the natural process of frog reproduction. . . .

"Bluebottles" still baffles me—finally looked it up in the dictionary and it's a blowfly that's blue that makes a loud buzzing sound. I've never seen one, but at least that section makes sense.

The last line of the poem seems very significant; he was so scared and intimidated by the masses of ugly creatures that he was afraid that the frogs might capture and torture him for stealing any more of their "babies." Scared him so much that he apparently decided not to gather frogspawn any more—didn't want anything to do with it he was so scared. The experience rather "killed" his interest in that aspect of nature as a whole or else abolished his possible ideas of becoming a true naturalist—either way it means about the same.

Third reading:

Reading it through for the final time it all goes together and makes perfect sense to me. (Can't believe it—it's too easy—I *must* be missing something.) I looked specifically for major shifts this time. Biggest, most apparent shift is between two stanzas—goes from fascination with frogspawn and frog theory to the horrors of a densely populated area of grown frogs. "Sub-shift" in

> the first paragraph is between watching tadpoles hatch and learning about frogs in school—practical and theoretical.
>
> I liked this poem because it was pretty easy to figure out and it all made sense to me. Good descriptive writing—I can picture everything the author is saying.

Easy to figure out? Perhaps. But the response illustrates a complex and highly effective approach to reading the poem. The function of each reading is distinct: the first works through difficulty with vocabulary and locates a major problem; the second works through the problem; the third consolidates the analyses of the earlier readings and makes them "all go together."

Through these readings the reader circles the fundamental problem posed by the title with its two key terms, "death" and "naturalist." In what sense is the child a naturalist? And in what sense does he die? After all, as the student notes at the end of her first reading, "He's not DEAD." In her second reading, she develops two alternative definitions for "naturalist": either the boy will become a naturalist by profession or he is a naturalist now because of his interest in frog reproduction. With this definition in hand she can test it to see how either or both of these "naturalists" dies and concludes again that the final experience could kill off both; the experience could shake his ambition to become a naturalist, or it could "kill" his interest in frog reproduction. This protocol particularly illustrates the capability of this approach to show how understanding emerges, how a reading is composed.

Once students and instructor had completed the narrative accounts of their readings, these accounts were shared to open the discussion. In each case it became apparent that specific words and images caused problems for almost all the readers, and these common problems became the focus for discussion. For example, much of the discussion of "The Grace of Geldings in Ripe Pastures" focused on the final line: "that repeats them." Both the instructor and many students noted problems with this line in their narrative accounts. When it became clear that this was a common problem, the instructor read from her narrative:

> The meaning eludes me—I can't connect "rich nitrogen" with "repeating" of either the horses or their penises (not sure what "them" in the last line refers to, which is connected to not clearly knowing what last line is about).

In her account the instructor specified a difficulty sensed (but sometimes not clearly defined) by many students. The discussion then focused on ways of resolving this difficulty. This procedure led to an openness in the discussion because the working assumption was that all readers experience difficulty. Students were less likely to blame their own problems on an inability to read poetry.

In my initial trial of this procedure the reading accounts were used solely to initiate discussion. Subsequently (with a group of students who were prospective English teachers) I added a further step. After students in the class had written four narrative accounts, I asked them to use these accounts as data and write a profile of themselves as readers of poetry. In James Moffett's (1968) terms, they were to move from "what happened" to "what happens." This task was more than an exercise in abstraction, though; the assignment pushed students to define themselves as readers and to take inventory of the useful conscious strategies that they employ.

I will quote from the profile of one student:

> I always must size up a poem before I read it, check out its length, its shape. I'm like a general examining the battlefield. Next, read the title, and that always sets up an expectation of what's going to happen. I felt at ease with "Blackberry Picking." It is straightforward, clear. On the other hand, "Mother Ruin" made me cautious and ready for some imagery that might not be clear.

The first reading she describes as a technical reading, usually done out loud, slowly, paying attention to spots that may give her difficulty. If there is a word she doesn't know, she looks it up in her first run through the poem. In the second reading she moves faster, conscious of the problems encountered in the first reading, testing her solutions if she came up with any. Her next reading is a time for savoring the poem:

> At this point, I don't feel finished with the poem. In fact, I haven't experienced it in two readings. This next reading is my favorite. This is where I start to let the poem go. I experience it now by noticing all the marvellous details that give the poem life: "Big dark blobs burned like a plate of eyes," "a rat-grey fungus," and "a glossy purple clot." These are the images that I linger over in these later readings. I appreciate their power. In these later readings (I cannot say final readings because there are no such things) I see the poem as a film with narration. I am the narrator, reading off the script, and having come to a better

> understanding of specific problems by looking closely at them, I see the poem. The eye of my mind watches what I read.

In these profiles the text is no longer the poem; rather the writer is "reading" the reading self. The new "text" to be deciphered is the act of reading depicted (imperfectly, of course) in the narrative reading accounts.

In this and almost all the other accounts of readings we can see a mingling of the "subjective" and "objective" responses—to the point that it is difficult to distinguish between the two. Students felt free to express feelings of frustration, confusion, even anger, but these feelings were connected to the text (the extensive marking up of the poem helped here). Similarly, students often referred to personal associations that might help them interpret the poem, but again usually with reference to the poem. Expressions of feeling or personal association rarely floated free of the text. To use Bartholomae's expression, the procedure "opens up" the discourse to allow for the expression of confusion and difficulty in a way that the thesis-controlled critical paper does not. But it also directs the student to specify ways in which the text gives rise to difficulties. It is more text-based than are approaches that direct attention almost exclusively to the reader's feelings and personal associations.

But, most importantly, procedures like the one I have described allow us all, teachers and students, to drop the masks that can inhibit learning. We can all act as the fallible, sometimes confused, sometimes puzzled readers that we are. We can reveal ourselves as learners, not always the most graceful of positions. To borrow from the response of one student, we can "show what the hell is going on" with us, and we can ask students to do the same.

References

Bartholomae, David. 1983. "Writing Assignments: Where Writing Begins." In *Fforum: Essays on Theory and Practice in the Teaching of Writing*, ed. Patricia L. Stock. Portsmouth, N.H.: Boynton/Cook.

Bernstein, Jeremy. 1981. "Profiles: Marvin Minsky." *The New Yorker*. December 14.

Dewey, John. 1933. *How We Think.* Boston: D.C. Heath.

Flower, Linda. 1981. *Problem-Solving Strategies for Writing.* New York: Harcourt Brace Jovanovich.

Moffett, James. 1968. *Teaching the Universe of Discourse.* Boston: Houghton Mifflin. Available from Boynton/Cook Publishers, Portsmouth, NH.

Polanyi, Michael. 1958. *Personal Knowledge: Toward a Post-Critical Philosophy.* Chicago: University of Chicago Press.

Steiner, George. 1978. *On Difficulty and Other Essays.* New York: Oxford University Press.

Time for Questions

Nancie Atwell encourages students to choose their own books. I'm afraid students wouldn't be able to choose well. What can the teacher do to help students choose?

Teachers, first of all need to read and to share their enthusiasm for particular books with students, perhaps through reading aloud excerpts from the book. Just as teachers of writing should be writers, teachers of reading should be readers.

Books also need to be available, and not solely in the school library. Teachers should establish classroom libraries that are bigger than the normal size. In Nancie Atwell's class, for example, there are several hundred books for students. The National Council of Teachers of English has published excellent guides for selecting books; see particularly *Your Reading* and *High Interest—Easy Reading.*

There should also be an opportunity for students to share readings, not through formal book reports, but through more casual sharing periods when they may talk briefly about the book, read an interesting passage, and answer questions from other students. This kind of sharing is usually missing in the Uninterrupted Sustained Silent Reading periods that are becoming common in many schools. Classrooms can also publish annotated listings of good books where students might write a three- or four-sentence description that might interest someone else in reading the book.

As teachers become familiar with books that appeal to students, they will come up with some "sure winners," books that seem to overpower the most reluctant reader. E. H. Hinton's *The Outsiders* is probably supreme in this category.

Atwell regularly writes letters back and forth with students. What exactly does she do when she responds to a student's letter?

She does a number of things. She suggests new books. She talks about reading experiences she has had that are similar to those of the student. She talks about reading habits and processes. But, perhaps most importantly, she helps students view themselves as readers capable of thinking perceptively about books they read. This push toward critical thinking can be seen in a series of letters written early in her course. Her student Tom writes:

> Dear Ms. A.,
>
> I just finished *Jeff White Young Woodsman.* I think it's a good book. It tells about Jeff, born up north then after his parents died at the age of four, moved in with his "so-called" aunt untill he was fifteen. But because he didn't like it their in the city and he didn't like his aunt an uncle he moved up north again with an old friend of his father.
>
> Tom
>
> P.S. Is this too "Book Reportish" Is it what you want to hear or read.

> Dear Tom,
>
> As letter stands, it's a little "book reportish," yes. Could you jot me another postscript about what made *Jeff White* good?

Atwell is pushing Jeff to define his criteria for good reading and show *why* the book is good. This pushing soon begins to pay off. Later in the month Tom writes:

> Dear Ms. Atwell,
>
> I just finished *Jeff White Young Trapper.* It's the second book in the Jeff White books. If I could cut off the realy mysterious parts I think it would be better. A little mystery is nice but it gets a bit scarry in the hight of it. But other than that it's a good book.
>
> Tom

Though Tom has not fully explained why the scary parts should be cut, we have the sense that he is a different kind of reader than he was earlier in month. He's not simply someone who gives plot-summary book reports.

My students read so passively. When it comes time to write or discuss, they seem to barely remember what happened in the book. How can I make them more active readers?

Paradoxically, to read well one must forget much of what has been read. If we were to take everything in, we would go crazy. So, students must learn to *assign significance;* in a practical sense this means marking up a book. The little checks, the underlinings, the yeses in the margins are all ways of saying, "This is important. I'll remember this." We put some information in the foreground and put the rest in the background.

There are a number of ways we can encourage students to actively assign significance. David Bleich (1975) asks students to select the key words of key sentences in a piece of literature. For example, in the short story "A Rose for Emily" someone might pick the word "rose" in the title, a word that does not appear in the story. Why "rose?" Who is giving the rose to Emily? Why does she deserve a rose? Is the story itself the rose? My point is that by looking at this word the student has a way into the story.

David Bartholomae and Tony Petrosky (1986) suggest that students begin by listing major characters and major events in a story. By determining, for example, what the critical events are in *I Know Why the Caged Bird Sings* the student can begin to analyze Maya Angelou's growth. The student has highlighted some events and ignored others—which is what active readers do.

David Bartholomae is quoted as criticizing "the tyranny of the thesis." Isn't there a place for the thesis control paper about literature?

My view of this question is probably a minority one. I feel that the disadvantages of the thesis-control paper outweigh the advantages—especially for the student who has not had much experience writing about literature. I remember that when I had to write these papers, I would pick a thesis that I could support and would ignore aspects of the poem or story that went counter to my thesis because the purpose of the paper was to *support* that thesis, not call it into question. Furthermore, the act of channeling my reading into this kind of writing felt most unnatural; my reading bristled with questions, paradoxes, perplexities, but none of this seemed to fit the form I was required to use.

I also feel that literature does not reduce itself easily into single-sentence theses. Think of those embarrassing interviews on T.V. where the commentator asks someone like Igor Stravinsky, "How would you describe yourself in a sentence?" It's a question that makes a silly assumption: that complex human beings and human behavior are reducible to something only a bit longer than a bumper sticker message. Reading is a continual dialogue with the text, and our generalizations are provisional; like sand castles, they don't last for long. My late colleague Gary Lindberg (1986) put it well:

> There is something to be said for those truths about texts that supposedly hold their shape independent of the biases of particular readers. They satisfy our wish for something stable, authoritative, and pure. But they are also dead. By their very nature they are irrelevant to the human needs of readers. There is much more to be said for those messier truths that we formulate, undo, and remake again in the human gesture of coming to words. Such truths never last. They are too tentative to connect in elaborate systems of meaning. But they renew our acquaintance with things of the world, they loosen our bondage to a fixed perspective, and they open us to the endless surprise of dialogue with someone else. (156)

The essays in this chapter suggest a number of possibilities for making and unmaking the "messier truths" that Lindberg is talking about.

Are there other forms of writing that can help students work toward these "messier truths"?

Students can keep double-entry journals in which students comment on their own understandings of what they read. Ann Berthoff (1981), a major proponent of this type of journal, describes it as follows:

> What makes this notebook different from most, perhaps, is the notion of the double entry: on the right side reading notes, direct quotations, observational notes, fragments, lists, images—verbal and visual—are recorded; on the other (facing) side, notes, summaries, formulations, aphorisms, editorial suggestions, revisions, comment on comment are written. The reason for the double entry format is that it provides a way for the student to conduct that "continuing audit of meaning" that is at the heart of learning to read and write critically. The facing pages are in dialogue with each other. (45)

A student writing on the character Huckleberry Finn might use one side of the journal to make notes about what Huck does and says; on the other side the student could comment on the meaning of these actions—what they tell us about Huck.

John Dixon (1985) suggests a variation of this procedure to encourage students to think about dramatic action. The student selects a section of a play and then keeps a director's notebook on that section. One side of the notebook consists of directions to actors—how they would move, what tones of voice they would use to speak to each other, how they would be positioned on the stage, how their behavior toward each other would change in the section. On the other side the student writes a rationale for this action: why do the characters act as they do?

A third approach, similar to that used by Maureen Barbieri in chapter 13, is to suggest possible openings for students to use in their responses to literature. Audre Allison, an eleventh-grade teacher at Shoreham-Wading River (New York) High School, gave her students the following list of openers (Perl and Wilson 1986, 45):

1. I began to think of . . .
2. I wonder why . . .
3. I know the feeling . . .
4. I noticed . . .
5. I love the way . . .
6. I was surprised . . .
7. I really can't understand . . .
8. I thought . . .
9. I can't believe . . .
10. If I had been . . .

Each of these openings suggests a different mode of response. "I began to think of" encourages the reader to make mental associations. "I wonder why" encourages an exploration of motives. "I really can't understand" encourages the reader to clarify difficulties in reading the text. And so on. This simple list can elicit a range of responses.

Should literature be used as models for writing?

It depends on how the models are used. I don't think professional writing should be used to provide models of "patterns of development" such as compare/contrast, cause-effect, and so forth. This approach misses the quality that makes the writing good in the first place and instead asks students to view the writing as examples of static patterns. But I do think that literature can provide models of looking at experience; from reading E. B. White we do not get a formal sense of the essay so much as a sense of what it is to view the world like E. B. White.

I like to use short excerpts of literature as models for writing, and one that invariably has an effect is the opening to John Yount's novel *The Trapper's Last Shot.* The novel is set in rural Georgia where, on a sweltering day, five boys go swimming in a river. The first does a cannonball into the water:

> The surface all around, even to the farthest edge, roiled when he hit as if the pool were alive, but they didn't see the snakes at first. The boy's face was white as bleached bone when he came up. "God," he said to them, "don't come in!" And though it was no more than a whisper, they all heard. He seemed to struggle and wallow and make pitifully small headway though he was a strong swimmer. When he got in waist deep water, they could see snakes hanging on him, dozens of them, biting and holding on. He was already staggering and crying in a thin wheezy voice and he brushed and slapped at the snakes trying to knock them off. He got almost to the bank before he fell, and though they wanted to help him, they couldn't help backing away. But he didn't need them then. He tried only a little while to get up before the movement of his arms and legs lost purpose, and he began to shudder and then to stiffen and settle out. One moccasin pinned under his chin, struck his cheek again and again, but they could see he didn't know it, for there was only the unresponsive bounce of flesh. (3–4)

When students first read this passage, they think that it is the event itself that causes the horror they feel. But I ask them to point to language in the passage that affects them strongly—"face as white as bleached bone," "the unresponsive bounce of flesh," and others. In the discussion students come to see that much of the horror comes from the dispassionate stance of the narrator. In fact, it is *more horrible* because the writer does not use words like "tragic" or "horrible"—the accurate detail creates that feeling of horror in us.

I conclude this short discussion by reading some advice from Anton Chekhov:

> In the second story, if you have not forgotten, huntsmen wounded an elk. She has the look of a human being and no one has the heart to kill her. Not a bad subject, but dangerous in this respect, that it is hard to avoid sentimentality; the piece has to be written in the style of a police report without words that arouse pity, and should begin like this: "On such and such a date huntsmen wounded a young elk in the Daraganov forest." But should you moisten the language with a tear, you will deprive the subject of its sternness and of everything deserving attention. (quoted in Macrorie 1985, 83–84)

I also use literary models to show students how they can expand time—develop fully an incident that may have taken only a few minutes. Time expansion is a new idea for many students who write what I call "and then" narratives where the account of an experience is more an inventory of what happened with nothing highlighted or developed. To introduce the idea of time expansion I read from the climax of George Orwell's essay "Shooting an Elephant." Although the initial shooting takes only a few seconds it is described in painful detail. After the reading I ask students to think of an experience lasting no more than three or four minutes that they remember vividly. During the next class I ask them to write about this experience *leaving nothing out.* The writing that comes out of this assignment has an intensity often missing in their other work.

Should students' papers be used as models?

This will occur naturally if there is regular sharing in a class. In fact, student papers are often the best models because they seem within reach, while professional models may seem beyond students' capacity to emulate. I would even argue that the major virtue of sharing writing in small groups is not to offer constructive feedback, but to help all students in the group see various ways of approaching various topics.

References

Angelou, Maya. 1971. *I Know Why the Caged Bird Sings.* New York: Bantam.

Bartholomae, David, and Anthony R. Petrosky. 1986. *Facts, Artifacts, and Counterfacts: Theory and Method for a Reading and Writing Course.* Portsmouth, N.H.: Boynton/Cook.

Berthoff, Ann E. 1981. *The Making of Meaning: Metaphors, Models, and Maxims for Writing Teachers.* Portsmouth, N.H.: Boynton/Cook.

Bleich, David. 1975. *Readings and Feelings: An Introduction to Subjective Criticism.* Urbana, Ill.: National Council of Teachers of English.

Dixon, John. 1985. "What Counts as Response." In *From Seed to Harvest: Looking at Literature,* ed. Kathleen B. Whale and Trevor J. Gamble. Urbana, Ill.: National Council of Teachers of English.

Hinton, E. H. 1968. *The Outsiders.* New York: Dell.

Lindberg, Gary. 1986. "Coming to Words: Writing as Process and the Reading of Literature." In *Only Connect: Uniting Reading and Writing,* ed. Thomas Newkirk. Portsmouth, N.H.: Boynton/Cook.

Macrorie, Kenneth. 1985. *Telling Writing.* 4th ed. Portsmouth, N.H.: Boynton/Cook.

Matthews, Dorothy, ed. 1988. *High Interest—Easy Reading.* Urbana, Ill.: National Council of Teachers of English.

National Council of Teachers of English Junior High and Middle-School Booklist Committee and Jane Christensen. 1983. *Your Reading: A Booklist for Junior High and Middle-School Students. Urbana, Ill.: National Council of Teachers of English.*

Orwell, George. 1956. "Shooting an Elephant." In *The Orwell Reader: Fiction, Essays, and Reportage,* ed. Richard Rovere. New York: Harcourt, Brace, Jovanovich.

Perl, Sondra, and Nancy Wilson. 1986. *Through Teachers' Eyes: Portraits of Writing Teachers at Work.* Portsmouth, N.H.: Heinemann.

Yount, John. 1973. *The Trapper's Last Shot.* New York: Random House.

Suggestions for Further Reading

Atwell, Nancie. 1985. "Writing and Reading from the Inside Out." In *Breaking Ground: Teachers Relate Reading and Writing in the Elementary School,* ed. Jane Hansen, Thomas Newkirk, and Donald Graves. Portsmouth, N.H.: Heinemann.

———. 1987. *In the Middle: Writing, Reading, and Learning with Adolescents.* Portsmouth, N.H.: Boynton/Cook.

Bartholomae, David, and Anthony R. Petrosky. 1986. *Facts, Artifacts, and Counterfacts: Theory and Method for a Reading and Writing Course.* Portsmouth, N.H.: Boynton/Cook.

Berthoff, Ann E. 1981. *The Making of Meaning: Metaphors, Models, and Maxims for Writing Teachers.* Portsmouth, N.H.: Boynton/Cook.

Bleich, David. 1975. *Readings and Feelings: An Introduction to Subjective Criticism.* Urbana, Ill.: National Council of Teachers of English.

Corcoran, Bill, and Emrys Evans, eds. 1987. *Readers, Texts, Teachers.* Portsmouth, N.H.: Boynton/Cook.

Fillion, Bryant. 1981. Reading as Inquiry: An Approach to Literature Learning." *English Journal* 70 (January): 39–45.

Fish, Stanley. 1980. *Is There a Text in This Class?: The Authority of Interpretive Communities.* Cambridge: Harvard University Press.

Moran, Charles. 1981. "Teaching Writing/Teaching Literature." *College Composition and Communication* 32 (February): 21–29.

Nelms, Ben F., ed. 1988. *Literature in the Classroom: Readers, Texts, and Contexts.* Urbana, Ill.: National Council of Teachers of English.

Newkirk, Thomas, ed. 1986. *Only Connect: Uniting Reading and Writing.* Portsmouth, N.H.: Boynton/Cook.

Perl, Sondra, and Nancy Wilson. 1986. *Through Teachers' Eyes: Portraits of Writing Teachers at Work.* Portsmouth, N.H.: Heinemann. See particularly chapter 2.

Petrosky, Anthony. 1982. "From Story to Essay: Reading and Writing." *College Composition and Communication* 33 (February): 19–36.

Probst, Robert. 1988. *Response and Analysis: Teaching Literature in Junior and Senior High School.* Portsmouth, N.H.: Boynton/Cook.

Richards, I. A. 1929. *Practical Criticism: A Study of Literary Judgement.* New York: Harcourt, Brace.

Rosenblatt, Louise. 1978. *The Reader, the Text, and the Poem.* Carbondale: Southern Illinois University Press.

Smith, Frank. 1983. "Reading like a Writer." In *Composing and Comprehending,* ed. Julie Jensen. Urbana, Ill.: National Council of Teachers of English.

Tompkins, Jane, ed. 1980. *Reader-Response Criticism: From Formalism to Post-Structuralism.* Baltimore: Johns Hopkins Press.

Writing Across the Curriculum

16

Language Across the Curriculum

Examining the Place of Language in Our Schools

Bryant Fillion
Fordham University
New York, New York

"LANGUAGE across the curriculum" and "school language policies" have become familiar phrases among Ontario educators, at least since the publication of the 1977 Ministry of Education guidelines for English at the Intermediate and Senior levels. Following the lead of the 1975 Bullock Report, *A Language for Life,** both Ontario guidelines refer to language across the curriculum, with the Intermediate Guideline (1977a) stipulating that the school principal "recognizes the role that language plays in all areas of the curriculum and provides the initiative for a school language policy" (6). The Senior Guideline (1977b) notes that "in all subject areas, the use of language involves the student in the formation of

*One of the key recommendations of the report is that "each school should have an organised policy for language across the curriculum, establishing every teacher's involvement in language and reading development throughout the years of schooling" (514).

concepts, the exploration of symbols, the solving of problems, the organization of information, and interaction with his or her environment. Teachers need to recognize and reinforce the central role of language in this learning process" (5). A forthcoming Intermediate Guideline supplement, titled *Language Across the Curriculum,* will provide additional information to teachers and administrators trying to find out just what "language across the curriculum" means, and what they are expected to do about it.

While providing considerable impetus for schools to improve their work with students' language, such official mandates can lead to problems as well. Undoubtedly, more than a few English department heads have been caught off guard by a principal's request to "get a school language policy to me by next week." And Gerald Haigh's *Times Educational Supplement* parody of the situation (1976) must ring true for many Ontario schools:

> *Monday.* Arriving at school in a decisive mood, I wrote on my 'Things to do' pad:
>
> 1. See the caretaker again about that funny sticky stuff behind the radiator in room three.
> 2. Remove the outdated notices from the board in the corridor.
> 3. Institute a language policy across the curriculum. (231)

A School's Language Policy

The theoretical basis of language across the curriculum derives largely from the Bullock Report, and the work of people like James Britton (1970), Nancy Martin et al. (1976), and Douglas Barnes (1976). Three central tenets of the concept are that (1) language is more than surface structure, (2) the entire school as an environment influences students' language development, and (3) language plays a key role in virtually all school learning. Based on these assumptions, a school language policy is concerned with more than the elimination of errors in spelling, punctuation, sentence structure, and usage conventions. It involves broadening teachers' notions and awareness of language, helping students learn to use language, and helping them use language to learn. As one publication (National Association for the Teaching of English, 1976) succinctly states:

> One of the major functions of language . . . is its use for learning: for trying to put new ideas into words, for testing out one's thinking on other people, for fitting together new ideas with old ones, and so on, which all need to be done to bring about new understanding. These functions suggest active uses of language by the pupil as opposed to passive reception. A 'language policy' is more accurately described, therefore, as a 'language and learning policy.' (7)

Language across the curriculum, interpreted as a concern for improving surface structure, usually results in a somewhat grudging agreement from non-English teachers to pay more attention to spelling and sentence structure in their students' papers. The "policy" which results deals largely with the evaluation and marking of student papers.

Interpreted in the broader sense of "language *and learning*," language policies become considerably more radical, raising fundamental questions about learning and teaching. For example, a 1971 discussion document from the London Association for the Teaching of English (Barnes, Britton, and Rosen 1971) includes a sample "Language Policy" containing the following items:

> We need to find ways of helping pupils without putting words in their mouths. We could perhaps be less concerned to elicit from them verbatim repetitions of time-honoured formulations than to ensure that pupils engage in a struggle to formulate for themselves their present understanding. Discussion is an essential part of that process. . . .
>
> Many school activities should be carried out by small groups which can use their talk to move towards understanding by means which are not present in the normal teacher-directed classroom. . . .
>
> Written work asks for the teacher's attention and interest more than (perhaps, instead of) his marks. If prior and exclusive attention is given to spelling, punctuation and correctness (in its narrowest sense) then all too easily the writer feels that the message itself and his efforts to communicate it are of less importance. (163, 165)

Even though these statements, and the entire L.A.T.E. document, are intended as tentative guides for discussion, such a policy obviously goes far beyond an agreement to mark spelling and sentence errors in students' papers. And it poses some very difficult problems for implementation, especially in the secondary school, as Nancy Martin (1976) indicates:

> . . . the general pattern of the organisation of secondary schools works against it. . . . Apart from pressures of time there are implicit assumptions that a specialist will be able to manage his own affairs—including of course, the language proper to his subject. . . . This problem is compounded by the fact that most secondary teachers (other than some teachers of English) think of language as something to be corrected and improved.

Existing (Implicit) Policies and "Rules"

Faced with these difficulties, a secondary school staff might well decide to do without a language policy. However, the question is not really whether or not to have a language policy, but whether or not to make the policy explicit. Through the attitudes and actions of individual teachers, the shared assumptions of departments, and the demands and constraints placed on students' language use, every school already has a policy toward language and learning, even though the policy and its effects have probably never been articulated or discussed. For example, the policy in some classes, if not in entire schools, might be something like the following:

- Students will learn by listening and reading, rather than by speaking or writing.
- Students will be quiet, unless given permission to speak by and to the teacher.
- Students will ask very few questions about the subject.
- Students will write down only the words and ideas given to them by the teacher or the textbook.
- Students will only speak or write in correct, final-draft language, to demonstrate that they have learned the information given.

This is a parody, of course. But it may be closer to the truth than we suppose. Arno A. Bellack and others (1974), summarizing extensive research into classroom language, indicate that there are several unstated but powerful "rules" which seem to control "the classroom game" for most teachers and students. Among the rules for the pupils are the following:

- The pupil's primary task in the game is to respond to the teacher's solicitations.

- In general, the pupil will keep his solicitations to a minimum.
- Even more important than the *don't* solicit rule is the *don't* react evaluatively rule. Under no condition is the pupil permitted to react evaluatively to a statement made by the teacher; that is, the pupil does not tell the teacher he is right or wrong, that he is doing well or doing badly.
- A corollary of the "don't react evaluatively" rule is the general principle, "within the classroom, teachers speak The Truth." (351)

To the extent that Bellack's findings characterize classroom practice, these rules of the game constitute a language policy very much at odds with current theory and research. Among other things, they quite explicitly deny a key principle of the Bullock Report, that "language has a heuristic function; that is to say a child can learn by talking and writing as certainly as he can by listening and reading" (50). A language policy which severely restricts pupils' language use in the classroom impedes both language development and learning for a great many students. One major function of a school language policy is to bring such limitations to teachers' conscious awareness for examination and possible change.

In my work with school principals, I have tried to indicate the primary concerns of a school language policy from the point of view of a concerned and informed parent seeking a linguistically adequate school for my daughters. The following questions suggest the kind of information I think schools should be seeking about their own language policies and practices:

Some Questions for the Principal (From a Troublesome Parent)

- In what ways do you want students' language to be different as a result of time spent in this school?
- What evidence do you have that students can speak, write, or read better when they leave the school than when they entered?
- How much writing do students do in this school? What kinds of writing, and in which subjects?
- How many teachers in this school take class time to teach students how to do the kind of writing they require? How many provide opportunity for students to "practice" writing (i.e., without being marked)? How many provide students with models of "good" writing in their subjects?

- How many teachers encourage students' "exploratory talk," to put new ideas and information into students' own language?
- In an average day (or week) in this school, how much opportunity will an average student have to question, talk, or write about the things she or he is expected to learn? How much opportunity does she or he have to *use* and *apply* knowledge (except on tests)?
- How readable and interesting are the textbooks? What additional material is available for students to read about the subjects?
- How many students in this school read (or write) for pleasure? What do they read? How many read newspapers regularly? How many are non-readers?

Perhaps it goes without saying that such questions make many principals feel somewhat uncomfortable. But most principals agree that the questions are reasonable, and perhaps even worth the time and energy to find some answers.

Examining Present "Policies" on Writing

During the 1977–78 school year, I was involved with several schools attempting to establish language policies, especially with regard to writing. In each case, we began by asking questions about present practices, and in three Toronto-area schools we conducted "writing surveys" to obtain answers to three questions: How much writing are students actually doing? What kinds of writing are they doing? In which subjects? The results of the surveys have been illuminating, both to the schools involved and to others as well. They indicate, I believe, both the need for and potential of language policies which involve teachers in gathering data and reflecting on their own practices.

In each of the three schools, the survey was conducted for a two-week period (ten school days), during which time we Xeroxed daily all of the writing done in and for school by a sample of students. Insofar as possible, we copied every bit of writing these students did: notes, tests, homework, worksheets, rough drafts, and papers.

The three categories devised to describe the kinds of writing found in the first survey also proved adequate for the two later surveys: *copying* (where the student was simply "taking down" information directly from some source), *directed writing* (where stu-

Table 16–1 School A (Grades 7 and 8)

n = 21 (random sample)

Amount of Writing in 10 School Days (average pages per student)

Grade 7	9.3 pages
Grade 8	9.4 pages

Note: In tabulating these data, we counted as a "page" any piece of paper with some student writing on it, often just a few words. Therefore, on the basis of this sample, students in this school write considerably less than a page a day.

Kinds of Writing

Copying:	46 pages (21% of total)
Directed writing:	96 pages (43% of total)
Undirected writing:	81 pages (36% of total)

Note: The sample of writing included very few rough drafts, no examples of informal or "personal" writing, and no examples of extended writing going on for more than two pages.

Writing by Subjects

English and math (taught together in this school):	90 pages (40% of total)
Science:	66 pages (30% of total)
History and geography:	56 pages (25% of total)
Others:	11 pages (5% of total)

dents were writing out answers to teacher or textbook questions primarily dealing with the recall of information, summarizing, or making notes in their own language), and *undirected writing* (involving some degree of original thought or creativity, as in stories or reports on students' own topics, where the writer was involved in manipulating information, ideas, and language. "Open ended questions" involving students in the interpretation and manipulation of content would also presumably result in undirected writing.).

The First Survey

The first survey (Table 16–1) was conducted in a senior public school (grades 7 and 8) in a middle-class area of Toronto. Perhaps the only additional comment necessary here is that the teachers in this school were quite surprised at how little writing was being done, and at the dearth of writing in the *undirected* category. Subsequent informal observation indicated that both the total amount of writing and the proportion of undirected writing increased in the school following discussion of the survey results by the teachers.

The Second Survey

The second survey (Table 16–2) was conducted in a junior high school (grades 7, 8, and 9) in a middle class neighborhood. In an attempt to simplify data collection, the survey was conducted using a small number of "able, cooperative" students, reasoning that this would produce "best case" findings. Presumably other students in the school would be writing less than these good students were. To provide more precise findings, words were counted rather than pages. On the average, students write about 275 words per page of lined notebook paper.

Because of the small number of students, and the sampling procedure used, we cannot generalize from this sample to the school population as a whole. Nevertheless, as in the first school, teachers were quite surprised at the limited amount of writing done by these "able" students, and the small proportion of it which could be identified as undirected writing. Following the survey, teachers reportedly worked to increase the amount of undirected writing done in various subjects.

The Third Survey

The third survey (Table 16–3) was conducted in a secondary school (grades 9 to 13), using a random sample of 36 students (approximately 2.25% of the student population). Given the random sampling, and the fact that the school is on a semestered system, not all subjects were covered for all grade levels. However, with the exception of art (2 students), family studies (3 students), and geography (8 students), all subjects were represented by at least 10 students at various grade levels.

To the extent that School C's findings accurately reflect actual practices, they do indicate a clear "language and learning policy" with regard to writing. Writing is done primarily to improve and demonstrate the retention of information. Writers seldom deal with

Table 16–2 School B (Grades 7–9)

n = 11 ("Good" Students)

Amount of Writing per Week (average number of words per student per week)

	Words in Continuous, Related Sentences	Isolated Words, Sentences, Phrases	Total Words per Week
Grade 7 (n = 4)	223	117	340
Grade 8 (n = 4)	616	210	826
Grade 9 (n = 3)	580	760	1340

Kinds of Writing (average words per student per week; % of total for grade)

	Copied	Directed	Undirected
Grade 7	92 (30%)	32 (10%)	190 (60%)
Grade 8	187 (23%)	590 (71%)	47 (6%)
Grade 9	741 (55%)	595 (45%)	0

Note: The sample contained very few rough drafts and no cases of students writing about or reflecting on their own experiences or commenting informally on the subject matter. Directed writing here consisted almost entirely of summarized or paraphrased information. Undirected writing was primarily play scripts and stories for English. In computing these averages, occasional isolated words which had been included in the "amount" tally were disregarded.

Writing by Subjects (total words by all students in two weeks)

c = copied
d = directed
u = undirected

	English	History Geography	Science	Others
Grade 7	u: 1520	c: 100 d: 260	c: 76	c: 564
Grade 8	c: 50 d: 2420 u: 350	c: 660 d: 2195 u: 25	c: 639 d: 49	c: 145 d: 50
Grade 9	d: 1693	c: 4445	d: 200	c: 1680

Table 16–3 School C (Grades 9–13)

n = 36 (random sample)

Amount of Writing

In two weeks, these students wrote a total of 98,890 words, an average of 2746 words/student, or slightly more than one page per day. However, amounts varied widely among students, teachers, and subjects. Most students wrote considerably less than a page a day.

Amount by Subject (average words per student per 10 days; average pages per student @ 275 words per page)

	English	History	Geography	Science	Technical	Business
avg. wds/10 days:	1323	1962	1640	1360	687	650
avg. pages/ day:	½+	¾	⅔	½	¼	¼

Kinds of Writing

In this survey, the "undirected" category was subdivided into subject-related, personal, and imaginative.

In the total sample, 37% of the writing was *copied*;
43% was *directed*;
19% was *subject-related undirected*;
1% was *personal undirected*, and
0.05% was *imaginative undirected.*

Note: Three long grade-13 papers in English and history account for more than half (55%) of all the *subject-related undirected writing*. Most *directed writing* involved answers to factual, recall questions, or longer "reports" which were largely paraphrased versions of encyclopedia or textbook information.

Kinds of Writing by Subjects (percent of total writing done in the subject)

	Copied	Directed	Subject-Undirected	Personal Undirected	Imaginative Undirected
English	14%	37%	47%	2%	0.08%
History	47%	39%	14%		
Geography	18%	77%	4%		
Science	50%	46%	4%		
Technical	76%	24%			
Business	35%	41%	24%		
Family studies	38%	38%	6%	18%	
Math	71%	25%	4%		
Art		26%	57%		17%

their own ideas, language, or understanding of material to demonstrate some degree of independent thought and work with the content, and they virtually never write imaginatively, or about their own experiences.

Perhaps predictably, when teachers in this school saw the survey results, their initial concern was that the "quality" of writing had not been reported. They were much more in favor of a policy which would "correct" writing than one which would deal with its uses for learning.

Learning to Use Language

The primary interest in "language across the curriculum" and "school language policies" has come from a concern with improving students' language, rather than from a concern with language and learning. However, the popular concern with young people's language development has had a narrow focus which invites a correspondingly limited response from schools. So long as the concern with language is limited to such surface specifics as spelling and grammatical correctness, attention is focused on direct instruction and teacher correction, rather than on the larger problems of language functions, intentions, and use.

Linguist Courtney Cazden (1977) argues, "The most serious problem facing the language arts curriculum today is an imbalance between means and ends—an imbalance between too much attention to drill on the component skills of language and literacy and too little attention to their significant use." The same pressures which have given needed attention to the importance of language development have done so in such a way as to impede the very progress desired:

> Responding to real or imagined community pressures, able and conscientious teachers all over the country are providing abundant practice in discrete basic skills; while classrooms where children are integrating those skills in the service of exciting speaking, listening, reading, and writing activities are becoming rare exceptions. (40–41)

Ultimately, of course, such exclusive emphasis on discrete skills will be self-defeating, though it does answer the immediate demand for action in a relatively painless and socially acceptable way. It is certainly far easier to teach (once again) a lesson on run-on sentences and fragments than to follow the advice of the Bullock Report:

> The kind of approach which we believe will produce the language development we regard as essential . . . involves creating situations in which, to satisfy his own purposes, a child encounters the need to use more elaborate forms and is thus motivated to extend the complexity of language to him. (67)

Once we accept as a basic premise that intention and use are essential elements in the development of language, there are important implications for a school as a language environment which promotes or inhibits development. In addition to asking "What are students being taught about language?" we must ask "What opportunities do they have to use language in meaningful ways for a variety of purposes?" The results of our school writing surveys suggest that these opportunities may be very limited indeed. There were very few instances where a student clearly encountered "the need to use more elaborate forms" and virtually none where a student wrote "to satisfy his own purposes."

As Joan Tough's research indicates, children arrive at school from homes which have provided markedly different opportunities for language use. (For a summary introduction to Joan Tough's work, see Shafer 1978.) The Bullock Report notes the implications of these findings for schools:

> If a child does not encounter situations in which he has to explore, recall, predict, plan, explain, and analyse, he cannot be expected to bring to school a ready made facility for such uses. But that is not the same thing as saying the ability is beyond him. What is needed is to create the contexts and conditions in which the ability can develop. (54)

When we concern ourselves with students' opportunities to use language in purposeful ways, rather than in dummy-run exercises divorced from context, we can raise some very powerful and practical questions about school practices. In my work with teachers, I have encouraged them to consider questions such as the following:

How much opportunity do your students have to use their own language to discuss and make sense of your subject; to talk and write to a sympathetic, encouraging audience, interested as much in what they have to say as in correcting what they say; to use language for such logical operations as explaining, describing, defining, giving options, inferring, speculating, comparing and contrasting, questioning, and paraphrasing?

In an average week in your classroom, how often do you *use* an idea or comment volunteered by a student? How often do you encourage a student to elaborate on what he or she has said? How often do you, or your students, ask questions you are genuinely interested in? How many students speak or ask questions voluntarily about the subject? How much voluntary reading do students do? How frequently and how much do students write? How often do they discuss and question what they have read or written?

There is nothing subject-specific to English or language arts in such questions, and in fact teachers of science, geography, family studies, and other subjects seem to find them useful ways to approach the topic of language development in their own subjects. Once teachers see that language use is as important to development as direct instruction and correction, their own role in students' language development becomes much clearer. We must begin, I think, by encouraging teachers of all subjects to look at what they and their students are doing with language, and at the relationship of these language uses both to learning and to language development.

Using Language to Learn

One major obstacle to the serious consideration of language in schools is that language is so obvious and all-pervasive that it often escapes our attention. Until teachers examine carefully the relationships of language to learning, understanding, and intellectual development, they are unlikely to take seriously their own responsibilities toward language development or to realize the potential of language for all learning. The Bullock Report says, "For language to play its full role as a means of learning, the teacher must create in the classroom an environment which encourages a wide range of language uses" (188). But this principle was clearly not operating in the writing collected in our surveys.

Two key points teachers need to understand about language and learning are that language plays a key role in understanding new information, and language plays a key role in intellectual development. This first point is nicely summed up in the NATE document on language across the curriculum:

> . . . theory and practice suggest that if a learner at any level is able to make his own formulations of what he is learning, this is more valuable to him than taking over someone else's pre-formulated language. In practice, this means that pupils often need to have the opportunity to say or write things in their own ways, in their own styles, rather than copying from books or taking notes from dictation. (8)

Douglas Barnes (1976) among others, offers theoretical and research evidence to support the idea that by putting ideas into our own language we come to understand them (see also Barnes and Todd 1977 and Barnes 1971). When students are denied the opportunity to use language in this way, learning suffers.

Perhaps more important than the immediate role of language in making sense of new information is the part it plays in developing mental operations and intelligence. A decade ago, James Moffett pointed out the relationship in *Teaching the Universe of Discourse* (1968):

> . . . a pedagogy based on provoking or eliciting thought presupposes that a child is already capable of generating the required kinds of thoughts. Asking "stimulating" questions and assigning "stimulating" reading invites the student to put out but does not give him anything, as teachers of the disadvantaged know well. In order to generate some kinds of thoughts, a student must have *previously* internalized some discursive operations that will enable him to activate his native abstracting apparatus. . . .
>
> Elicitation has a place certainly at some stage of instruction, but more basic is to create the kinds of social discourse that when internalized become the kinds of cognitive instruments called for by later tasks. (70)

Although the exact relationship of thought and language remains a largely uncharted area, there is little doubt that restricted language development is associated with restricted mental operations of the type most called upon by schools. At the very least, language must be accepted as our point of access to students' thinking. Despite many controversies, there are two key points of general agreement, cited in the Bullock Report:

> (a) that higher processes of thinking are normally achieved by the child's language behaviour with his other mental and perceptual powers; and
> (b) that language behaviour represents the aspects of his thought processes most accessible to outside influences, including that of the teacher. (49)

In James Britton's telling phrase, language is "the exposed edge of thought."

It is obviously possible to by-pass a good deal of students' language use in our teaching, by extensive use of teacher lectures and audio-visual presentations, short-answer recitation sessions, workbook "fill in the blank" exercises, "copy from the board" note-taking, and objective tests. Unfortunately, such teaching deprives students of two major means of learning—talking and writing—and it may result in limited intellectual growth as well. As Donald Graves (1978) points out in his study of the diminishing use of writing in schools:

> A far greater premium is placed on students' ability to read and listen than on their ability to speak and write. In fact, writing is seldom encouraged and sometimes not permitted, from grade one through the university. Yet when students cannot write, they are robbed not only of a valuable tool for expression but of an important means of developing thinking and reading skills as well. (30)

The language across the curriculum movement has great potential for improving both language and learning, by leading us to examine and reflect on the place of language in our schools in light of such admonitions. If they are not trivialized to an exclusive concern for surface correctness, school language policies may yet provide a salutary outcome to the "back to basics" controversy.

References

Barnes, Douglas. 1971. "Language in the Secondary Classroom." In *Language, the Learner and the School* by Douglas Barnes, James Britton, and Harold Rosen. Harmondsworth, England: Penguin.

———. 1976. *From Communication to Curriculum.* Harmondsworth, England: Penguin.

Barnes, Douglas; James Britton; and Harold Rosen. 1971. *Language, the Learner and the School.* Harmondsworth, England: Penguin.

Barnes, Douglas, and Frankie Todd. 1977. *Communication and Learning in Small Groups.* London: Routledge & Kegan Paul.

Bellack, Arno A., et al. 1974. "The Classroom Game." In *Teaching: Vantage Points for Study.* 2nd ed., ed. Ronald T. Hyman. Philadelphia: J. P. Lippincott.

Britton, James. 1970. *Language and Learning.* Harmondsworth, England: Penguin.

Bullock, Sir Alan, Chairman, Committee of Inquiry appointed by the Secretary of State for Education and Science. 1975. *A Language for Life.* London: HMSO.

Cazden, Courtney. 1977. "Language, Literacy, and Literature: Putting it All Together." *National Elementary Principal* (October).

Graves, Donald H. 1978. "Balance the Basics: Let Them Write." *Learning* (April).

Haigh, Gerald. 1976. *Times Educational Supplement.* March 26. Quoted in Nancy Martin, "Initiating and Implementing a Policy," in *Language Across the Curriculum,* by Michael Marland et al. London: Heinemann Educational Books, 1977.

Martin, Nancy. 1976. "Language Across the Curriculum: A Paradox and its Potential for Change." *Educational Review* 28 (3) (June): 206–19.

Martin, Nancy, et al. 1976. *Writing and Learning Across the Curriculum, 11–16.* London: Ward Lock Educational.

Moffett, James. 1968. *Teaching the Universe of Discourse.* Boston: Houghton Mifflin.

National Association for the Teaching of English. 1976. *Language Across the Curriculum: Guidelines for Schools.* London: Ward Lock Educational.

Ontario Ministry of Education. 1977a. *Curriculum Guideline for the Intermediate Division English.* Toronto: Ministry of Education.

——. 1977b. *Curriculum Guideline for the Senior Division English.* Toronto: Ministry of Education.

Shafer, Robert E. 1978. "The Work of Joan Tough: A Case Study in Applied Linguistics." *Language Arts* 55 (March): 308–14.

17

Journals Across the Disciplines

Toby Fulwiler
University of Vermont
Burlington, Vermont

When I write a paper I make it personal. I put myself into it and I write well. It bothers me when people tell me to make it more personal—to take *me* out of it, I'm afraid I can't write unless I am in the paper somehow.

Jody S.

STUDENT writing will not improve by simply increasing the number of writing assignments in a course, adding a term paper, or switching to essay tests. While these changes may be appropriate for some disciplines, they are not for others; in any case, such changes alone will not significantly alter the quality of student writing. Students do need to write often, and in every discipline, but equally important is the *kind* of writing students are asked to do.

Research by James Britton and his colleagues at the University of London (1975) suggests that the writing taught in schools today is narrowly conceived. Britton describes writing according to three "function categories": "transactional," language to get things done—to inform, instruct and persuade; "poetic," language as an art medium—poetry and fiction; and "expressive," language written for oneself—thinking and speculating on paper (88–105). In looking at two thousand pieces of writing from sixty-five secondary schools, Britton found that 84 percent of the writing by high school seniors was transactional. Poetic writing accounted for less than 7 percent of school writing, and expressive less than 4 percent (197).

Few teachers ask their students to write in the expressive mode, which may suggest that few teachers value this form of writing. Britton believes this must change, insisting that expressive writing is both the matrix from which other forms of writing take shape and the language closest to thought. Expressive writing "may be at any stage the kind of writing best adapted to exploration and discovery. It is the language that externalizes our first stages in tackling a problem or coming to grips with an experience" (165). Expressive writing characteristically is unstructured; it finds shape most often in letters, first drafts, diaries, and journals.

Janet Emig's (1971) research in the United States parallels Britton's work in England. Emig points out that first-utterance, expressive writing, which she calls "reflexive," is essentially a form of thinking, "a unique mode of learning," different from talking, reading, and listening (1977, 122). As an aid to learning, the writing "process" is even more important than the written product. The "process" of writing exercises and influences the process of thinking, while the product of writing—the term paper, lab report, and essay exam—evaluates and measures student performance. Britton and Emig agree that some forms of student writing need to be evaluated; however, they also suggest that the current school practice of stressing only the transactional product-oriented writing has a negative effect on the writing and learning abilities of students.

One writing activity which focuses both student and teacher on the learning process of writing is the student journal. In *Hooked on Books* (1966), Dan Fader urged all high school teachers to use journals in their classrooms: "I have seen journals in public schools used for continuing book reports in English classes, for observations upon municipal government in civics classes, and as diaries in social studies classes" (26). Journals offer a variety of writing activities to college students in all disciplines. Field notes jotted in a biology notebook and sifted through the intellect can become an extended observation written in a "biology journal"; this entry, in turn, might become the basis for a major project. Personal responses by history students in their journals may increase the understanding of distant and confusing events. Social work students might use journals for role-playing exercises to understand their client's situation. The journal can become the first articulation for any idea or experiment.

Journals Across the Curriculum

When I began teaching in 1967, I sometimes assigned journals in composition and literature classes, but used them sparingly in the classroom itself, preferring to let students write on their own; some students used them well, while most never really understood what they were about. I no longer trust to chance. Journals work now for most students because we use them actively, every day to write in, read from, and talk about—in addition to whatever private writing the students do on their own. These everyday journal sessions take the place of other routine writing assignments from pop quizzes to homework and book reports. Journal writing in class stimulates student discussion, starts small group activity, clarifies hazy issues, reinforces learning experience, and stimulates student imagination.

Journal writing works because every time students write, they individualize instruction; the act of silent writing, even for five minutes, generates ideas, observations, emotions. It is hard to daydream, doze off, or fidget while we write—unless we write about it. Journal writing will not make passive students miraculously active learners; however, regular writing makes it harder for students to remain passive.

At Michigan Technological University where I teach writing, the Humanities faculty coordinates a "writing across the curriculum" program to encourage teachers from every discipline to incorporate more writing in their classroom instruction. We conduct off-campus writing workshops which last from two to four days and introduce our colleagues, inductively, to a variety of ideas for using writing to enhance both learning and communication skills. Workshop topics include invention and brainstorming, rewriting and revision, editing, peer-response groups, evaluation, and journal writing.

We ask teachers of history, chemistry, and business to keep a journal, themselves, for the duration of the workshop. Sometimes we start with a journal writing session asking participants, for example, to write down their opinion about the causes of poor student writing. Other times we ask the teachers to summarize or evaluate the worth of a particular workshop session by writing about it for five minutes in their journals. And still other times we ask them to "free-write" in order to generate possible paper topics which will be expanded, later, into short papers. These five- and ten-minute writing exercises allow teachers to experience firsthand the potential of journal writing as an aid to learning.

Teachers who find value in journal writing at the faculty workshops often incorporate student journals into their subsequent classes. A professor of American history now uses journals as a regular part of his course in Michigan History. Periodically, he interrupts his lectures to ask students to write for a few minutes on a particular lecture point. In discussing the railroad system of the state, for example, he asks students to write for five minutes about their knowledge of trains—whether from personal experience, movies, or books. He uses this brief writing time to engage his students more personally with the topic of his lecture. Later in the term, he will base an exam question on the midterm or final on one of the in-class journal sessions.

A geography professor uses journals in two large lectures classes. In Recreational Geography, he asks students to keep journals to stimulate their powers of observation. By requiring students to write down what they see in their journals, he finds that they look more closely and carefully and, hence, begin to acquire the rudimentary techniques of scientific observation. He also requires students in Conservation to keep journals; specifically, at the beginning of new course topics, he asks them to write definitions of terms or concepts which they misuse or misunderstand. At the conclusion of each topic he requests another written definition to discover how their initial perceptions have changed. During the final week of the ten-week course, he asks students to compose an essay about their attitude changes toward conservation as a result of the course; the journal is the primary resource for this last assignment.

A political science professor who has been skeptical of journals throughout most of his twenty years of teaching has begun using journals in his course on American Government and Politics. He asks students to record frequently their opinions about current events in the journals; he also requests students to write short personal summaries of articles in their journals, thereby creating a sequential critical record of readings accomplished during the term. While both of these activities may be conducted through other written forms, using the bound journal is simple and economical.

A teacher of music asks her students to keep "listening journals" in which they record their daily experience of hearing music. Periodically, she conducts discussion classes which rely heavily on the subjective content of the journals, and so involves the students both personally and critically in her course content. In similar fashion, a drama teacher asks his actors to keep a journal to develop more fully their awareness of a character or scene in a play. He has found that his student actors write their way into their characters by using journals.

Professors in the technical curriculum have also found uses for journals. One metallurgy professor has prepared a full-page handout with suggestions to students about using journals in Introduction to Materials Science. He uses journals to encourage thoughtful reflection upon important topics, practice writing answers to possible exam questions, and improve writing fluency. More specifically, he asks students to write about each day's lecture topic prior to attending class; after class, they are asked to write a class summary or questions about the lecture. Periodically, these journals are checked to monitor student progress; they are not graded. In reading his first batch of one hundred journals he was surprised to discover few charts, diagrams, or drawings among the student writing. As a consequence he has introduced a section on "visual thinking" into his course, as he believes that metallurgical engineers must develop visualization to a high degree. The journal was useful as it indicated the thinking processes of his students and so changed a part of his pedagogical approach.

In my own literature and composition classes I use journals daily. I may ask students to define "romanticism" in their own words, for five minutes, before talking about American romantic authors Emerson, Thoreau, or Whitman. Sometimes I stop a class early and ask for a few minutes of journal writing to allow students to reflect on the class discussion just completed. I assign journal writing as homework to prep students for the next class discussion: "How would you react if you were a Harvard divinity student and you just heard Emerson's 'Divinity School Address'?" These short exercises engage students directly with the material being read. Sometimes, when a poem or story is particularly difficult, I will ask students to write about the line or passage which they do *not* understand, for example "Write out in your words the meaning of 'Do not go gentle into that good night' or 'What if a much of a which of a wind'." By next class, students who have taken this suggestion seriously will have written themselves toward understanding.

So far I have talked about the journal as a pedagogical catalyst; an equally valuable function focuses student attention on language use. By reading passages out loud, or reproducing passages to share with the class, students become more conscious how their language affects people. Students in my freshman humanities class actually suggested that duplicated journal passages should become a part of the "humanistic" content of the course; we mimeographed selected journal entries, shared them for a week, and all learned more about each other. Passing journal entries around class suggested new writing possibilities to students; in this case, the stimulus to experiment came from classmates rather than teacher and so had the validity of peer education.

I am not concerned with *what* students write in their journals, nor even if they respond to all my suggestions. One student felt she wasn't doing the journal "correctly" because she kept drifting off into personal reflections—writing about her own religious convictions instead of, for example, role-playing an imaginary Harvard divinity student, as I had requested. What could I say? She made the material her own in the most useful way possible. I suspect that the best journals deviate far and freely from the questions I pose. In some disciplines, line electrical engineering or physics, homework questions might be less open-ended than those in liberal arts courses, but even in the most specialized fields some free, imaginative speculation helps. And when that speculation is recorded in the journal, students have a record to look at, later, to show where they have been and perhaps suggest where to go next.

Teachers find it easy to add more writing to a class by using journals. Regardless of class size, informal writing need not take more teacher time; journals can be spot-checked, skimmed, read thoroughly, or not read at all, depending on the teacher's time, interest, and purpose. Journals have proved to be remarkably flexible documents; some teachers call them *logs,* others *commonplace books,* still others *writers' notebooks.* While I prefer students to keep looseleaf binders, science teachers who are conscious of patient rights often require bound notebooks. While I suggest pens (pencils smear), a forestry teacher I know suggests pencils (ink smears in the rain). And so on. Individual permutations appear to be infinite.

Academic Journals

What does a journal look like? How often should people write in them? What kinds of writing should they do on their own? How should I grade them? These questions often occur to the teacher who has not used or kept journals before. Here are some possible answers.

I describe journals to my class by explaining that journals exist somewhere on a continuum between diaries and class notebooks: whereas diaries are records of personal thought and experience, class notebooks are records of other people's facts and ideas. Like the diary, the journal is written in the first person; like the class notebook, the journal focuses on academic subjects the writer would like to learn more about. Journals may be focused narrowly, on the content of one discipline, or broadly, on the whole range of a person's experience. Each journal entry is a deliberate exercise in expansion: "How accurately can I describe or explain this idea? How far can I take it?" The journal demands the students expand their awareness of what is happening, personally and academically, to them.

Student writers should be encouraged to experiment with their journals, to write often and regularly on a wide variety of topics, to take some risks with form, style, and voice. Students should notice how writing in the early morning differs from writing late at night. They might also experience how writing at the same time every day, regardless of mood, produces surprising results. Dorothy Lambert (1976) relaxes students by suggesting that "a journal is a place to fail. That is, a place to try, experiment, test one's wings. For the moment, judgment, criticism, evaluation are suspended; what matters is the attempt, not the success of the attempt" (151). She asks students to pay attention to writing as a process and quit worrying about product perfection—in this case, spelling, grammar, punctuation, form, diction, and style. For better or worse, the journal is the student's own voice; the student must know this and the teacher must respect it.

Peter Elbow (1973) urges students to engage in the process of discovery through "free writing," a technique that encourages writers to free associate while writing as fast as they can. Elbow writes: "You don't have to think hard or prepare or be in the mood: without stopping, just write whatever words come out—whether or not you are thinking or in the mood" (9). This process illustrates immediately, for most writers, the close relationship between writing and thinking. The journal is a natural place to free-write. Students can practice it on their own to get their mental gears moving toward a paper topic; teachers can assign free writing to brainstorm new research projects. Keeping these exercises in journals guarantees a written record of the ideas generated, which may prove useful during the term of study or, later, to document intellectual growth.

Some teachers insist on not reading student journals, arguing they have no right to pry in these private academic documents. They have a point. However, I believe for a number of reasons that teachers ought to look at students' journals. First, for students just beginning to keep journals, a reading by a teacher can help them expand their journals and make them more useful. Sometimes first journals have too many short entries; a teacher who notices this can suggest trying full-page exercises to allow the writers more space to practice developing ideas. Second, some students believe that if an academic production is not looked at by teachers it has no worth; while there is more of a problem here than reading journals, the teacher may decide at the outset that looking at the journals will add needed credibility to the assignment. Third, students feel that journals must "count for something"—as must every requirement in an academic setting. "If teachers don't look at these things how can they count 'em?"

One way to count a journal as a part of the student's grade is to count pages. I know a teacher who grades according to the quantity of writing a student does; one hundred pages equals an A; seventy-five a B; fifty a C; etc. Other teachers attempt to grade on the quality of insight or evidence of personal growth. Still other teachers prefer a credit/no credit arrangement. To complete the requirements for the course the students must show evidence they have kept a journal; these teachers need only to see the journal pages for evidence of use and do not read the entries. But this last method precludes the *teacher* from learning through the student's writing.

To resolve this apparent paradox between the student's need for a private place to write and the benefit to both student and teacher from at least a limited public reading, I ask students to keep their journals in a loose-leaf format with cardboard dividers to separate sections of the journal. This way, I look at sections dealing with my course, but not at the more personal sections. If portions of the student's commentary about a particular class would prove embarrassing, the loose-leaf allows the student to delete that entry prior to my perusal.

Reading students' journals keeps teachers in touch with student frustrations, anxieties, problems, joys, excitements. Teachers, regardless of discipline, who understand the everyday realities of student life may be better teachers when they tailor assignments more precisely toward student needs. Reading student journals humanizes teachers.

Personal Journals

A student's journal can be a documentary of both academic and personal growth, a record of evolving insight as well as the tool used to gain that insight. In classes which explore values, such as philosophy, sociology, and literature, the journal can be a vehicle to explore the writer's own belief system. (For a thorough discussion of the possible therapeutic uses of personal journals, see Progoff 1975.) In like manner, writing classes may benefit from using the journal for self-discovery. In *On Righting Writing,* Robert Rennert (1975) reports using a journal for deliberate values-clarification purposes throughout the semester. He asks students to use journals to rank their values, to make lists of "important human qualities," and to write their own obituaries. He confronts students and makes them objectify, to some extent, their own biases through responses to topics such as "What I want my clothes to say about me." Rennert reports encouraging results from his journal-focused class: "Confronted with significant questions and problems, students moved off dead center and were stimulated to discover, through writing, knowledge about their values and attitudes" (106).

The journal is a natural format for self-examination. The teacher can initiate the process of suggesting journal writing on traditional value-clarification questions: What color clothes do you usually wear and why? If your house was on fire and you could only save one object, what would it be? If you had only two more days to live, how would you spend them? These questions, and dozens of variations, force the writers to examine their lives closely and to find words in order to do so.

In *Composition for Personal Growth,* Hawley, Simon, and Britton (1973) offer teachers suggestions for posing developmental problems for their students. Under the heading "Journal-Synthesizing Activities" Hawley lists a number of imaginary situations which require journal writers to move outside their writing and experience it from a different perspective. In an exercise called "Time Capsule" students are given these directions: "Your journal is discovered one hundred years from now (or three hundred years ago). You, your other-time counterpart, find the journal. Write a description of the person and the way of life revealed in the journal" (142). Tasks such as these provide students with the means to witness their own progress and, as such, are useful concluding exercises in any class using journals.

Teachers who have not done so should try keeping a journal along with their students. Journals do not work for everyone; however, the experience of keeping one may be the only way to find out. Teachers, especially, can profit by the regular introspection and self-examination forced by the process of journal writing. The journal allows sequential planning within the context of one's course—its pages become a record of what has worked, what hasn't, and suggestions for what might work next time—either next class or next year. Teachers can use journals for lesson plans, practice exercises, and class evaluation. The journal may become a teaching workshop and a catalyst to generate new research ideas as well as a record of pedagogical growth.

Teachers should consider doing journal writing daily, in class, along with their students. Teachers who write with their students and read entries out loud in class lend credibility to the assignment and test the validity of the writing task. If the instructor has a hard time with a given topic, it provides insight into difficulties students may encounter and so makes for a better assignment next time.

The teacher-kept journal provides an easy means to evaluate each class session. The journal is not the only way to do this, of course, but it provides a handy place to keep these records, alongside the planning sessions and the in-class journal. "Why was that discussion on Walt Whitman so flat today? If I had waited longer, instead of answering my own question, others might have spoken and deflected some of the attention away from me." Jottings like this may help teachers understand better their own teaching process and sometimes result in insights about what should or shouldn't have been done. These evaluations also act as prefaces for the next planning session, pointing toward more structure or less. And when a class, for one reason or another, has been a complete failure, writing about it can be therapeutic. I can objectify what went wrong and so create the illusion, at least, of being able to control it the next time.

Journals are interdisciplinary and developmental by nature; it would be hard for writers who use their journals regularly and seriously not to witness their own growth. For teachers in most disciplines, however, the personal nature of journals may be of secondary importance—at least to the teacher—with the primary focus remaining the student's grasp of specialized knowledge. However, the importance of coupling personal with academic learning should not be overlooked; self-knowledge provides the motivation for whatever other knowledge an individual learns and absorbs. Without an understanding of who we are, we are not likely to understand fully why we study biology rather than forestry, literature rather than philosophy. In the end, all knowledge *is* related; the journal helps clarify the relationships.

References

Britton, James; Tony Burgess; Nancy Martin; Alex McLeod; and Harold Rosen. 1975. *The Development of Writing Ability, 11–18.* London: Macmillan.

Elbow, Peter. 1973. *Writing Without Teachers.* New York: Oxford University Press.

Emig, Janet. 1971. *The Composing Processes of Twelfth Graders.* Research Report no. 13. Urbana, Ill.: National Council of Teachers of English.

———. 1977. "Writing as a Mode of Learning." *College Composition and Communication* (May).

Fader, Daniel N., and Morton H. Shaevitz. 1966. *Hooked on Books.* New York: Berkley.

Hawley, Robert; Sidney Simon; and D. D. Britton. 1973. *Composition for Personal Growth.* New York: Hart.

18

No Smoke, No Magic

John B. Ferguson
Exeter AREA High School
Exeter, New Hampshire

"THANKS to you, we have to write a math autobiography," a student snarls as she takes her seat in my English class. *Another* teacher has asked her to write. She senses some sort of conspiracy. But her tone suggests that she is not wholly displeased by the assignment her math teacher has given her.

I don't know exactly what a math autobiography is, but I do know that the math teacher is trying to use writing to help her students understand mathematics better. And I do know that it is working. The math teacher had attended a seminar on writing across the curriculum that Terry Moher and I taught at Exeter AREA High School, and even though the seminar has been over for more than a year, most of the participants still talk with us about their classes and their attempts to use the ideas we explored. We are excited because the seminar didn't simply teach a set of facts. It changed the way people teach.

Linda was dubious about enrolling in our "Learning Across the Curriculum" seminar because she was not sure there would be very much offered for a math teacher. A year later, she has a different perspective on her classes and her tests. Earlier, for example, she might have asked a question about absolute numbers this way:

> Given the equation $2\,|x| = -2x$. For what, if any, values of x is the statement true?*

She could mark the answers to this question right or wrong, and if she found that many of her students gave an incorrect answer, she could review absolute numbers.

On a more recent quiz, Linda gave a slightly different question:

> Given the equation $2\,|x| = -2x$. For what, if any, values of x is the statement true? Explain.

The "explain" at the end changed her answers. Although one student answered simply, "I don't understand," which told Linda no more than the old test had, many of the other students were more daring in their answers. One said, "The statement can't be true because any # put inside the absolute value sign will end up positive. Therefore $-2x$ can't be an answer."

What a wonderfully clear explanation. The response is wrong, but look at the reason it is wrong. There is no confusion about absolute numbers. This student understands that concept perfectly. What he doesn't understand is that multiplying two negative numbers results in a positive number.

Most of the students who took this test got this problem wrong, but Linda now understands why. She will not have to spend unnecessary time reviewing absolute numbers. Instead, she will be able to focus on the real problem, multiplying negatives. Eventually, all of her students may be able to express themselves as clearly as one of them did on this test:

> The statement is true for any # less than or equal to zero because the $|x|$ is always positive. A neg. # times a neg. # = a pos. #. If a positive # were used each side of the equation would have opposite signs. ex.

$$2\,|-1| = (?)\ -2(-1) \qquad 2\,|0| = (?)\ -2(0)$$
$$2 = 2 \quad \text{yes!} \qquad 0 = 0 \quad \text{yes!}$$
$$2\,|2| = -2(2)$$
$$4 = -4 \quad \text{no!}$$

Teachers who took the Learning Across the Curriculum seminar all began to have new insight into what their students were think-

*This equation can be translated as "two times the absolute value of x equals minus two times x." The absolute value is the value of the number disregarding the plus or minus sign. For example, the absolute values of +4 and −4 are the same.

ing. Even the teachers who were skeptical at the beginning, as Linda was, found that there were things that writing could accomplish in their classes that would make their teaching easier and make them more aware of their students' understanding of the content.

Concern about being in charge of the classroom became an important issue for many of the teachers. We were challenging the traditional model of the teacher's dispensing knowledge to the student. We urged the teachers to look at the ideas the students already had and to find their curriculum within those ideas. Some of the teachers were very nervous about this. Kathy, one of the Spanish teachers, gave a long lecture about fossilization, the idea that once a student writes down an incorrect Spanish word, she will remember that incorrect form forever. The notion of letting students experiment in Spanish, with all of the inherent misuse of the language, was contrary to this current theory of teaching foreign languages.

Kathy looked like the kind of teacher administrators dread having in the classroom—small, young, innocent, a pushover for any student interested in causing a problem. A few weeks into the seminar, however, she showed what she was really like. She began by describing a "typical" class. Suddenly, she was jumping up and down and pointing at us, demanding answers:

"You, do you know what this is?

"You, tell me the tense of this verb!

"You. Sit up. Explain the meaning of this word!"

We woke up, sat up, and realized that Kathy had a lot more control of her classes than we had imagined. But she was no longer completely happy with this control. She could jump around in her classes and demand attention and learning from her students, but writing gave her a simpler method. As Kathy put it:

> I can't believe that writing is actually one of the best and easiest ways to accomplish student involvement in course content, and that you don't need to use smoke and magic to obtain it.

She began to use student journals and projects to explore different aspects of Spanish culture. A student essay on bullfighting accomplished more to incorporate some of the life of the language into her classes than any "magic" could ever have done.

Jeannette, who teaches French, had some of the same fears Kathy had about students taking control, but she also realized that there was a need for something more. She had been assigning a chapter and vocabulary words from *Le Petit Prince* each night and then explaining the chapter to her class the next day. "They never had to really think, analyze, or do any type of problem solving when puzzled. . . . They were always looking to me for answers." This changed when she asked the students to use a *Petit Prince* journal. They were to read a chapter and record important facts to help their comprehension. Then they had to annotate their journals with themes, vocabulary, and questions and feelings about particular passages. Class time was no longer used for teacher lecturing but for group work. Students would share ideas with each other for the first five minutes and then one group would write its summaries and observations on the board and explain them to the rest of the class. "There was a lot of interaction, sharing of ideas, agreement and disagreement on their interpretation of the text, but more importantly, there was thinking, analyzing, and commitment on their part." Each week Jeannette would come to our seminar more and more excited about her students' efforts. Her only concern now was that the students were doing everything and she was simply sitting back and watching them learn. The conclusion of her final project for the seminar best explains her feelings:

> I am no longer the center of the classroom: the students are, the pressure is on them to perform. I am still available for clarification when they meet a road block. Usually the students help each other understand the episodes of the story. They challenge each other and are so excited when another group has similar findings. They defend their points of view and give reasons for their beliefs, they test their ideas against the other groups' responses, they pressure the silent groups to respond to their findings. There is a greater commitment to the task at hand when they interact with each other in French. They seem to respect each other more now than at the beginning of the year. They realize that each member has something important to contribute to the class. This course came at the right time for me. Thank God, I no longer have to discuss the *Petit Prince* with myself in front of a passive audience.

Wallace, another French teacher, now uses personal journals to allow his students to explore ideas in French. When they are stuck for a word, they simply substitute the English. The danger of fossilization is ever present, but he feels that the involvement of the students is far more important. Consider how much more exciting this passage is than anything found in a second-year French text:

> Sara (ma amie) a un petit ami. Ils'appelle Sean. Il est penioble, mais il est sympatique. Il est grand, et il est beau.
>
> Debbie (ma amie) n'a pas un petit ami. Elle aime un garçon. Ils'appelle John et il est *tres* grand.
>
> J'aime un garçon. Ils'appelle Dan, et il est tres tres beau, et tres sympatique. Il n'est pas mon petit ami (yet) mais (he will be!)

The student is discussing her own life, and the life of her friends, much as she might over lunch in the school cafeteria. The final desperate return to English allows her to complete her thoughts. She is not trapped by her lack of vocabulary into writing only what she can already say. (In a previous entry, she has described her horse as "sympatique." In this entry it is her boyfriend who is "sympatique." She has already demonstrated a real need for a wider vocabulary.)

Karen had returned to teaching after ten years and was unsure of her position in the classroom. Her students were performing experiments in biology and keeping lab journals, but most of their information was technical. She was not sure there was room in her courses for students to explore their own ideas. She worked through this in several different ways.

Buried in her attic, Karen found her own journals from her university biology courses. She brought these into her classes and let the students read them. They were a record of her own uncertainties, her own discoveries about biology. They showed her students that science was not a static field with right answers already available to the teacher.

Her assignments changed as well. She offered the students more room to explore. One of her test questions asked, "Through examples and definitions, explain how you would determine whether an unknown substance is an element, compound, or mixture." Dawn's answer begins with a scientific tone, but there is a much more valuable insight at the end:

> I could measure the mass of a substance, and measure its volume in order to calculate the density.

> Once I found the density, I could determine if it is an element. If not, I could find out if it is a mixture.
>
> Since a mixture is a group of one or more substances grouped together by physical means, I could try to separate it by non-chemical methods.
>
> Magnetism is one method, or I could boil the mixture since most substances have different boiling points.
>
> I could also try to separate it by sight: picking out the different parts.
>
> If it was a compound, which is a substance combined chemically, I could burn the substance to separate it.
>
> There are many different tests I could do to figure out what it is. There are many others however, that I don't know about, but it surprises me to know that there are enough I *do* know that I could answer this problem.

"It surprises me [that] . . . I *do* know. . . ." Writing about scientific principles has led to discovery, not only about the process of analyzing a substance but also about the student's own awareness of her ability to figure things out. No longer is this student simply following the directions of the teacher to reach foregone conclusions.

Marion initially thought she might be out of place in our seminar. She is a teacher of special needs kids, and she thought that her efforts to deal with students reading and writing well below grade level were not comparable to the work many of the rest of us were doing. "There are momentous differences between the special needs students I work with and the average high school student."

Marion found, however, that there were many important ideas available to her to make her students think more about what they were doing. She used *My Brother Sam Is Dead,* by James L. and Christopher Collier, a novel set at the time of the American Revolution, to teach a whole language unit that included English, social studies, music, math, and other subjects. Her questions became much broader. For example, she asked her students to define *principles* and then asked them to explain their own principles. Another question picked up on a metaphor in the book: "How does it feel to be 'all sparkly inside'? Write about a time when you had that sort of feeling." Finally, she had her students work on group projects that extended the knowledge they had gained from the book. They had to write their own Constitution. One group created the world of Gubusta. Some of their ideas demonstrated their knowledge of the U.S. Constitution; others showed the main concerns of today's students.

Constitution for Gubusta

Adopted June 15, 1987

> We, the people, are the government of Gubusta. Gubusta's main goal is to get the people to vote. The people defend their own country. The people take care of themselves. Gubusta is a very mountainous country that has approximately 5 million people including 4,854,977 eligible voters.
>
> . . .
>
> A citizen becomes an adult at the age of 18. He or she can vote, drink, drive, get married, smoke, run for office, and do other things adults generally do.
>
> Laws: There will be no capital punishment.
> Punishment will be fines and/or imprisonment.
> Lost and Found Laws—if a citizen finds something and returns it the Government will give him or her a reward.
> If convicted of killing someone else while under the influence of drugs or alcohol there is an automatic life sentence in prison with no chance of parole.
>
> . . .
>
> This constitution is designed to encourage government of the people, by the people and for the people. We believe the only way to do this is through voting. There will be public voting every six months plus any more deemed necessary, by the people. In an emergency, voting can (and will) be held within 24 hours. Conviction of voting fraud will have a mandatory jail sentence of at least five years with no chance of parole.
>
> Signed, this 15th day of June, 1987

Carla teaches in the vocational center. Many of our students go there to get hands-on experience instead of the more academic training we give them at the high school. Carla added a journal to the work her students were doing in child services. She gave them a quotation from E. M. Forster for inspiration: "How do I know what I think until I see what I've written." Then she asked them to note ways they had interacted with children, something they had learned about children, situations they had or had not handled well, situations that had made them laugh. Some of the entries simply chronicled the frustrations of working with children:

> Today I was stationed in snack. What a mess that was! I hate to cook and of course I had to make playdough. Well, everyone was trying to eat the flour right out of the bowl. The dust was flying

> everywhere and I kept saying, "We need to keep the flour in the bowl." No one was listening to me. Amy even tried to drink the food coloring. No wonder parents don't let them cook at home. They don't listen. I was so mad. Mad at them and mad at myself. You know who does snack and cooking easily? Cathy. Somehow she gets children over there and they listen. I'll talk to her and see if she will give me her secret. At reading time, Brian came over to sit on my lap and he plopped right down on my lap and I thought I was going to die. I told him that hurt me and he stuck his tongue out at me. And the day did not get any better. Outdoor time, you looked at the window and saw me talking to Sherri while Ryan and Brian were on the climbing structure. I ran over to them but not before Brian bumped his nose on the bar. You know how some days you should just stay in bed? Today was the day.

Five entries later, the same student expressed more of her frustrations, but ends on a poignant note that should have taught her more than any reprimand from the teacher could ever have done:

> It finally dawned on me. You know, that quote you gave us about not teaching a child, about letting the child discover it for herself? You know? Well, it happened today. I was rushing Andrew to get him dressed because I am sick of putting on snowsuits and I guess I was going too fast. And he looked up at me and said, "I can do it myself. And I have been doing it myself for a long time. Didn't you know?" Well, if I had spent time with him, the kind of time you want us to spend with children, I could have seen him work on this for a couple of weeks. Instead I've been so upset about taking off snowsuits, putting them on, taking them off, putting them on (we *do* this a lot). I could have enjoyed his progress toward learning how to do it himself instead of doing it for him. So what have I taught him? I taught him that he is slow, that he can't do anything for himself. And I did not want to teach him that.

Jeff is the chairman of the guidance department, and one of the people in the course who felt he would not have any particular opportunity for students to write since he did not have any classes. We wanted him in the seminar anyway, partly because we felt the guidance department should understand how teachers are attempting to teach their students, but also because we were pretty sure he would have some use for writing across the curriculum.

Jeff's final project for the seminar was notable for several reasons. It was just a plan when he first presented it to the group in May. He was obviously very excited about it, but also unsure of how all of his ideas would fit together and how successful the final result would be. He hoped to collect a group of freshmen who were just finishing their first year at the high school and have them put together a guide for the following year's incoming freshman class.

By September, he was ready to hand out a small blue booklet full of survival tips:

> ***"Hey, Freshman!"***
>
> This somewhat derisive shout may be directed at you and your friends during the first few weeks. Try not to let it bother you, because it is usually only a big-mouthed sophomore who is trying to intimidate you . . . his way of trying to protect his turf from the new arrivals, we suppose. A shrink once described it as a "ritualistic display of fundamental insecurity."
>
> ***Watch Out for This Teacher!***
>
> She's great in the classroom, but she's terrible in the halls. If you don't have a hall pass, and you see her coming, we suggest that you hide in the nearest locker. [This caption appears under a sketch of a teacher in combat gear who's saying, "Ekstrom's my name. Passes are my game."]
>
> ***Bullies?***
>
> New freshmen often worry about being stuffed in a locker, or otherwise bullied. Forget it. The only way someone gets stuffed in a locker is if a friend does it. Actually, the upperclassmen are not likely to bother you. Don't worry about them, for they have other things to worry about (like getting nailed with quiet study).

Jeff had thought at first that he was in charge of this group and was pleased that he was channeling their energies so effectively, but the students managed to put him in his place and gain control of the project:

"We know what we're talking about, Mr. Hillier, so pay attention to what *we* say!"

Students do know what they are talking about. They do have answers to questions. The answers may not be our answers. The questions may not even be our questions. But there is an incredible amount of knowledge buried within our students; and if we see our job as not simply to impart knowledge but to draw out what is already there, then writing is a tool that can lead us into completely new areas, and writing can make our students know that they are a part of their own education.

Appendix

Guidelines for Using Journals in School Settings

In recent years teachers in elementary and secondary schools, as well as in college, have been asking students to keep personal notebooks, most commonly called journals but also known as logs, daybooks, thinkbooks, and even diaries. These informal notebooks serve a range of educational purposes, from practice in self-expression to figuring out problems in science classes. Some teachers encourage students to write about whatever they want, while other teachers carefully specify topics. In most cases, students are encouraged to express honestly their personal opinions, take some risks with their thoughts, and write in their own natural voices.

Because journals provide students considerable freedom to express their thoughts and feelings, students often write about private and intimate subjects—subjects that more properly belong in personal diaries than school journals. The problem for teachers is how to encourage students to write personally and frankly about ideas and issues they care about without at the same time invading their private lives.

This document will outline some of the assumptions behind journal assignments and suggest guidelines to help teachers avoid the problems of privacy which journals occasionally present.

Assumptions About Language and Learning

Students are asked to keep journals for strong pedagogical reasons, based generally on the following assumptions about the connections between thought and language:

1. When people *articulate connections* between new information and what they already know, they learn and understand that new information better (Bruner 1966).

2. When people *think and figure things out,* they do so in symbol systems commonly called languages, which are most often verbal but also may be mathematical, musical, visual, and so on (Vygotsky 1962).

3. When people learn, they use all of the language modes—reading, writing, speaking, and listening; each mode helps people learn in a unique way (Emig 1977).

4. When people *write* about new information and ideas—in addition to reading, talking, and listening—they learn and understand them better (Britton et al. 1975).

5. When people *care* about what they write and see connections to their own lives, they both learn and write better (Moffett 1968).

Writing to Learn in Journals

Teachers assign journals—and logs and thinkbooks and daybooks—for a variety of specific and practical reasons, including the following: (1) to help students find personal connections to the class material they are studying; (2) to provide a place for students to think about, learn, and understand course material; (3) to collect observations, responses, and data; and (4) to allow students to practice their writing before handing it in to be graded.

Teachers in all subject areas, from history and literature to psychology and biology, have found that students who write about course readings, lectures, discussions, and research materials better understand what they know, what they don't know, and what they want to know—and how all this relates to them. In elementary classes, as well as in high school and college, when students study science, math, and reading, they log what they are learning about science, math, and reading in their journals. Teachers commonly ask students to read aloud voluntarily from their journals to help start class discussions or to clarify for each other points of confusion or differing interpretations. In short, journals are active, methodical records of student thought and opinion during a given term, and are meant to help students prepare for class discussions, study for examinations, understand reading assignments, and write critical papers.

In addition, English and language arts teachers commonly assign journals to help students learn to write formal assignments. In these classes, student writers keep journals for many of the same reasons as professional writers: to find and explore topics; to clarify, modify, and extend those topics; to try out different writing styles; to sharpen their powers of observation; to attain fluency; and in general to become more aware of themselves as writers.

In most instances, teachers consider journals to be the students' territory, a place where students can experiment and try out ideas without being corrected or criticized for doing so. Consequently, while most teachers periodically collect and read journals, they neither correct them for spelling nor grade them for ideas. Instead, they respond personally and positively to selected entries, usually in soft erasable pencil. Sometimes teachers simply respond positively to selected entries; other times they ask questions or make suggestions in response to student questions. In many cases the journals provide an opportunity for non-threatening dialogue between teacher and student. In short, journals are useful tools for both students and teachers.

The following section presents some guidelines for assigning journals which teachers have found helpful in the past.

Guidelines for Assigning Journals

1. Explain that journals are neither diaries nor class notebooks, but borrow features from each: like diaries, journals are written in the first person about issues the writer cares about; like class notebooks, journals are concerned with the content of a particular course.

2. Ask students to buy loose-leaf notebooks. They can then hand in to you only those pages which pertain directly to your class, keeping their more intimate entries private.

3. Suggest that students divide their journals into several sections—one for your course, one for another course, another for private entries. When you collect the journals, you need only collect that part which pertains to your own course.

4. Ask students to do short journal entries in class. Write along with the students, and share your writing with them. Since you don't grade journals, the fact that you also write gives the assignment more value.

5. Every time you ask students to write in class, do something active and deliberate with what they have written. For example, have volunteers read whole entries aloud, have everyone read one sentence to the whole class, have neighbors share one passage with each other, etc. (In each case, students who don't like what they have written should have the right to pass.) Sharing the writing in this manner gives credibility to a non-graded assignment.

6. Count, but do not grade, student journals. While it's important not to qualitatively evaluate specific journal entries (for here students must be allowed to take risks), good journals should count in some quantitative way: a certain number of points, a plus added to a grade, or an in-class resource for taking tests.

7. Do not write back to every entry; it will burn you out. Instead, skim journals and write responses to entries that especially concern you.

8. At the end of the term ask students to put in (a) page numbers, (b) a title for each entry, (c) a table of contents, and (d) an evaluative conclusion. This synthesizing activity requires journal writers to treat their documents seriously and to review what they have written over a whole term of study.

Of all writing assignments, journals may be the most idiosyncratic and variable. Consequently, good reasons exist to ignore any of the above suggestions, depending on teacher purpose, subject area, grade level, or classroom context. However, these suggestions will help many teachers use journals more positively and efficiently in most school settings.

References

Britton, James, et al. 1975. *The Development of Writing Abilities, 11–18.* London: Macmillan Education.

Bruner, Jerome S. 1966. *Toward a Theory of Instruction.* Cambridge: The Belknap Press of Harvard University.

Emig, Janet. 1977. "Writing as a Mode of Learning." *College Composition and Communication* 28:122–28.

Moffett, James. 1968. *Teaching the Universe of Discourse.* Boston: Houghton Mifflin.

Vygotsky, Lev S. 1962. *Thought and Language.* Cambridge: MIT Press.

Note

This document was drafted by Toby Fulwiler, University of Vermont, with considerable help from the members of the NCTE Commission on Composition, including Glenda Bissex, Lynn Galbraith, Ron Goba, Audrey Roth, Charles Schuster, Marilyn Sternglass, and Tilly Warnock.

Time for Questions

Bryant Fillion found that writing was not used to foster learning, but his conclusions come from work in Canadian schools. What do surveys of U.S. schools reveal?

Sadly, the pattern Fillion found does seem to be representative of U.S. schools as well. The most extensive study of U.S. classrooms is John Goodlad's *A Place Called School* (1984). Goodlad found that while many teachers claimed that the purpose of instruction was to develop intellectual abilities, their teaching practices did not match their goals. I'll quote from his chapter "What Schools and Classrooms Teach":

> What the schools in our sample did not appear to be doing in these subjects was developing all of those qualities commonly listed under "intellectual development": the ability to think rationally, the ability to use, evaluate, and accumulate knowledge, a desire for further learning. Only *rarely* did we find evidence to suggest instruction likely to go much beyond mere possession of information to a level of understanding its implications and either applying it or exploring its possible applications. (236)

In another survey, Arthur Applebee (*Writing in the Secondary School,* 1981) found that the most common type of writing in mathematics, science, and social studies classes was note taking. Even writing assignments that seemed to push students beyond the recall of information probably did not. Applebee gives these examples:

> Select some phase of 20th century American literature and discuss it in a theme of 300–500 words. Turn in polished draft only. (Eleventh Grade English)

> Explain the ability of the Constitution to change with the times. (Eleventh Grade American History)
>
> Write a brief essay describing a building (or type of building) which best represents 20th century American culture. (Ninth Grade World History)

Applebee notes that these assignments "become reasonable tasks only when they are interpreted by students as requests to summarize material previously presented in lessons or texts" (74).

What kind of writing should *be done in the subject areas?*

A big question. Students should be encouraged to use what James Britton calls "expressive language" to work through key questions. Expressive language resembles speech (see examples in the letters in Nancie Atwell's article and in the reading narratives in my own article). We can see it at work in the following journal entry, where a student works toward an understanding of what the humanities are:

> At first I thought about just human behavior but when I think of the humanities I think of English and that doesn't fit in. It seems that human creative expression or communication might be a good short definition. Because I consider photography, drawing, painting, writing, building, and lots of other stuff to be creative expression. Humanities has to be a very general topic; so the definition would also have to be general. When someone mentioned subjective, I agreed with that a lot. I think that separates it pretty well with the sciences. Scientists all seem to be very objective people with objective purposes. (Quoted in Fulwiler and Young 1982, 19)

The writer is using writing to think aloud, to work toward a definition. A teacher could respond to a journal like this by raising questions: what does "creative" mean? what are the "subjective" purposes of humanists? Isn't a writer like Lewis Thomas a "humanist" too?

Writing can also be used to support the thinking process that are central in each discipline. I grew up with a biologist, and I was always made aware of how important careful observation was. The famous biologist Louis Agassiz began his biology classes by having his students look at a fish—for three full days. Students should be encouraged to use writing to hone their own capacity to observe. The historian must interpret documents and, if the subject is recent, conduct interviews. Students can also compile oral histories involving interviews with people who experienced history. Studs Terkel's *The Good War* could be used as a model.

Aside from journal writing, what other forms of informal writing might be useful in classes across the curriculum?

1. *Writing to initiate discussion.* Discussions often founder because students haven't engaged with the content or issues to be discussed. Even "good" classroom discussions often involve only the teacher and five or six students. It is often useful to have all students write on a question or issue *before* the discussion begins. After a few minutes the teacher might ask students to summarize what they've written as a way to begin the discussion. I know that I'm reluctant to simply call on students during a discussion, but if they've written something, I find it easier to get contributions from the more reticent students.

2. *Writing questions.* Students are very used to the passive position where they must answer the questions posed by the teacher or the textbook. But they can be encouraged to come up with discussion and essay questions. I've found that student questions often address a difficulty in reading that I would never have known to ask about.

3. *End-of-class responses.* Often lectures or discussions go right to the end of the class. These final minutes might better be spent in the students summing up what they have and have not understood. This type of writing pushes students to assess their own learning—and it provides valuable information for the teacher.

4. *Progress reports.* If students are engaged on a project, they might be asked to report back to the teacher on how things are going. What has gone well? What difficulties are arising? How do you plan on solving them? What is the next step? Students can use progress reports to assess their progress during a marking period, the effectiveness of a group collaboration, or the process of writing a research paper. Again, such reports, besides giving writing practice to the student, can provide valuable information for the teacher.

Does a heavy reliance on the textbook limit the kinds of writing students do in the content areas?

I think so. Textbooks clearly have a major part to play, but other kinds of reading may be more useful in eliciting interpretation, analysis, and evaluation. Part of the problem, especially in the social studies area, is that the edges of controversy are blunted; Frances Fitzgerald presents a chilling picture of this process in *America Revised.* And textbooks in all areas seem designed on a "transmission" model of learning, where information is passed on to the student.

Students in science classes could profit from reading essayists like Stephen Gould, Lewis Thomas, and Loren Eisley. Students in computer classes could enjoy Tracy Kidder's *Soul of a New Machine* and students in a biology class could learn a great deal about diseases from Berton Roueche's *The Medical Detectives.* Students in history classes could read books like Barbara Tuchman's *Guns of August* to understand the origins of World War I or A. J. P. Taylor's controversial *Origins of the Second World War* to understand how the world stumbled into that war. The list could go on.

Books of this kind provide the challenge of sustained reading that textbooks (particularly those that have, in Jean Chall's words, been "dumbed down") do not. Because they probe more deeply into particular topics they lend themselves to interpretation more easily than textbooks. Most importantly, they provide a model of writing that includes a human voice. Too many textbooks provide a neutral voice; there is no contact with a writer. If the only kind of exposition students have read is the textbook, they will, I feel, try to write like textbooks when they attempt to analyze or present information. We all know the dreary result.

Most school curricula define areas of knowledge that must be covered. Can teachers still cover the prescribed material and *do the reading (outside the text) and writing you suggest?*

This is the dilemma. How are we to define the objectives of our teaching? I feel that we often think about curriculum as *material* to be covered rather than as *processes of thought.* The Goodlad study suggests that schools are emphasizing coverage of factual material at the expense of developing skills in interpreting, analyzing, and applying information. But if schools are to emphasize these intellectual capacities, they may need to scale down the range of information students are to master.

After all, the teacher's job is not to cover, but to uncover.

References

Applebee, Arthur. 1981. *Writing in the Secondary School: English and the Content Areas.* Urbana, Ill.: National Council of Teachers of English.

Fitzgerald, Frances. 1980. *America Revised.* New York: Random House.

Fulwiler, Toby, and Art Young, eds. 1982. *Language Connections: Writing and Reading Across the Curriculum.* Urbana, Ill.: National Council of Teachers of English.

Goodlad, John. 1984. "What Schools and Classrooms Teach," Chapter 7 of *A Place Called School.* New York: McGraw-Hill.

Kidder, Tracy. 1982. *Soul of a New Machine.* New York: Avon.

Roueche, Berton. 1984. *The Medical Detectives,* Volume II. New York: E. P. Dutton.

Taylor, A. J. P. 1962. *Origins of the Second World War.* New York: Atheneum.

Terkel, Studs. 1984. *The Good War: An Oral History of World War II.* New York: Pantheon.

Tuchman, Barbara. 1962. *The Guns of August.* New York: Pantheon.

Suggestions for Further Reading

Applebee, Arthur. 1981. *Writing in the Secondary School: English and the Content Areas.* Urbana, Ill.: National Council of Teachers of English.

———. 1984. *Contexts for Learning to Write.* Norwood, N.J.: ABLEX.

Barnes, Douglas. 1976. *From Communication to Curriculum.* Harmondsworth, England: Penguin.

Britton, James, et al. 1976. *The Development of Writing Abilities 11–18.* London: Macmillan.

Emig, Janet. 1983. "Writing as a Mode of Learning." in *The Web of Meaning: Essays on Writing, Teaching, Learning and Thinking,* ed. Dixie Goswami and Maureen Butler. Portsmouth, N.H.: Boynton/Cook.

English Journal. April 1978. This issue is devoted to teaching scientific writing.

Fulwiler, Toby, ed. 1987. *The Journal Book.* Portsmouth, N.H.: Boynton/Cook.

Fulwiler, Toby, and Art Young, eds. 1982. *Language Connections: Writing and Reading Across the Curriculum.* Urbana, Ill.: National Council of Teachers of English.

Gere, Ann, ed. 1985. *Roots in the Sawdust.* Urbana, Ill.: National Council of Teachers of English.

Goodlad, John. 1984. *A Place Called School.* New York: McGraw-Hill. See especially chapter 7, "What Schools and Classrooms Teach."

Maimon, Elaine. 1985. "Maps and Genres: Exploring Connections in the Arts and Sciences." In *Composition and Literature: Bridging the Gap,* ed. Winifred Horner. Chicago: University of Chicago Press.

Maimon, Elaine, et al. 1981. *Writing in the Arts and Sciences.* Cambridge, Mass.: Winthrop Publishers.

Martin, Nancy. 1983. *Mostly About Writing: Selected Essays.* Portsmouth, N.H.: Boynton/Cook.

Martin, Nancy; Pat D'Arcy; Bryan Newton; and Robert Parker. 1976. *Writing and Learning Across the Curriculum 11–16.* Portsmouth, N.H.: Boynton/Cook.

Martin, Nancy, et al. 1983. *Writing Across the Curriculum Pamphlets.* Portsmouth, N.H.: Boynton/Cook.

Mayher, John S.; Nancy B. Lester; and Gordon M. Pradl. 1983. *Learning to Write/Writing to Learn.* Portsmouth, N.H.: Boynton/Cook.

Medway, Peter. 1980. *Finding a Language: Autonomy and Learning in the School.* London: Writers and Readers Publishing Cooperative.

Sizer, Theodore. 1984. *Horace's Compromise: The Dilemma of the American High School.* Boston: Houghton Mifflin.

Young, Art, and Toby Fulwiler, eds. 1986. *Writing Across the Disciplines: Research into Practice.* Portsmouth, N.H.: Boynton/Cook.

Style and Grammar

19

Breaking the Rules in Style

Tom Romano
Formerly of Edgewood High School
Trenton, Ohio

THIRD-GRADER Justin is one of the best writers in class. He loves reading, is sensitive to language, enjoys crafting stories. In his latest piece, one sentence reads, "I ate blugurt in the morning."

"What's blugurt?" I ask him.

"You know how you can put two words together to make one?" Justin says. "Like *can* and *not* make *can't?*

"A contraction."

"Right. Well, *blugurt* is my combined word for *blueberry yogurt.*"

Ninth-grader Dianna's paper about the Cleveland Browns' miserable losing streak has received an 82 percent. Nine errors are marked; no teacher comments appear on the paper.

In one spot Dianna has written, "When asked about the Browns' record, quarterback Brian Sipe said, 'I don't know. There's just something wrong with the Browns.' Something wrong indeed!"

Something wrong indeed! That nicely timed rhetorical phrase revealing Dianna's voice and ironic sensibility—had been dutifully labeled "SF."

Patty, a high school junior, is reading *The Color Purple,* written primarily in protagonist Celie's rich black dialect. One day I ask the students to explain what they have learned about writing from the novels they are reading. Patty writes, "Alice Walker taught me that you can break the rules of writing I learned in tenth grade and write one of the best books ever."

Justin, Dianna, and Patty are not the first writers to realize that conventions of standard writing may be altered or broken for the sake of meaning. Walt Whitman knew it, too.

So did

Emily Dickinson	e. e. cummings
John Dos Passos	D. H. Lawrence
Jack Kerouac	Virginia Woolf
Tom Wolfe	Richard Brautigan

et al.

And so does Winston Weathers, author of *An Alternate Style: Options in Composition,* a book for all who love linguistic innovation, rhetorical experimentation, boundary-breaking written expression, and, above all, glorious human diversity. Through the work of many writers, Weathers offers numerous examples of effective writing that has broken the rules of convention style, or "Grammar A," as he calls it. Yes, he shows us, you can break the rules of writing and still write exceedingly well.

For centuries now some of our best authors have done that. They have not written exclusively in Grammar A, but have, instead, employed an alternate style, a "Grammar B."

Weathers identifies and explains about a dozen traits or stylistic devices that he attributes to Grammar B, among them *sentence fragments, labyrinthine sentences, orthographic variations, double-voice, lists,* and *crots.* I'll illustrate these concepts through the writing of my high school juniors and seniors.

Early in our study of Grammar B, Chris experimented with sentence fragments, creating a poem in the tradition of Gertrude Stein:

I. Once. No. Many times.
Tried to ignore it.
But woke still. With my cat.

> Walking. On my chest.
> Licking. My face.
> *Chris Hardin, senior*

I asked Chris why he decided to take sentence fragments to such extremes. "I wanted to slow readers down," he told me. "I wanted them to read every word."

The students also tried labyrinthine sentences. Erin, whose writing was often characterized by a cautious restraint, used this lengthy, meandering sentence type to cut loose on a roller coaster ride that rose with fond description, plunged to righteous indignation, and leveled off to a hard-won tranqulity. In addition, she took purposeful liberties with spelling and sentence fragments in order to highlight double meanings and communicate her quiet commitment.

> The waves are crashing down on white, sandy beaches as we take our morning walk, for the third day in a row, to celebrate the spring break and a get away from the city, schools, and familiar neighbors who seem to know all that happens whether at school, on a date, or inside our house, where no body should interfere, especially not those that are jealous because we get a Florida vacation while they sit at home, dreaming about the palm trees, the shining sand, glistening water and savage tans.
>
> The sights fill me with memories of things I might never see again. Return soon though. Eye will never forget these seven daze of onederful sites, clear beautiful sees, and a gorgeous state. Can't wait to come back. Will come back. Planning.
>
> *Erin Kash, senior*

Standard English already permits some orthographic variation: dialogue/dialog, judgment/judgement, theater/theatre. In the alternate style, however, variations in spelling are not used only when dictionaries permit. Orthographic variation is created to make a jolt of meaning (*e.g.*, "If a student's paper contained three spelling errors, the teacher assigned it an F—automaniacally").

Erin's use of *eye, daze, onederful, sites,* and *sees* makes me stop and take note of multiple meanings. And these multiple meanings emphasize the vast visual difference between coastal Florida and southwestern Ohio with its cornfields and low rolling hills. Because Erin has made me look closely, by the time I get to the word *state,* I no longer think *Florida* alone. I think *mental state, emotional state, state of being.* I don't know if Erin intended these meanings, but her serious playfulness has alerted me to language. I'm aware of an intellect at work that expects me to think.

Although teachers often press students to straddle no fences in their writing, to argue either one side of an issue or the other, Weathers notes that sometimes contrasting ideas are valid and opposing points of view are equally interesting. In fact, psychologist Jerome Bruner (1986) maintains that often "depth is better achieved by looking from two points at once" (10).

Instead of dealing with one point of view or idea, then the other, or minimizing one in favor of the other, a writer may choose to employ *double-voice,* a stylistic maneuver that presents the points simultaneously. Scott, for example, engages double-voice to indicate a hormonal dilemma and the probability of double dealing:

> Girl friend . . . . . Girl friend
> I love you.
> Only one for me
> Always and forever.
> Who's she?
> Always be together.
> Is she new here?
> Spend eternity together.
> Do you know what her name is?
>
> *Scott Robinson, senior*

Double-voice may appear many ways. One voice may be italicized or placed in parentheses. The voices may alternate sentence by sentence or paragraph by paragraph. Often the double voices are set side by side in paragraphs or columns to emphasize the duality of the two ideas or points of view. Such arrangement further suggests *synchronicity,* "all things present in the present moment" (Weathers 1980, 35)—another characteristic of the alternate style, one that accounts for its plentiful use of present tense.

I write with students as often as I can, although I can't write every day with every class. A teaching load of six classes and anywhere from 125 to 150 students makes that impossible. With these alternate style techniques, however, I felt obligated to get into the pool with the students, to try each of the assignments. I wrote my double-voice assignment the period before my writing class met, while my American Literature students were answering an essay prompt.

The room is silent. Twenty-five American Literature students ponder, dig into their minds, working hard to formulate coherent thoughts that will impress me with their extensive knowledge of Henry David Thoreau.	Oh, Jesus! Thoreau—what a conceited ass. He's plagued me for weeks. I shoulda read those essays.
Thoreau believed in the power of the mind to plumb the depths of thought and imagination, to deal with intellectual subjects.	God, did Jenny look good last night, her hair, her eyes, her wonderfully luscious mouth, her
Radical political ideas, the individual's relationship to his government. That's what Thoreau dealt with in his seminal essay, "Civil Disobedience." And my astute essay question will lead the students to confront crucial issues.	My stomach is rumbling like a distant thunderstorm. Pepsi for breakfast! Why did I do that?
Nothing can stop an individual who is determined, who advances confidently in the direction of his will, who leaves material possessions behind and seeks to know truth.	Time's awastin'. Better crank up the B. S. machine.

The list, simple, unexplained, sometimes poetic, is usually presented in a column with one item per line, much like a grocery list. It may be used to present abundant detail, enabling readers to see an untainted, holistic picture. Weathers compares the list to a "still life" (20).

Chad, who thought highly of Tom Wolfe and who dismissed the columnar list as "too much like a poem," incorporated a list of items into a narrative about his visit to a college at the behest of its soccer coach.

> So after the coach leaves, I get a feel for what a college dorm room is like: Snipped-snaps of Jordan, Kareem, Bird, Tony Perez, a goldfish tank, paper, an Algebra III text, Diadora's crusted with dry mud, phone hung upside down on the wall, stereo singing softly with four speakers, a picture of a girl, Athens license plates tacked to the wall, Mousse and soap and toothpaste, and speed-

vedged tightly into a basket, draped with a towel like warm , a nerf basketball hoop jutting from the wall, a dead sock ng on a makeshift clothesline, Tide.

Chad Pergram, senior

The *crot* is the concept of Grammar B that gave my students the most trouble. "Crot," Weathers explains, "is an obsolete word meaning 'bit' or 'fragment.' . . . A basic element in the alternate grammar of style, and comparable somewhat to the stanza in poetry, the crot may range in length from one sentence to twenty or thirty sentences" (14).

In a piece of writing, crots are not connected by transitional words or phrases. In fact, they are nearly always "separated one from the other by white space." And although a series of crots is meant to create a cumulative effect, each crot in the series may often stand alone, ending abruptly, making a point in itself, possessing "some sharp, arresting, or provocative quality." A piece written entirely in crots, writes Weathers, "is similar to a slide show" (15), each slide unique in composition, clear in image, precise in idea.

Chad's list of the dorm room, ending abruptly and ironically with "Tide," qualifies as a crot. And I opened this article with three crots: the self-contained literacy sketches of Justin, Dianna, and Patty.

Weathers' book excited me. I told a friend about it and explained my intentions of introducing high school students to the alternate style. "I'm hoping it will spur them to take some chances," I said. "I want them to cut loose in their writing."

"Looks like you're going to do what you've always done," he said.

I blinked. He was right. For years I've sought to free students from restrictions, to create an atmosphere that removes impediments to exploration and communication. But in all my efforts to help students to write effectively, I'd never actively pushed students to break conventional rules of writing, to systematically employ specific stylistic devices as a means of liberating their voices and driving home their ideas.

Even so, my best students over the years gave me persistent instruction in the discipline of possibility. These students were the ones with irrepressible voices who ever surprised me with risks and originality. They knew intuitively that any rule of writing could be broken if the end result was writing that works.

David was one of those students. I wrote a final essay exam that asked my modern American literature students to discuss five pieces of literature they had read during the semester: one that revealed something of America's past, one that helped them gain sympathy for a character, one that challenged their ideas or beliefs, one that was artfully written, and one they enjoyed the most. Here is an excerpt from David's essay:

> Another book that shows just how much change has happened is *The Electric Kool-Aid Acid Test* (your probably tired of hearing me talk about it). It was well written. I liked the way it looked on paper. How many books can you say *that* about? It looked good on paper. It had run on sentences in parts where the action seemed like it could go on forever and he just kept dragging the sentence out to keep you reading on, and on, and on. Then. All of a sudden. He would toss in a fragment sentence. He also had poems, songs, and the thoughts of the characters thrown into a fully italisized paragraphs.
>
> *David Van Cleave, junior*

I hadn't been teaching the alternate style in that class, but David had read Tom Wolfe as part of his independent reading. That was enough. David learned writing through reading. Wolfe had become his "distant teacher" (John-Steiner 1985, 37), showing him possibilities for supercharged prose.

In the same batch of papers that hot June day, I read Becki's superb essay, a double-twisting, one-and-a-half in the pike position, written in twenty-five minutes:

> The reality. The pain. The loneliness.
>
> All the endurance and loyalty involved with war is what I got from the novel *Johnny Got His Gun.* I never realized the true horror of war until this story. I cried when he did, laughed when he laughed, and felt the pain of being abandoned. Which is why "Richard Corey" ended his life. He wasn't happy with all his material things, no, not by far. He needed and so desperately yearned for love. And all he got was a lot of "oohs and ahs" by the peasants. He was at the end of his rope in the cold damp basement. His son witnessed his murder. Then, shortly, his own. His wife lay sobbing in her bed awaiting death, as did her daughter. Her daughter turns her face to the wall so as not to look death in the face then BANG. The cold hard iron doors shut. Shutting out the rest of the world His brother never wrote

> him. His parents were dead and he was in jail. Sitting, and thinking, thinking and sitting. I felt sorry for the poor guy. Growing up in the city can change a man for the worst. Unless you're Stony Decoco. Then you deal with life the best way you can. Day by day. Not getting too attached to anyone or anything for fear of change. Raising hell and earning money are two of the most important things to Stony. Who cares about love? Stony did. He loved Cheri so much that every breath he took reminded him of her. Then she left him alone to face the world and being a survivor, he did.
>
> *Becki Strunk, junior*

It took me awhile to catch on to Becki's nontraditional essay, her sophisticated discussion, which deftly blended one piece of literature into the next, one character into another. At one point, jumping the gun, I said to myself, "Wait a minute—'at the end of his rope in the cold damp basement'? Richard Corey didn't hang himself." But I backed up, read further, and was rewarded by Becki's subtle creation of language, interpretation, and compassion. She had connected powerfully with Dalton Trumbo, Edwin Arlington Robinson, Truman Capote, James Baldwin, and Richard Price.

You *can* break the rules of writing. My students had been showing me the way. And Winston Weathers had provided a solid academic discussion of alternate style techniques that are available to us all. I hadn't pushed before, but I would now, so "that all the 'ways' of writing be spread out before" my students (Weathers 1980, 2). Options in composition.

I created a handout that defined many Grammar B concepts and included examples of them from Weathers' book and from my own reading and writing.

"When you first gave us that packet to read," wrote one student, "I could've hit you. But when we talked about it together & tried some stuff, things became clear (even though I hate the word 'crot.')"

For homework we wrote lists, double-voice pieces, and series of crots. We experimented with orthographic variation and sentence form, both fragmentary and labyrinthine. Each day we shared, sometimes reading in a circle, sometimes putting our efforts on the chalkboard, opaque, or overhead.

The sharing became an instructive delight, for the students' enthusiasm often turned those brief assignments into satisfying pieces of writing. Some were later published in the school magazine. A creative current flowed in the classroom, and everyone tapped into it. Yes, my students were discovering, you can break the rules of writing.

After the positive experience of sharing homework, I asked the students to compose longer pieces in the alternate style. As always, they were free to choose their own topics. We began the processes of drafting, conferring, revising, editing, and publishing. The work was exhilarating, surpassing any idea of success I'd hoped for when we began exploring the possibilities of Grammar B. The students invested themselves in the writing. Most wrote their longest, most effective pieces. There were book reviews, short stories, exposés, meditations, essays, remembrances, satires, travel pieces—all singularly original in form, all ranging more freely in language experimentation and vision than any of the writers had ever ventured before.

Here is an excerpt from Karen's exposé of high school education titled "The Art of Learning Nothing":

> Biology—How to etherize tine bugs so we can stare at their tails and wings and guess. Male or female? Which is more dominant?
>
> 25% chance of wrinkled winged female 25% wrinkled winged male 25% red-tipped female 25% red-tipped male . . . except red-tipped is a female trait so your whole experiment is now screwed up.
>
> ***Reasons Why My Experiment Screwed Up***
>
> 1. bugs etherized to death
> 2. bugs reproduced so much they changed color
> 3. bugs friend to death in incubator
> 4. bugs (male) were fags
> 5. stupid lab partners' fault—give them the F—not me
> 6. I don't have any idea
>
> What Was Avogadro's number again? Kelvin's number? Melvin's number?
>
> H'm'ny MOLES . . . Molality. Malarity. Molecule. Molecular. Mole Method. What's the difference? I forget.
>
> Charles' Law
>
> Boyles' Law put them in a pot and mix laws together and you get a V that equals , and Dalton's Law says the total pressure of a mixture of gases is the sum of partial pressure and I'm totally drowning in the sum of equations.

American Indian history.

"It is difficult to comprehend the proposition that the inhabitants of either quarter of the globe could have rightful original claims of dominion over the inhabitants of the other, or over the lands they occupied or that the discovery of either, by the other should give the discoverer rights in the country discovered . . . "

You said it. Great book you picked for us. Slam.

English can be fun. GRRammar!

We, us, them, they, their, there, they're, are, our, idea, idear, ideal.

Students scrunch over their desks scribbling and scratching their papers.

With pencil in hand and mouth, I nibble on the eraser and I sit . . .

and sit . . .

and sit . . .

"Birds chirp at my bedroom window. . . . " No. "Love, like a cancer—never a full recovery . . . " Yuck. No. "To be or not to be, that's not my question." That won't work. Nibble . . . Nibble . . .

Chomp!

I spit the eraser from my tongue and stare at the dammed paper.

Let's try clots

CROTS!

crots, crots

SORRY

"autonomous unit characertized by the absence of any transitional device . . . "

huh?

D. H. Lawrence

my work my crot
my crot my life
my life my crot
my crot might rot

Karen Ballinger, senior

For many of the students the alternate style was a liberation akin to the women's suffrage amendment. It was long overdue; it emboldened them; they were never the same after it. One girl echoed the sentiments of her classmates when she wrote:

> The alternate style adds freedom to do what we've always wanted to do but we always felt we'd get an F. This style enabled me to get what I really thought down on paper without worrying about structure. All of our class' pieces came out more truthful and, I think, interesting in the process.

The students broke rules of writing and began ruling writing. In their alteration of standard style, they wrote with more purpose than ever before, paying closer attention to punctuation, word choice, and the structures they created. In paper after paper I saw evidence of intellect and intent, of students vitally aware of their role as writer, as maker and shaper of meaning through language.

One student kept calling the alternate style the "ultimate style." For many it was. They saw Grammar B as a genre in itself. I looked upon it differently. I saw the alternate style as a resource, offering writers further stylistic options—nontraditional ones, to be sure, but no less legitimate and with ample precedent in our diverse literary heritage. I wanted the Grammar B techniques to become part of a versatile rhetorical repertoire that each of my students possessed.

The three weeks of actively breaking some rules of standard English, of creating with an alternate style, increased my students' confidence. Their vision became expansive, their language adventurous, their use of line and page inventive. Instead of wearing ruts in safe, beaten paths, my students broke new trails when their purposes demanded. In addition, writing and reading in the alternate style made them more open-minded about literature. "This taught me that there are 'alternate' styles in writing," wrote one student. "As a writer I see that there isn't just one 'way' of doing things."

The most important aspect of the alternate style, however, has little to do with crots, orthographic variation, or labyrinthine sentences. The important thing is the spirit of the alternate style and its implications for nurturing all student writers, elementary school through college.

High school or university students whose writing reflects their reading of Faulkner and Ginsberg are employing alternate styles and evolving original voices. Elementary school students whose writing repertoire includes invented spellings, drawings, speech marks, and supplemental talk are also employing alternate styles—eminently appropriate ones—and they, too, are evolving original voices.

Some English teachers have admonished me for encouraging rule breaking in my students, for neglecting to stress standard grammar, usage, and form. One contended that my students will create "maverick" essays that will earn them poor grades once they leave my classroom.

Our foray into the alternate style lasts only three weeks. Many times during a semester I remind students that readers have expectations about the way print should look and that we must weigh our violations of those expectations against the results we hope to achieve.

But I must confess, I'd like to see students using the techniques of Grammar B and purposefully breaking other rules of standard style a lot more often in their future writing. I'd much prefer they do whatever necessary to generate original thinking and language than to slavishly heed to the grammatical amenities of Grammar A.

As writing teachers, we don't have to worry much about socializing most students to the conventions of standard style. That socialization will occur if they engage often in real literacy activities—writing frequently for their own purposes, reading frequently from the vast world of print. The bulk of what students read will be written conventionally. Combine that reading with the patient, persistent teaching of editing skills within the context of their own writing, and students will gradually move toward mastery of many standard conventions of composition.

What we writing teachers should worry about, however, is our students' linguistic confidence. I want students to develop a willingness to be bold with language, to press forward with words. I want them to be versatile and practiced enough to readily interact with the writing they create, and to do so with imagination, logic, and originality.

One of my students pointed out that the alternate style "really helps writers understand their voices." I think he's right. My students pushed beyond self-imposed boundaries of written expression. They surprised themselves and learned something about limits. Such understanding of the power and range of their own voices is crucial to students' maturation as writers. Voice is the vitality of a writer, both the root and point of growth. We write about personally important matters and through a lifetime develop our voices. We extend them, we adapt them, we learn with them.

The alternate style options explained by Winston Weathers let my students participate in this development in ways new and exciting to them. They trusted both instinct and intellect, practicing possibilities, evolving their voices. Yes, my students broke rules of writing. With style. And learned.

References

Bruner, Jerome. 1986. *Actual Minds, Possible Worlds.* Cambridge: Harvard University Press.

John-Steiner, Vera. 1985. *Notebooks of the Mind: Explorations of Thinking.* New York: Harper & Row.

Weathers, Winston, 1980. *An Alternate Style: Options in Composition.* Portsmouth, N.H.: Boynton/Cook.

Time for Questions

Arguments about the place of grammar instruction often go awry because "grammar" has so many meanings. How can these various meanings be distinguished?

Patrick Hartwell (1985) has identified five different meanings generally given to the word *grammar.* In abbreviated form these are:

1. Grammar in the head. Speakers of any language internalize the syntax of the language. A child of five has internalized most of the language's grammatical rules. This knowledge is almost entirely tacit—users cannot articulate the grammatical rules they apply when they speak. For example, a child will know that we would say "three fat men" and not "fat three men" even though he or she had never thought about the rule for placing adjectives in a series. We are not "taught" this kind of grammar; we learn it, Chomsky would argue, because we are biologically predisposed to learn it.

2. Grammar as linguistic science. Linguists attempt to construct models of "grammar in the head." These models are necessarily complex and are not designed to help the language user. Attempts during the late 1960s to teach watered-down versions of transformational grammar were generally unsuccessful and were mercifully abandoned.

3. School grammar. This is the grammar derived from Latin grammars found in textbooks like the Warriner series. In fact, Charlton Laird has referred to school grammar as "the grammar of Latin ingeniously warped to suggest English" (quoted in Hartwell 1985, 110). Some of the definitions in school grammar are ridiculed by

linguists as hopelessly fuzzy. School grammar texts inform students that "a sentence expresses a complete thought" and then later that a paragraph has "one main idea" and that an essay has "one point." Linguists recoil at this imprecision. But school grammars do not really claim to be scientifically precise—only generally useful.

4. Grammar as etiquette. Written language has certain conventions, and when writers (or speakers) deviate from these conventions, they use "bad grammar." Writing instruction in this century has been driven by an almost neurotic concern for this problem, but the argument that we should be concerned only with meaning (and not with mechanics) is equally misleading. Errors do matter. Mina Shaughnessy (1977) writes:

> Errors . . . are unintentional and unprofitable intrusions upon the consciousness of the reader. They introduce in accidental ways alternative forms in spots where usage has stabilized a particular form. . . . They demand energy without giving any return in meaning. They shift the reader's attention from where he is going (meaning) to how he is getting there (code). (12)

The reader, after all, is a buyer in a buyer's market.

5. Grammar as style. A number of books stress the conscious manipulation of sentences in order to help students become aware of stylistic options. Some of these presuppose that the writer understands school grammar (see Christensen 1978); other proponents of grammar as style (many of the sentence-combining texts) do not presuppose this knowledge.

These distinctions help clarify the debate about grammar. Grammar in the head is something we possess as a member of our species. Grammar as linguistic science is essentially unteachable except at high levels of education. The question usually comes down to this: does school grammar improve grammar as etiquette?

I've read statements that claim that research has proved that grammar instruction does not improve writing ability. If this is the case, shouldn't grammar instruction be entirely eliminated from the curriculum?

The most widely quoted statement about the ineffectiveness of grammar instruction comes from a 1963 publication, *Research in*

Written Composition. Based on a review of almost seventy years of research, the authors claim:

> In view of the widespread agreement of research studies based on many types of students and teachers, the conclusion can be stated in strong and unqualified terms: the teaching of formal grammar has a negligible or, because it displaces some instruction and practice in composition, even a harmful effect on improvement in writing. (37–38)

Many have used this conclusion to claim that grammar should not be taught at all.

In the past few years, though, there has been some skepticism about this sweeping claim (see Kolnn 1981). Many of the studies cited in the 1963 survey do not meet current standards for experimental control, many failed to define what "instruction in formal grammar" meant, and many came up with ambiguous results. It is fair to say, however, that formal grammar instruction, while it may not be as harmful as the 1963 survey claims, is clearly not as essential to writing instruction as many programs seem to suggest it is. There is *no* reason to place any student in a writing class where actual-experience writing is limited so that formal grammar might be taught.

Many have difficulty accepting the sweeping claim for no grammar because at times grammatical knowledge seems useful. Take for example a student who writes:

> She came in like she always did. Taking her good sweet time.

I've always found it easier to explain the fragment error to a student if that student could find the subject and verb in a sentence. Without that minimal formal sense of what constitutes a sentence, a student has, I feel, a much harder time determining the problem and the solution.

The problem with most grammar instruction is that it is not limited to the kinds of knowledge that might come in useful to the writer. I've never had occasion to use the distinction between transitive and intransitive verbs, yet I can remember a string of teachers trying to beat that into my head.

If you accept that minimal grammar instruction might be useful, how should it be taught—in grammar units?

It should be taught in small doses. I've found few things more tedious (for students and for teachers) than grammar units that last for a period of weeks. Beside the obvious motivational problems, there is the problem of transfer. Even those students who may learn grammatical principles in the unit will often not transfer this learning to their own writing.

If grammar is to be taught it should be taught in mini-lessons of five to seven minutes at the beginning of some writing classes. The lesson should deal with an issue that relates to the writing that students are doing. If students are overusing particular descriptive words—or using words like "awesome" to describe just about anything—a mini-lesson could focus on finding substitutes for these overworked adjectives. By relating grammar instruction to actual writing problems, the instruction has a better chance of sticking.

Why do students make grammatical errors?

For many students, writing is a slow process that strains the writer's memory. To get something of a feel for this slowness, try writing with your nonwriting hand. Most people, when asked to make this switch, find it difficult to maintain the sense of what they write because so much of their attention is given over to letter formation. Under these conditions, it is easy to see how a writer may get lost within a sentence and how grammatical errors are sometimes caused by breakdowns in attention.

Another obvious cause is the reliance on oral speech patterns in spelling. Words that are said as a unit (for example, "used to"/ "useto") are written as a unit. Verb endings that are not pronounced (I walk[ed] downtown) are not represented in the word. In a more general way, the composition of basic writers often have an oral quality. I remember one paper that began, "Well,. . . . "

Writers also get lost when they try to convey complex meanings that require the use of subordinating constructions that the writer initially mismanages. For example, a sentence quoted in Mina Shaughnessy's *Errors and Expectations* (1977):

> If he or she feels that they would prefer going to college to take a course and major in something that has any doubt about whether or not they will be employed in the field that they have chosen then they should. (61)

The thought behind this sentence is not simple. I would translate it as: A person going to college should be willing to take a course that may not lead to employment if he or she wants to. Shaughnessy argues that attempts to consolidate ideas in sentences like this, "though the attempts lead to ungrammaticality, may show a responsiveness to the writing situation that should be encouraged and not checked by a permanent retreat into simple sentences" (51). Errors of this kind might be referred to as "developmental errors" not caused by carelessness but by an attempt to tackle complex grammatical structures.

What can a teacher do when confronted by such convoluted sentences?

A first step would be to have the student read the paper aloud; students who have difficulty writing often do not reread what they have written. Some of these difficulties may become apparent when the student hears the sentences aloud. An audience for the writing can also help the student re-enter the text. A student listening to the sentence about picking courses might ask: "Are you saying people should or shouldn't take courses that won't lead to jobs?" This might push the writer to reformulate the sentence—at first orally and then, perhaps, in a revision.

Is there anything that can be done for high school students with spelling problems?

Poor spellers often think that the problem is unmanageable. If they make thirty spelling errors in a 500-word paper, they often see these thirty errors as thirty distinct problems. In fact, most poor spellers spell the vast majority of the words they use correctly, and even their misspellings are usually off by no more than a letter or two. These misspellings often fall into two or three categories; for example, a student may frequently leave off the sound at the end of words because he or she doesn't hear it. One of the teacher's main jobs is to show the student a pattern in these errors so that the problem does not seem so hopeless.

Poor spellers, like students who make grammatical errors, often do not reread what they have written. Students should be asked to read aloud their writing and to note words they are not sure of. Most adults, I believe, correct their misspellings not by applying a rule, but by seeing if the word "looks right"—we match the word against some visual representation of that word. If the student has located a word that seems misspelled he or she should note the *part of the word* that seems questionable. The student can then look the word up.

If students are to master spelling lists, the words should be taken from their own misspellings. Standardized spelling lists seem less useful because students usually know how to spell most of the words on them. Why use valuable time testing students on words they already know? And the fact that a student has used a word is some indication that he or she will use it again. It makes more sense to concentrate on these words than to ask students to learn to spell words they are not likely to use.

Are some spelling problems really handwriting problems?

I think so. Some students write so illegibly that it may be difficult for many of them to clearly *see* the words they have written. These students should be given access to word processors, if they are available. The screen of the word processor will give them a clearer picture of what they have written—and it will give them a way of correcting misspellings that won't require constant smudgy erasing.

I believe that many of the mistakes my students make are catchable. If students would take time, they could find them. But they don't. The problem isn't that they don't understand the rules of correctness—it's that they don't apply this knowledge to their papers.

This sounds like a description of me. I set out with the best of intentions to proofread my writing. But within paragraphs, my pace picks up and I begin reading exactly what I intended to write. My guess is that students reread their papers right after they finish writing them. They are tired and want to be finished.

I've begun using class time for a final rereading. Students should do this final reading with a ruler or other straightedge that forces them to read a line at a time. I have dictionaries in the class for them to check words. At times I have them trade papers and ask the partner to be a "copyeditor." I remind them that if mistakes pass unnoticed by the copyeditor, someone loses a job.

I've also worked other editing exercises into this time before papers are handed in. One is to have each student read his or her paper and find twenty words that can be cut. At first students moan politely, but once they start, they find it's easy.

References

Braddock, Richard; Richard Lloyd Jones; and Lowell Schoen. 1963. *Research in Written Composition.* Urbana, Ill.: National Council of Teachers of English.

Christensen, Francis. 1978. *Notes Toward a New Rhetoric: Nine Essays for Teachers.* Rev. ed. New York: Harper & Row.

Hartwell, Patrick. 1985. "Grammar, Grammars and the Teaching of Grammar." *College English* 47:4 (February): 105–27.

Kolnn, Martha. 1981. "Closing the Books on Alchemy." *College Composition and Communication* 32 (May): 139–51.

Shaughnessy, Mina. 1977. *Errors and Expectations.* New York: Oxford University Press.

Suggestions for Further Reading

Christensen, Francis. 1978. *Notes Toward a New Rhetoric: Nine Essays for Teachers.* Rev. ed. New York: Harper & Row.

Daiker, Donald; Andrew Kerek; and Max Morenberg. 1982. *The Writer's Options: Combining to Composing.* 2nd ed. New York: Harper & Row.

DeBeaugrand, Robert. 1984. "Forward to the Basics: Getting Down to Grammar." *College Composition and Communication* 35 (October): 358–67.

D'Eloia, Sarah. 1977. "The Uses—and Limits—of Grammar." *Journal of Basic Writing* 1 (Spring/Summer):1–20.

Elley, W. B.; H. Lamb; and M. Wyllie. 1976. "The Role of Grammar in a Secondary School English Curriculum." *Research in the Teaching of English* 10:5–21.

Farr, Marcia, and Harvey Daniels. 1986. *Language Diversity and Writing Instruction.* Urbana, Ill.: ERIC/National Council of Teachers of English.

Hairston, Maxine. 1981. "Not All Errors Are Created Equal: Non-Academic Readers Respond to Lapses in Usage." *College Composition and Communication* 43 (December):794–806.

Hartwell, Patrick. 1985. "Grammar, Grammars and the Teaching of Grammar." *College English* 47:4 (February):105–27.

Kolnn, Martha. 1981. "Closing the Books on Alchemy." *College Composition and Communication,* 32 (May):139–51.

Lanham, Richard. 1987. *Revising Prose.* 2nd ed. New York: Macmillan.

Moffett, James. 1983. "Grammar and the Sentence." Chapter 5 of *Teaching the Universe of Discourse.* Portsmouth, N.H.: Boynton/ Cook.

Shaughnessy, Mina. 1977. *Errors and Expectations* New York: Oxford University Press.

Weathers, Winston. 1980. *An Alternate Style: Options in Composition.* Portsmouth, N.H.: Boynton/Cook.

Weaver, Constance. 1979. *Grammar for Teachers.* Urbana, Ill.: National Council of Teachers of English.

Williams, Joseph. 1981. "The Phenomenology of Error." *College Composition and Communication* 32 (May):152–68.

———. 1989. *Style: Ten Lessons in Clarity and Grace.* 3rd ed. Glenview, Ill.: Scott Foresman.